THE ETHICAL BUSINESS

The Ethical Business

Challenges and Controversies

Kamel Mellahi

Kevin Morrell

and

Geoffrey Wood

Second Edition

palgrave
macmillan

First published 2002
Reprinted three times
Second edition 2010

Published by
PALGRAVE MACMILLAN

Palgrave Macmillan in the UK is an imprint of Macmillan Publishers Limited, registered in England, company number 785998, of Houndmills, Basingstoke, Hampshire RG21 6XS.

Palgrave Macmillan in the US is a division of St Martin's Press LLC, 175 Fifth Avenue, New York, NY 10010.

Palgrave Macmillan is the global academic imprint of the above companies and has companies and representatives throughout the world.

Palgrave® and Macmillan® are registered trademarks in the United States, the United Kingdom, Europe and other countries.

ISBN 978–0230–54693–6

This book is printed on paper suitable for recycling and made from fully managed and sustained forest sources. Logging, pulping and manufacturing processes are expected to conform to the environmental regulations of the country of origin.

A catalogue record for this book is available from the British Library.

A catalog record for this book is available from the Library of Congress.

Kamel

To my parents for their guidance in the early years, and my wife Shanaz and children Ismail, Hamza and Leyla for their love and support

Kevin

To my wife Sarah and daughters Emily and Ruby for the joy they bring me, and to my mother Angela and mother-in-law Sheron for their love

Geoff

To my wife Vicky and daughter Alice for their patience and support, and to my father Bob for showing me how to be a scholar

Contents

Part 2 Issues facing management

List of tables, figures and cartoons

Tables

Figures

Cartoons

Cartoons by Kevin Morrell

Preface to the second edition

How to use this book

Business ethics is an applied activity. We have eight 'applied' chapters at the heart of this book, and at the heart of our approach. There are four chapters on major themes in business ethics: Governance and Compliance, Social Partnerships, Green Issues, Globalization and Trade (Chapters 3 to 6). There are also four chapters on major business domains: Accounting and Finance, Organizational Behaviour and Human Resource Management, Marketing, Supply Chain and Operations Management (Chapters 7 to 10). These chapters are designed to stand on their own and we encourage tutors and students alike to take a modular approach to this book. With that in mind, we strongly suggest that Chapter 1 is required background reading. It outlines the most influential theories in 'business ethics'. For those unfamiliar with, or new to, the topic, please read this chapter first. To get the most from the many cases we discuss, a decent understanding of the ideas in Chapter 1 is essential.

Chapter 2 is more specifically about our approach to 'business ethics'. It is not crucial to read this to interpret the following chapters, but it does make the case for why this book is different from some other texts, and it is placed deliberately as a bridge between the theories in Chapter 1 and the applied nature of Chapters 3 to 10. Chapter 11 is a reflective and integrative summary.

We hope you enjoy working with this book.

KAMEL MELLAHI
KEVIN MORRELL
GEOFFREY WOOD

Acknowledgements

The authors and publishers wish to thank the following for permission to reproduce copyright material:

Peter and Sarah Stanwick at Auburn University for the introductory case study, 'Tyco International: Dennis Kozlowski – Certainly a Man to Watch'; available at: http://www.auburn.edu/~stanwsd/tyco.html.

Agence Global for the closing case study, 'Rebuilding the Social Contract at Work: Saturn', from T. Kochan, *Le Monde Diplomatique*, 2004.

The Independent for the introductory case study, 'Fury at Private Equity Merger of AA and Saga', *Independent*, 26 June 2007.

The Washington Post for the closing case study, 'Returning to Lighter Regulation?', C. Johnson, *The Washington Post*, 29 November 2009.

Oxford University Press for the introductory case study, 'The Sweet Factory and the Ethics School', from F. Wilson, *Organizational Behaviour: A Critical Introduction* (1999).

The Guardian for the introductory case study, 'The Rise of the Machines', Eric Clark, *Guardian*, 4 May 2007; and for the closing case study, 'Top Fashion Brands Accused Over Failure to Ensure Living Wage' Karen McVeigh, *The Guardian*, 14 September 2007.

Ethical Corporation for the introductory case study, 'Facing Up to the Child Labour Challenge', *Ethical Corporation*, 16 August 2005.

RiskMetrics Group for the closing case study, 'Pay for "Fat Cats"', from Stephen Deane, 'Exit Pay Best Practices in Practice', RiskMetrics Group, 2007.

Transparency International for Table 6.1, 'Ten least and most corrupt countries', from 'Corruption Perceptions Index', http://www.transparency.org/policy_research/surveys_indices/cpi/2007. Copyright 2007 Transparency International: The Global Coalition against Corruption. Used with permission. For more information visit: http://www.transparency.org.

Springer for Figures 6.1 and 6.2, from J. B. Hamilton and B. S. Knouse, 2001, 'Multinational Enterprise Decision Principles for Dealing with Cross Cultural Ethical Conflicts', *Journal of Business Ethics*, 31,1: 77–94.

Sage for Table 8.1, 'Sisson's model of rhetoric and reality in HRM', from K. Legge, 1998, 'Is HRM Ethical? Can HRM Be Ethical?', in M. Parker (ed.), *Ethics and Organizations*, London: Sage.

Every effort has been made to trace all copyright-holders, but if any have been inadvertently overlooked the publishers will be pleased to make the necessary arrangements at the first opportunity.

Introduction

Ethics concerns attempts to distinguish 'right' from 'wrong', 'good' from 'bad' and what constitutes desirable conduct in a particular set of social circumstances. In the field of business ethics there is a startling variety of theories, approaches and philosophies, each professing to offer fundamental insights into what constitutes business ethics. Over the years, the subject of business ethics expands, making it increasingly difficult to oversee the subject area. To make things worse, many of the ethics theories and perspectives propounded are conflicting in both outlook and remedies. This explains, partially, why some managers are sceptical about business ethics and the value of being ethical altogether, opting instead for a 'pragmatic' approach when dealing with ethics. In this volume, we take the view that business ethics seeks to understand what constitutes ethical behaviour on the behalf of the firm, why firms should act ethically, and what the outcomes of ethical conduct should entail.

There is little doubt that business ethics has become an increasingly fashionable area of enquiry over the past twenty or so years. Today, firms face considerable consumer pressure to be seen to be acting in an ethical manner, while legislation designed to ensure 'good' corporate behaviour – in areas ranging from marketing to the environment – has proliferated. Ironically, these pressures have been partially offset by others, including increasingly mobile investor capital, the rise of speculator-driven economic activity, and rapid changes in technology and market compositions, all of which encourage managers to take a short-term profit maximization point of view. It is thus no coincidence that the 1990s and 2000s have seen firms placing increasing emphasis on developing 'green' consumer products, on reducing waste and encouraging recycling, but also persistent financial scandals and ongoing allegations of misconduct by major multinational firms in the developing world. It is generally recognized that business ethics matters. More contentious are questions such as where the primary duty of management lies – to shareholders, all members of the organization, stakeholders, society, or the entire biosphere? Similarly, if managers act only in an ethical fashion to stay out of trouble with the law, or to placate consumers, are they really acting in an ethical fashion at all? In other words, is a 'good' action only 'good' if prompted for the 'right' reasons. These issues represent central themes in the contemporary literature on business ethics, and indeed, in this volume.

This book is divided into three closely interrelated parts. In the first, entitled 'Theoretical Foundations', we introduce key concepts and issues related to business ethics, and ground the field of business ethics within the classical philosophical tradition. In the second part, 'Issues Facing Management', we go on to explore a range of contemporary ethical issues and policy options facing management, ranging from corporate governance to green issues. In the third part, entitled 'Ethical Management in Practice', drawing on many of the constructs and issues discussed in the earlier parts, we outline key ethical questions and debates facing the different functional areas of management, ranging from finance to marketing.

Whatever one's ideological orientation and to whatever philosophical tradition one is most drawn, it is clear that business ethics matters, for legal, marketing and productivity reasons, but, perhaps, above all, in order to provide the basis for advancing the human condition. More contentious is the question of priorities, and whether ethical questions should, at times, be sacrificed in the interest of realizing other goals, such as maximizing stockholder value. However, it is recognized increasingly that ethical management has a value of its own, both in terms of making the world 'a safe place in which to do business', and in contributing to the general well-being of wider society and the natural environment.

Part 1
Theoretical foundations

Introducing business ethics

Chapter objectives

- To understand what constitutes ethics, and the relationship between ethics and specific moral guidelines.
- To introduce the principal philosophical frames of reference and their relevance to ethical practice in the real world.

1.1 Introduction

Business ethics can mean different things to different people (Jones *et al.*, 2005). Here we want to suggest that it is an attempt to apply the tools and concepts developed by philosophers to distinguish 'right' from 'wrong' and the desirable from the undesirable, to the corporate world. Ethics is an applied form of philosophy because it places a greater emphasis on human and organizational behaviour and on action in the world. At their heart, ethical questions include studies of the nature and origin of our concepts of good and bad, the just and the unjust (Lamsa, 1999: 346). These questions have been debated for thousands of years and they are continually contested. 'Business ethics' is a comparatively new development – or at least the phrase 'business ethics' is comparatively new. Essentially it can be thought of as the study of business from an ethical point of view. It is worth saying at the outset that we think it is legitimate to question whether there is a need for a separate term like business ethics at all. In an important sense, 'ethics' should apply equally to life in business as it does to life in general. We even have some sympathy with those who suggest that there is a basic tension between the terms business and ethics, and that bringing them together is a mistake. Of course, business decisions have ethical implications, but then so does any sphere of human activity – does the phrase 'business ethics' imply there is a different set of rules for ethical behaviour in business that we otherwise don't have to follow? Is business ethics the 'get-out clause' we look for if we want to continue to profit and compete in the marketplace? We don't think so, but it is true that many of the questions we think of as being at the core of 'business' (how profitable something is, how efficient, how it will survive in the marketplace and so on) involve very different sorts of considerations from basic ethical questions that are related to justice, fairness, and right and wrong. You may already have heard the rather tired phrase that business ethics is a contradiction in terms, an oxymoron. Although it's often said in an intellectually lazy manner – to dismiss, rather than encourage further thought – it does signal a basic challenge that books such as this engage with in different ways. You may also have heard a completely contradictory assertion that is almost as empty – namely, 'good ethics is good business'. That is even less helpful, because it is such a vague generalization. It becomes a nonsense when we learn how highly profitable companies engage in commercial espionage, union busting, unethical outsourcing and a host of other questionable practices. Or when we consider those legitimate businesses that do exceptionally well from manufacturing products with repugnant consequences, such as tobacco and arms manufacturers. Plenty of illicit organizations do good business precisely because they deal in drug trafficking, people smuggling and counterfeit goods. Where, then, does all this leave business ethics?

In the past few years, there has been a proliferation of courses at business schools which deal with business ethics. Critics have charged that such courses can easily fall into the trap of being seen as little more than a soft and easy option, lacking both theoretical depth and practical nuance (Freeman, 1991: 17). None the less, there is little doubt that there is a rapidly burgeoning body of critical literature on the subject. Alongside this, practical courses have tried to address the challenges of providing worthwhile ethical tools relevant to the rapidly changing business environment of the 2000s. In the first half of this chapter, we explore in general terms what really constitutes ethical behaviour. More specifically, we examine whether there can be any definite and fixed standards about ethical behaviour, or whether moral standards will always change according to different social contexts. This is often referred to as being a debate about ethical relativism. To illustrate, consider two different explanations for how and why we have ethical standards (that is, shared beliefs about what is right and what is wrong). First, some people believe that ideas of right and wrong are social constructs – that is, they are purely and simply the product of whatever society or community created them. If you believe this, or if you believe that what counts as right and wrong depends on the circumstances, then either of those beliefs would put you firmly on the ethical relativist side of the debate. You would feel that ideas about good and bad are relativist because they always need to be understood relative to the context (either the community or the situation): there is no absolute right and wrong. Second, and in contrast to this, some people believe that there are important moral absolutes. An example of one moral absolute might be that 'you must not kill another person whatever the circumstances'; or another might be 'you should never discriminate against someone purely on the grounds of their race, whatever the circumstances'. If you believe that this, or something like this, should be a moral principle, that had to be followed without exception, then you are on the anti-relativist (or absolutist) side of the debate.

Deciding on these issues is not by any means easy. You might want to allow some flexibility to determine what is right and wrong if you think life is too simple for moral rules. Some might think, for example, that the state, in protection of its citizens, should give some highly trained and qualified people the right to shoot a person who is a terrorist, if they think this can save other lives. As an individual, you might also feel that you want to respect moral systems from different cultures and traditions, and perhaps allow for the fact that your own opinions about morality may be culturally biased. Those kinds of beliefs seem to commit you to relativism. On the other hand, you might want a guarantee that some of the rights you enjoy as a human being (such as the right to life) should be protected, no matter what. That seems to commit you to absolutism. You might also be unhappy with some of the implications of relativism. For example, if two people disagree completely on a moral issue, a relativist stance would imply that they can both be right (or that neither is wrong). If you disagree, you may discover you are absolutist. At its heart, deciding where to locate yourself in this debate is perhaps less important than continuing to reflect on the basic question that prompts the debate in the first place. Does what is considered 'good' and 'bad' vary greatly from society to society, from business to business, or from organization to organization, or are there certain broader issues of 'right' and 'wrong' that have a global relevance? In the second half of this chapter we follow up such practical questions, by assessing the extent to which such dilemmas can be resolved through philosophical theory. We outline some of the main schools of philosophical thought that have been applied to understanding business ethics: utilitarianism, deontological ethics, virtue ethics, rights-based approaches, and some more contemporary contributions in what are sometimes collectively referred to as postmodern approaches.

As noted in the introduction, there is little doubt that contemporary firms are under considerable pressure – from both consumers and governments – to act (or perhaps at least to be *seen* to act) ethically. However, if they are motivated simply by external pressures, are such actions devoid of moral worth? Should we give credit to businesses for acting ethically, if they are doing it only for selfish motives? Proponents of the different philosophical traditions of utilitarianism, the rights-based approach, deontological and virtue theories, and the more contemporary theorists will differ radically in their responses to this and to other central questions.

1.2   Moral relatives and ethical absolutes

1.2.1   What is ethical conduct?

It may be useful to draw a distinction between ethics and moral codes; the latter are specific, and confined to particular sets of social circumstances (Singer, 1995: 2). Ethics can be seen as a more general term, denoting both ethical theories and day-to-day moral beliefs, though many make a more detailed distinction (Beauchamp and Bowie, 1997: 2). Thus moral codes differ greatly from society to society, an example being restrictions on sexual conduct or, for that matter, the use of particularly vulnerable categories of labour, such as children. In contrast, ethics are universal; central to our ideas of what it means to be human are some notions of 'good' and 'evil', and certain social taboos that are common to all societies.

There are problems in trying to decide what counts as ethical conduct. Let us look at the commonplace idea that ethical conduct is partly about putting someone else first. This could be: letting someone cross the road in front of your car, or holding a door open for someone; in more dramatic cases, it could be giving blood or donating organs. Such actions are often described as *altruistic* – acting for another's sake (in Latin *alter* = other). Now, some people have suggested that there is no such thing as genuine altruism. Even if we appear to be acting for the good of others, we are only doing so in because it is in our own self-interest: we like to feel good about ourselves, to act consistently with a favourable self-image and think we are nice people and so on. This theory – that all behaviour is motivated by self-interest – is known as *psychological egoism* (in Latin *ego* = 'I' or 'self') and it can be summed up by an exam question one of the authors of this book once encountered: 'There are altruistic actions, but there are always egoistic explanations for those actions'. If psychological egoism is true, how can we give credit for ethical conduct? Why should we reward someone who is doing what they want to do in any case and acting in their own interest? This has some quite wide implications. For example, is a bank being 'ethical' if it refuses to lend money to some types of companies (tobacco companies, say). If the same bank advertises an ethical lending policy as part of its business strategy, and makes money doing so, then how is it being ethical?

What makes the question of ethical conduct even more complicated is that even though many agree that altruism is the cornerstone of acting ethically, some people have suggested all individuals *should* try to act solely in their own self-interest. This position of self-ishness is even stronger and is sometimes referred to as *ethical* egoism. It has some wider implications too. For example, some people have suggested that the most efficient way for capitalism to work is for individual firms to pursue their own self-interest. Firms exist to make profits and (provided they act lawfully) by doing that they discharge their social responsibilities. The bank making money through ethical investing could say it is acting ethically simply because it is making money for shareholders. Even if the bank's motives were selfish, it could be said that it had a duty to act selfishly because it needed to offer its own investors a profit.

Self-interest and good ethics often coincide, as it is often in one's interests to act morally or altruistically (Ridley, 1996; Singer, 1995: 3). For example, to our knowledge, all societies have one or another taboo against the arbitrary killing of healthy adults belonging to one's own social unit. However, many societies tolerate some degree of euthanasia (commonly of the very old or the very young) or the slaying of 'outsiders' – those who have for some reason placed themselves beyond the pale of society.

Law is the public's agency for translating morality into specific social guidelines and practices, and specifying punishments (Beauchamp and Bowie, 1997: 4). However, it is often all too easy for firms simply to refer ethical problems to their legal departments, the assumption being that if it is not likely to run into trouble with the law, then an action is ethical (Beauchamp and Bowie, 1997). None the less, the law is not concerned with moral problems *per se*; the fact that an action is legally acceptable does not make it moral. An example cited by Beauchamp and Bowie (1997: 4) is the case of Pacific Lumber, the subject of a hostile takeover by Charles E. Hurwitz. Hurwitz took over the firm, in the teeth of managerial resistance, who feared that he would take a far more ruthless and short-term approach towards the firm's resources, both human and natural. Hurwitz immediately doubled the rate of tree-cutting in the country's largest private redwood forest, to pay off debts incurred in the takeover, an action many critics branded as immoral, though it was perfectly legal (Beauchamp and Bowie, 1997: 5).

It should also be recognized that while it may be very easy to draw ethical boundaries in theory, it is somewhat more difficult to do so in practice. This is partly why debates about relativism and absolutism are often very difficult to resolve. We have just seen that while the killing of fellow humans is generally seen as unethical across societies, in some circumstances it is tolerated, or even condoned. Again, most societies value truthfulness; in fact, some degree of truth-telling is necessary for basic social cohesion. However, as Singer (1995: 2) notes, an absolute prohibition on lies may be of little value in specific circumstances. For example, in Nazi-ruled Europe, in response to Gestapo enquiries, it would be surely right to deny it if you had a Jewish family hiding in your house. Similarly, in apartheid South Africa, should managers have co-operated with the authorities in the implementation of the pass laws aimed at restricting the movement (and civil liberties) of African workers? Indeed, hindering the agents of unjust authority wherever possible is surely an ethically commendable stance in life, even if it involves regular deception.

In deciding what constitutes ethical business conduct, it is even more difficult to draw firm distinctions between 'right' and 'wrong'. Perhaps all that can be hoped for is to make people more attuned to recognizing moral complexities (Solomon, 1992: 4), and better-equipped to deal with them. This is particularly important in that all business decisions do have an ethical dimension (Solomon, 1992: 4).

Two of the core disciplines of the management sciences – economics and accountancy – are centred on the basic assumption that all social actors (both individuals and groups) are 'utility maximizers' (Bowie, 1991: 29). In other words, in seeking to maximize the material benefits accruing to themselves, these actors are always looking after their own interests (utility can best be understood as the sum of benefits an individual or group may derive from a particular action). However, certain contradictions are inherent in these assumptions, the most obvious being the clash of interests between principals and agents (Bowie, 1991: 29); that is, between the owners of the firm (principals), and their employees (paid agents). This tension is apparent whether the employee is drawn from the highest ranks of senior management, or is the most junior hourly-paid worker. While it is possible to argue that the clash between personal and corporate interests can be reconciled, or that any differences that do arise can simply be factored in, in practice, the issue is often neglected (Bowie, 1991: 29). According to Ghoshal (2005) this problem is just one illustration of how the most influential perspectives on business and management come from disciplines whose view of social life is inherently 'gloomy'. The view of people and organizations as utility maximizing and self-interested may be useful in modelling behaviour in markets, but it does a poor job of addressing ethical behaviour. In practice, ethical conduct in the business world is likely to involve a casting aside of conventional wisdom and such crude assumptions of self-interested agents. Instead, it will involve taking the interests of others, rather than the firm, or the person of the manager, first (Bowie, 1991: 29).

1.2.2   Why does business ethics matter?

Business ethics became an increasingly fashionable field of study in the 1990s. There is little doubt that, in part, this represented a reaction to the excesses of the 1980s, to the central emphasis on individual financial gain – no matter how that was achieved – and the ostentatious display of wealth that characterized that decade. By the close of the 1980s, a range of factors, from repetitive financial scandals to objective evidence of global environmental damage, underscored the importance of ethical conduct in business (Vinten, 2000). However, as we have already touched upon, and as Solomon (1992) notes, it can be extremely difficult to define what constitutes ethical conduct. An often cited example of the kind of ethical dilemmas confronting managers would be dealing with the problem of downsizing a workforce of dedicated loyal employees as a result of a cost-cutting decision made by superiors (Solomon, 1992). This simple scenario illustrates three sets of competing interests: the principals who presumably wish to minimize labour cost to secure greater revenue (or, more charitably, to ensure the long-term success of the firm); their agents who have to face the fallout of such a decision at the front line, and attempt to manage it; and the redundant employees who have lost their livelihoods and income, and in all likelihood a large part of their identity. More importantly, it also suggests that some ethical problems may well have no solution. Managers in this case may well have to come to terms with the fact that the best they can do in such a scenario is to cause as little further pain as possible.

Given that a firm is legally defined in terms of its stockholders, executives and employees are placed in a morally ambiguous position: both as paid agents entrusted with the task of dealing with competitors, and maximizing profits. However, as Solomon (1992: 8) notes, competition is just one of a number of relationships that firms have with each other, and with members of the wider community. Focusing solely on being competitive can be disastrous for the community, and indeed for the underlying co-operation that is necessary for any successful business activity. Indeed, the emphasis on short-term profit maximization in the closing decades of the twentieth century, characterized by corporate raids and hostile takeovers – in the name of stockholder rights – and the resultant defensive downsizing bloodbaths crippled many firms and injured hundreds of thousands of loyal employees (Solomon, 1992: 8 and Lamsa, 1999). Instead, it can be argued that by according greater attention to ethical concerns, the firm can secure its role as a vibrant and creative part of society over the medium and long term (Vinten, 2000).

Solomon (1992: 258) argues that without a sense of community and co-operation there would simply be no firm; indeed, without individual and corporate virtue (virtue being 'goodness' likely to benefit society as a whole), all success would be empty and transient. However, in any less than perfect organization or society, there is no guarantee as to what virtue theorists would refer to as the 'unity of virtues' (Solomon, 1992: 260). 'Good' conduct is dependent on the context, and different contexts may overlap or they may clash with one another. This problem of the unity of virtues can be seen as another example of the problem of ethical relativism we introduced above. If we accept that context has a very strong influence on what people perceive to be ethical behaviour, it is possible to see how, in some situations, people can become so tied to their jobs, or to their company's way of doing things, that they become incapable of looking beyond the narrow horizons of what their company or their manager defines as ethical. This may explain why a stockholder view of the firm and its responsibilities means that people can become focused on profit, or the 'bottom line', to the detriment of other considerations. One feature of organizational life is that hierarchies can result in people behaving out of character, or with insufficient thought about the ethical implications of their actions. The combination of a focus on the bottom line and unthinking obedience to superiors can be an unhappy one. More recently, however, and particularly in the wake of a number of high profile corporate scandals, there has been something of a reaction against unethical business practice (Daily *et al.*, 2003; Lamsa, 1999). This reaction encompasses many of the topic areas we introduce in this book. For example, we discuss these and other issues in the remaining chapters: the role of corporations in marketing their products to vulnerable audiences (Chapter 9), the impact of corporations on the environment (Chapter 5), and on working conditions for those in developing countries (Chapter 6); the need for ethics in accounting practices (Chapter 7) and attention to governance mechanisms (Chapter 3); discomfort with organizations treating their employees as a disposable commodity or 'human resource' (Chapter 8). Some theorists suggest that firms today are more conscious of the importance of taking ethical issues seriously (Solomon, 1992: 261–6). Barry describes how, '[t]he world of global business is marked by a remarkable and growing concern with ethics' (Barry, 2004: 195).

1.2.3   Practice and theory

Despite, or perhaps even because of, this recent flurry of interest, there is a danger that business ethics can simply be deployed as a whitewash, without any real changes in conduct (Freeman, 1991: 12). For example, there is little doubt that *claims* of environmental good conduct can help to sell products; however, there is often little monitoring of environmental claims that can be ambiguous or bogus. Examples of the former could include claims that wood or paper products are from sustainably managed plantations. However, this could conceal the fact that the plantations in question may have been planted in the place of clear-felled tropical forests, or that thirsty alien species of trees may disrupt natural rainfall catchment areas, with negative consequences for human and natural communities downstream. Other claims may simply be bogus: the consumer has little chance of discovering, for example, if tropical hardwood products are indeed from sustainable sources, or from the uncontrolled timber 'gold rushes' that are currently taking in place in countries such as Cambodia, Mozambique and Brazil. Similarly, there is a high likelihood that wildlife products – ranging from ivory to skins – may be sourced from international poaching rackets, whatever the vendor's protestations.

Beauchamp and Bowie (1997: 11) argue that there are three basic approaches to studying business ethics: the prescriptive (an attempt to formulate and defend basic moral norms); the descriptive (focusing on describing practices, moral codes and beliefs); and the conceptual study of ethics (involving analysing central ethical terms, such as right, good, justice, virtue in an attempt to distinguish what is moral from what is immoral). Some critics of prescriptive approaches to business ethics argue that rule-setting erodes the freedom of the individual and entails a degree of inflexibility that means we are insensitive to the particular features of an ethical problem. However, while it is undoubtedly correct to argue that any regulation erodes the freedom of the individual, there is little doubt that a number of practical measures to enforce ethical conduct have been of great benefit to humanity (Beauchamp and Bowie, 1997: 9). For example, the banning of the use of chlorofluorocarbons (CFCs) represents a major step towards undoing damage to the ozone layer.

To proponents of ethical relativism (to recap, these are people who believe that what counts as good or bad varies so greatly from society to society that there can be no ethical universals) moral rules are culturally specific. It follows, then, that any attempt to enforce universal ethical codes represents little more than a form of cultural imperialism (one society imposing its will on another). Some Asian critics of attempts to promote Western democracy have suggested that democracy is neither in the interests of, nor desirable in, certain Far Eastern societies. This viewpoint is most associated with the governments of China and Singapore. However, despite considerable variance in moral rules and what different communities may see as desirable, there is little doubt that the underlying principles of morality are often similar. It is generally recognized, for example, that sometimes the interests of the individual have to be sacrificed for the good of society as a whole. It therefore follows that – at least in some cases – a distinction can be drawn between relativism in terms of judgements about a particular situation, and relativism in terms of underlying standards (Beauchamp and Bowie, 1997: 10). In other words, people may differ on how ethical standards may be best met, but certain basic underlying norms may still be common to all societies. A controversial illustration of this may be that some features of family life are often considered cultural universals (for example, taboos on incest and illegitimacy, or male dominance) (Hendrix, 1993). None the less, it should be recognized that moral disagreements are inevitable – by their very nature they provoke disagreement and diverse opinions. Also, they may not always be resolvable, because of, among other things, a lack of information, lack of definitional clarity, and selective use of evidence: 'Though there is a sense in which ethical issues in business can, and must, be resolved, this is a very different proposition from suggesting that there will be one, definitive solution "out there" that will be accepted by everyone' (Morrell, 2004: 390).

However, whether one's starting point is ethical relativism, or a more universalist approach, there is little doubt that, even outside the basic family unit, certain strictures (or social taboos) underpin ethical conduct within specific social settings. This can be in the form of laws, unwritten rules, or various codes of conduct relevant across firms, industries or professions. In academic life, for example, there is a strong taboo against plagiarism. Any false or malicious allegation of plagiarism will irreparably damage a relationship, as any half-competent academic will know. This is an example of a strong universal professional taboo. Sometimes, though, questions relating to ethical behaviour are set down explicitly, or codified. In terms of the relationship between the law and ethics, we saw earlier that laws can facilitate ethical behaviour but they cannot ensure ethical conduct by all individuals, all the time. There is little doubt that a degree of self-policing may be desirable. For many years, a number of professions (such as law and accounting) have upheld sets of professional standards. However, in a rapidly changing global environment, several professions have increasingly battled to maintain professional reputations given the consolidation of the industry. The accounting industry is often singled out in this regard, since conflicts of interest can arise with some of the larger accounting firms who simultaneously offer consultancy and auditing services. In the 1990s, there was a string of high-profile scandals which highlighted specific cases of auditing shortcomings (Daily et al., 2003). The most infamous recent example of this was the case of Enron in the United States (McCall, 2004). The firm's auditors, Arthur Andersen, also offered managerial consulting services to Enron. This situation resulted in senior partners being allegedly complicit in covering up malpractices, leading to the latter's demise, with 'fundamentally unfair and inaccurate portraits' of the management accounts (Jennings, 2004: 1). 'Enron collapsed when the market lost confidence in it...loss of market confidence was not so much the cause of the collapse as a symptom of the long-term inflated reporting of assets and expected earnings...compounded by the passive compliance of the auditors' (Morrell and Anderson, 2006: 123). High-profile corporate scandals such as Enron have led critics to argue that the setting of ethical standards is too serious a business to be left to the professions, and that more ethical conduct can only be engendered through both an overhaul of existing legislation and a sea-change in popular attitudes.

There are indeed people who advocate sweeping and systemic change. Goodpaster argues that creeping moral disorder in society can only be checked if the respect for persons is placed at the centre of our notion of corporate community (quoted in Gilbert, 1991: 111). This should be incorporated in the overall strategic vision held by senior management, leavening out the demands of corporate self-interest, profits and the law, to be enacted out through managerial processes (Gilbert, 1991: 111). It can be argued that Goodpaster's vision is a somewhat limited one; a more comprehensive approach to ethics should also incorporate an underlying 'respect for persons' alongside the grand strategic vision. Such an underlying ethos would include the organizational rank-and-file, allowing room for a firm-wide dialogue on values and introspection by non-executives (Gilbert, 1991: 111). From this viewpoint, the modern firm is perceived as an arena, within which interacting individuals have the opportunity to reconcile their relationships. This arena is a forum for the exchange of ideas, and a place where different opinions are listened to because of a shared respect and commitment to some underlying ethical values.

1.2.4   What is ethics practice?

Singer rejects the notion of ethical relativism and instead suggests that we should 'do what increases happiness and reduces suffering' (1995: 5). As we shall see, this is a utilitarian stance on ethics. Before we discuss this more fully, it is worth examining his rejection of relativism in more detail. He suggests that ethical relativism can provide a justification for situations that seem to us intrinsically unfair; for example, the use of child labour. Ethical relativists would argue that child labour could be justified if a particular community or society believed that it was the right thing to do. This is a 'global' argument for the rejection of ethical relativism, but there are individual and personal arguments against it as well. For example, self-interested acts should surely be compatible with more broadly-based principles if they are to be thought of as ethical (Singer, 1995: 10). This means that there has to be some basic commitment to shared standards, or else we would have chaos, with each person justifying their own choices with reference to the relativist argument that 'there are no absolute rules, so everything and anything is permitted'.

In the end, because it is an applied discipline, ethics should be about deeds, not about sterile philosophical debates. Both Immanuel Kant and Adam Smith repeatedly emphasized that our day-to-day actions should be guided by enlightened self-interest and altruism – a concern for others (Freeman, 1991: 19). It is from this position that many writers – and most other philosophers of ethics – postulate their theories (Freeman, 1991). A central practical concern which many of these theorists share is that we should have a fairer and more just world. Many ethical problems are about trying to redress instances of unfairness and inequity. This inequity can be seen in the way that governments or regimes control power, and in the way that goods are unfairly distributed in society. It is also evident in how most people's chances of success are allocated to them at birth, and in the way that, across all nations, power is concentrated in the hands of a few. The desire to promote greater equity does not have to be about such grand or abstract issues, nor does it have to be based on the assumption that all individuals are equal and with equal abilities. Instead, acting ethically should mean that we work on the notion that all individuals should be given fair opportunities to realize themselves to the best of their potential (Singer, 1995: 16–17). A contemporary illustration of this might be in relation to debates about positive discrimination or affirmative action (for example, large organizations may seek to promote women from minority ethnic groups on the grounds that they are under-represented). Some forms of affirmative action can be justified regardless of whether the beneficiaries are of superior, inferior or equal ability to the bulk of the populace, and regardless of whether such actions lead to greater profit. In the case of the under-representation of women from minority ethnic groups, we could argue that some organizations are set up in such a way that prejudice is built into their corporate structure. Breaking down such entrenched barriers to equality is an ethical stance that should be pursued irrespective of whether or not there is a 'business case'.

1.3   Different philosophical approaches to business ethics

1.3.1   Key perspectives

Bowie (1991: 33) argues that there are two major theories of business ethics: deontology, founded on underlying rules, and utilitarianism, which sees ethical behaviour in terms of desired outcomes. In addition, a further three frames of reference have had increasing influence. The first, virtue ethics, is founded on the philosophies of the ancient world and in particular on the writings of Aristotle and Plato. The second explores ethics from the issue of basic personal rights. The third reference frame (which is really a loose cluster of viewpoints), postmodernism, would blame ethical failings on the Enlightenment's emphasis on rationality, and on the pursuit of 'progress' and 'advancement', regardless of the subjective human cost. Beginning with a discussion of deontology and utilitarianism, we shall move on to discuss virtue ethics, rights-based approaches and postmodernism.

1.3.2   Deontology

From the ancient Greek *deon*, meaning duty, deontology has its foundations in the works of Immanuel Kant (1724–1804). In his influential *Practical Reason*, Kant argued that we should 'impose on ourselves the demand that all our actions should be rational in form' (quoted in Burns, 2000b: 28). Kant suggested that there are certain rules of morality that are binding on all rational beings (he was most definitely an anti-relativist). He went on to say that an action is only morally right if you were willing to have everyone act in a similar way in a similar situation (Lamsa, 1999: 347). In other words, 'maxims should be universalized' (Burns, 2000b: 28). What the phrase 'maxims should be universalized' means is that each of us should act as though our choice would become a moral law for everyone else. Though it is sometimes summarized in a trite way as the 'golden rule' or a 'do unto others as you would have them do unto you'; Kant's ideas are far stronger than that. He is not simply suggesting we treat others as we would want ourselves to be treated in return. He goes a lot further, by placing an obligation on us that almost requires the actions of a saint. His golden rule is more like, 'behave towards others as if the whole world was watching you, and as if from that moment on the whole world would behave in exactly the same way for the rest of time'. This was something that should be applied to all actions (so it was categorical) and it was a 'must' statement (so it was an imperative). In what was another implication following from his categorical imperative, Kant stated that people must never be treated only as a means, but always as an end in themselves (Lamsa, 1999: 347; Beauchamp and Bowie, 1997: 30). Kantianism has some very powerful and stringent implications. It implies that one should act in an ethical way because it is one's duty, regardless of the consequences (Kitson and Campbell, 1996: 13). Kantianism also lays down obligations that – if followed – are strong enough not be self-defeating, solving the problem of destructive individual 'freeriding' (a problem that, as we have seen, plagues utilitarianism) in the face of co-operative action (Kitson and Campbell, 1996: 15).

Of course, moral problems in the real world are extremely complex. Above all, there is the problem of uncertainty, and what really constitutes right and wrong. A decision to downsize the workforce in a company may, for example, be a product of forces beyond the manager's control. It may work out as the best course of action for those staff members who are retained, yet it may also inflict great misery on those who are made redundant (Lamsa, 1999: 347). As Kant argues, human nature is ultimately fallible and it is impossible to ensure perfect outcomes 'from the warped wood of human nature' (Kant, 2000: 55). Lamsa suggests that one way out of such moral dilemmas is often to behave according to custom, which can provide useful moral benchmarks (1999: 347). The problem with this approach is that any reliance on custom brings us back to a relativist standpoint, when the whole point about Kant is that his rule – the categorical imperative – is universal.

For Kant, people's motives for their actions are critical. People should make the right decisions for the right reasons; if people are honest only because honesty pays, honesty itself is cheapened (Beauchamp and Bowie, 1997: 30). In other words, if a firm acts in an ethical fashion to help it market its goods and services, and hence to enhance its profits, then such actions are devoid of moral worth. Absolute morality is a categorical imperative, with social interaction and civil society being dependent on moral action by all (Kant, quoted in Burns, 2000b: 28). Or, to give another example, managers are not really acting ethically at all, if they are simply prompted to do so out of fear of prosecution or by consumer pressures. This emphasis on motives is an important one. It is not a distinction that would necessarily trouble those in the utilitarian camp; to the latter, any increase in overall happiness, regardless of the rationale underlying the actions that led to this, would be desirable.

Kant believed that actions should respect underlying moral law; a person's motives should reflect a recognition of a duty to act – and that morality provides a rational framework of rules, which constrains and guides people (Beauchamp and Bowie, 1997: 33; Kant, 2000: 54–5). While certainly detailed, Kant's writings are somewhat open-ended and incomplete; contemporary deontologists use Kant's notion of respect for persons as a ground for providing ethical theories of justice and rights, and for distinguishing the desirable from the undesirable (Beauchamp and Bowie, 1997: 33). Even so, it is difficult to overstate the importance that his ideas have had on moral philosophy, and Kant is often considered to be one of the greatest philosophers to have ever lived, in part because of his ideas about ethics.

Ultimately, deontology hinges on a system of rules. This has led critics to argue that deontology is overly inflexible, and that any moral ambiguities may only be resolved by finding ever more complicated or specific rules, and by ranking them in a hierarchical way, so that they do not conflict with one another (Singer, 1995: 3). However, empirical research would seem to indicate that many managers do approach ethical decision-making from what is effectively a deontological starting point (Menguc, 1998).

1.3.3 Utilitarianism

Utilitarianism is based on a moral principle (the utility principle), but it is not really founded on moral rules (the means). Instead, it is founded on goals (the ends) (Singer, 1995: 3). The classic utilitarian view sees an action as right if it results in the greatest net utility (happiness) for the most people possible. So, out of a choice of several options, the one that should be pursued is always the one that maximizes happiness and minimizes pain overall. There are some problems with this view, as we shall see, but the main thing to bear in mind is that utilitarianism is concerned with the consequences of a particular action; hence it is consequentialist. This is in contrast with those who would try always to follow set principles. A utilitarian would not have a rule of 'you should never lie', for example. To a utilitarian, lying may be commendable in some circumstances (if you refuse to tell a drunk and abusive mother where her baby is, for example), but it may be bad in many others. Utilitarians argue that the 'goodness' of one's actions is to be understood in terms of the consequences; ethical conduct seeks to ensure the 'greatest good for the greatest number' (Lamsa, 1999; Maciver and Page, 1961: 55). This is sometimes referred to as the 'happiness principle' or 'hedonic calculus' for balancing pleasure versus pain, the overall good of any action versus the costs entailed (Solomon, 1992: 90). As John Stuart Mill (1964: 5) argues, the 'utility or greatest happiness principle holds that actions are right... if they tend to promote happiness, wrong if they tend to produce the reverse of happiness. By happiness I mean pleasure, by unhappiness pain and the privation of pleasure'.

In other words, individuals should seek to act in such a way as to maximize the net social benefits accruing from their actions (Lamsa, 1999: 346); a practice is good or right if it leads to the best possible balance of good consequences over bad ones (Beauchamp and Bowie, 1997: 22). This will entail measuring possible benefits and harm as best one can, and then weighing these up (Lamsa, 1999: 346). As noted earlier, utilitarianism has had a profound impact on classical theories of economics (for example, on the writings of Adam Smith), and, because of this, and because of its applied, practical nature, it has become a perspective held by many business people (Lamsa, 1999: 347). Prominent utilitarian theorists include David Hume (1711–76), Jeremy Bentham (1748–1832) and J. S. Mill (1806–73). Perhaps the most influential contemporary utilitarian philosopher is the eminent Harvard professor, Peter Singer, who has argued that the practice of genuine utilitarianism involves considerable reflection if the good of society – and the biosphere – is to be maximized. Unlike more conservative writers who make extensive use of utilitarianism – such as Milton Friedman – Singer places a great deal of emphasis in his writings on social good, rather than concentrating exclusively on economic growth.

Thus utilitarianism centres on the assumption that, when faced with a choice, the 'right' thing is to do is to try ensure the best possible outcome for the bulk of people affected as long as it does not result in a disproportionate amount of suffering by a minority; nothing is wrong which allows this, and nothing is right which fails to do so. As Mill (1964: 6) argues, 'pleasure and freedom from pain are the only desirable ends'. However, one of the most difficult challenges facing utilitarians is what constitutes happiness. Bentham appears to simply have seen happiness as the avoidance of pain (Kitson and Campbell, 1996: 7). This may be true, but what is sometimes neglected is that Bentham was advocating welfare reform, and writing at a time when vast numbers of the population suffered from poor sanitation, hunger and disease. In those settings, the idea that everyone should be happy and free from pain was truly radical. Mill, who was also a remarkable radical, did take some care in identifying different degrees of happiness and in trying to forestall some of the vulgar critics of utilitarianism. He differentiated human happiness from that of animals, for example, and famously wrote 'better to be Socrates dissatisfied than a fool satisfied'. Both these sentiments should have pre-empted some of the more rudimentary criticism of utilitarianism – though the problem of defining happiness still remains. In terms of the business world, and in how utility is most frequently operationalized, modern neo-classical economists tend to refer to expected utility as the key mechanism that drives individual choice. Consumers (and organizations) are thought to behave in such a way that, for each of their choices, they try to maximize utility (Kitson and Campbell, 1996 : 7). This view of consumers as utility maximizing is at the root of the most influential models of human behaviour – in what is sometimes understood as the rational choice paradigm. It informs the agency view of the firm with which we opened this chapter, for example. In these models, though, what is crucial is that consumers (and organizations) are understood as being self-interested. The utility they seek to maximize is their own, whether as consumers, citizens, employees, shareholders or organizations competing in the marketplace This is not at the core of utilitarianism though, since that concerns itself with utility for the greatest number. So, to confuse these two accounts – utilitarianism as a moral principle, and rational choice as a descriptive or explanatory account of choice – is misleading.

To recap: for utilitarians, the individual is faced with the dilemma of choosing what will benefit those affected by her or his actions the most; the maximization of good and the minimization of evil (Beauchamp and Bowie, 1997: 22). Invariably, the individual is confronted with trade-offs. For example, a 'green' energy source such as hydroelectric power may inflict great damage on river systems. Utilitarians also hold on to the key concept of intrinsic good, expressed variously as pleasure/happiness/utility. The implication of this is that profit *per se* is not intrinsically good, but, if increasing the prosperity of shareholders may contribute to increasing overall happiness of society, then the overall consequences of increased profit may be so (Beauchamp and Bowie, 1997: 23). Of course, if these come at the expense of exploitation, increased inequity or harm to the environment, such costs would need to be offset against the benefits of increased profit. While it is problematic to measure these things on the same terms, the benefit of a genuinely rounded utilitarian perspective is that it should get us to concentrate on costs overall. Part of the problem with environmental pollution is that, historically, companies have not had to factor in fully the cost to the environment. Though they may be forced to pay for catastrophes such as oil spills or chemical leaks, historically they have not been made to pay for costs to less visible by-products of their manufacturing processes (the rise in CO_2, for example).

Although the basic precepts of utilitarianism are relatively simple, they in fact represent the foundation of a sophisticated ethical paradigm. The latter is often ignored by 'vulgar utilitarians', seeking to defend the neo-liberal orthodoxy (in other words, a belief in the beneficial powers of unrestrained free markets). Conversely, utilitarianism can be attacked because it is seen as simply being the basis of this orthodoxy. Utilitarianism is often simply seen as a cost–benefit analysis (Solomon, 1992: 90). Commonly seen as the father of classical economics, Adam Smith is depicted as a defender of the profit motive, independent of moral considerations (see Maciver and Page, 1961: 36–7; Evensky, 2001: 497). Indeed, several prominent proponents of unrestrained free markets, influenced by the works of Milton Friedman (see Friedman, 1997: 57) have argued that at times profoundly amoral approaches to doing business may be desirable (Evensky,

2001: 497). If one is to argue for an amoral approach, this would imply that any consideration of whether something is ethical or unethical is irrelevant. Instead, businesses should act within the law and leave ethics to other kinds of institutions (governments, charities). For example, Albert Carr argues that, in poker, deception and concealment are virtues, as opposed to kindness and open-heartedness, and no one thinks the worse of the poker player for this; the same should be true for the entrepreneur (Bowie, 1997: 97). This is a rather shaky argument (as many arguments from comparison are) since it depends on the legitimacy of the comparison. Poker players do not usually employ other people or risk other people's money or livelihoods – which an entrepreneur will do. One could also argue that murder, violence and the ability to smuggle drugs are virtues for the Mafia, but that does not mean they apply in other businesses (and organized crime is a lot more like a business than is a poker game).

Similarly, Theodore Levitt, a marketing scholar at the Harvard Business School, argues that embellishment and distortion may be desirable attributes in business; consumers do want not only products, but also the 'tantalizing imagery' held out through creative advertising and ambitious claims (quoted in Bowie, 1997: 98). However, while claiming to be true to the neo-liberal traditions, such viewpoints represent little more than crude parodies of what Adam Smith really has to say. In *The Theory of Moral Sentiments* Smith stresses the importance of co-operation and trust, and the indispensability of a basic degree of social solidarity. Surprisingly, Smith mentions the concept of the 'invisible hand' – the forces of the market that will ultimately result in equilibrium – only once in his classic work, *The Wealth of Nations* (Solomon, 1992: 86). Indeed, as Solomon (1992: 87) argues, Smith's view was that the individual and firm should strive to be good citizens, contributing to the overall good of society, in an age when innovation was often stifled. Smith saw people as being naturally social and benevolent; justice provided the main pillar of society; our self-interest was constituted within society, and 'tied to that system of virtues that makes us good citizens' (Solomon, 1992: 87–9).

Indeed, Smith does not reduce altruism to a kind of ethical egoism that supports utilitarian results. His view is a long way from that of the market-based free-for-all that is sometimes attributed to him. He would reject the view that each person is the best judge of his/her own interests, and that consequently people should look out for themselves – with market mechanisms in some way sorting it all out for the best (Maciver and Page, 1961: 42–3). Smith really argues (in his own words) that 'society cannot exist unless the laws of justice are tolerably observed, no social intercourse can take place among men who do not generally abstain form injury of another...Man, it has to be said has a natural love of society, and desires that the union of mankind should be preserved for its own sake, and though he himself was to derive no benefit from it' (quoted in Bowie, 1991). Indeed, it is increasingly recognized that 'a society that only pursues individual self-interest is inherently unstable' (quoted in Bowie, 1991). Unlike many of his later admirers, Smith remained convinced of the importance of society, and of the need to take conscious steps to promote a general social good; issues that are echoed in the works of contemporary utilitarian philosophers such as Singer.

Similarly, another early proponent of utilitarianism, J. S. Mill, stressed the importance of virtue and of the general social good, concerned about the prosperity and well-being of society as a whole, arguing that a simple utilitarian happiness calculus (in other words, trying to calculate the possible social good stemming from a particular action) was insufficient to ensure ethical behaviour (Solomon, 1992: 93). As we have seen, utilitarianism is often held up by neoliberals as 'the business philosophy', the hard-headed, essentially quantitative approach that seeks to balance the material costs and benefits of any action. This has led critics of utilitarianism, such as John Rawls, to charge that utilitarianism legitimates behaviour such as the rich consistently exploiting the poor, as long as the rich are collectively happier than the extent of collective suffering by the less endowed (Solomon, 1992: 91). However, to many utilitarians, the right of the bulk of society to a basic quality of life receives primary importance. It can be argued that the relentless pursuit of individual profit desensitizes business, and has the capacity to eclipse the most basic ethical considerations (Solomon, 1992: 94).

As with most philosophical paradigms, there are considerable divisions in the utilitarian camp as to how the general good of society should be advanced. One such division is between those who can broadly be referred to as 'act' utilitarians, and 'rule' utilitarians. The former hold that, in all situations, one should perform acts that lead to the greatest good (Beachamp and Bowie, 1997). In contrast, the latter believe that there should be certain rules governing human conduct that are not expendable, nor subject to changes by the demand of individual circumstances, a possible example being rules aimed at protecting life. It could be argued that the differences between 'rule' utilitarians, in particular, and deontologists is simply one of style; both are committed to some basic rules governing human conduct (Solomon, 1992: 253). However, deontologists are rather more inflexible when it comes to rules; the latter to utilitarians are only valuable if they can be demonstrated to serve a practical purpose (Solomon, 1992: 253). Critics of utilitarianism have often questioned whether happiness can be measured, and how the best action may be selected when confronted with a range of alternatives (Beauchamp and Bowie, 1997: 26). Utilitarian responses have included the argument that, in the end, the choice between a number of seemingly equally valid alternatives is one that confronts all ethical theories. Alternatively, it could be suggested that this criticism is a 'pseudo-problem': in the real world, people are capable of making rough and ready comparisons of values on a daily basis (Beauchamp and Bowie, 1997: 27).

A more serious criticism could be that decisions that would be most beneficial to the bulk of members of society – for example, denial of health insurance (or even state health care) for those with HIV/Aids – may inflict a great deal of misery on a few. This scenario would strike many of us as unjust, and indeed countries such as the United Kingdom, which have a universal healthcare system, seem to be based on alternative principles. However, even where there is a universal healthcare system, some rationing of resources has to take place. Agencies responsible for such rationing – such as the National Institute for Health and Clinical Excellence (NICE) in the UK – use broadly utilitarian principles when deciding whether a particular drug or intervention should be funded by the state. Another example would be where companies use poorly paid subcontracted labour in some production processes. This may be exploitation of the few subcontractors but it could be beneficial to the firm as a whole (and its shareholders), because it could mean that greater security for those employed in secure contracts in core areas of the firm's business. An example of the latter would be the following, cited by Legge (1996): 'The case that caught my eye was that of a 16-year-old who was paid £30 for a 40-hour week in a garage. When he inquired about compensation for losing the top of a finger at work, he was apparently told he was a 'subcontractor'.' This seems a horrendous injustice – how could one defend a company that exploits a vulnerable child and then fails to offer adequate compensation following an industrial accident? Cases such as this may strike us as lying beyond the pale and not be justifiable on any grounds. While in law it is likely that there is a definite value given to a person's finger, there may be no excuse for what happened in terms of net utility. We might feel uneasy if faced with a utilitarian formula with 'lost top of finger' on one side apparently being balanced out by 'continued savings with using subcontractors + decreased insurance and liability costs + minimal costs through health and safety practices'. The classic utilitarian response – that all entailed costs must be properly weighted – does not absolve utilitarians from the task of making some very hard choices. However, it is important to note that Mill and others advocate utilitarianism as a principle of last resort, to be used where all other moral frameworks fail to result in an agreed course of action. It is the most important principle, but that does not mean that other moral principles are ignored. Instead, Mill argues at the very beginning of his essay that utilitarianism should be understood as 'the rule for deciding between the various principles *when they conflict*' (emphasis added) (Mill, 1964: 5). This important qualification is ignored almost universally by critics of utilitarianism, but it means that in the case of the injured subcontractor, utilitarianism might never come into the picture because we could all agree that such a situation was deplorable. Given the many ways in which utilitarianism is attacked and vilified, it is hardly surprising that the world's leading living utilitarian thinker, Peter Singer, has had to contend with ongoing, sometimes violent, protests. These have been mounted not only by religious fundamentalists, but also by others who find his views on various questions, such as euthanasia, unacceptable for other reasons. As Singer himself concedes, utilitarianism lacks obligations strong enough to produce the outcomes that it calls for – unlike the case of a religious commandment, there is no external power sanctioning or monitoring behaviour. In reality, what may shape the outcome of events and the overall net utility can depend on whether others act selfishly or not (Singer, 1995: 7). In other words, ethical conduct by a few, or even the majority, can be eroded through others 'free-riding'. One example of this can be that companies who want to reduce their operating costs may discharge untreated waste into the environment. If only a few organizations do this, it can prejudice the attempts by other companies to improve the environment.

1.3.4   Virtue ethics

Virtue theories draw on the classic Hellenistic (that is, ancient Greek) tradition to provide some guidelines as to desirable social conduct (Beauchamp and Bowie, 1997: 38). Virtue theory takes into account the nature of the agent making the decision, and her/his cultural context (Aristotle, 1952: vi). Moreover, unlike, say, deontology, virtue theory seeks to get away from either rule-making, or near-rules. In terms of its emphasis on individual accountability, a key principle within virtue ethics can be traced back to Socrates' admonition 'know yourself', since it emphasizes reflection on one's actions and character. A second key feature of virtue ethics is the realization that action is grounded in a context – a social context, but also a temporal one. To see whether someone is virtuous, it is not enough to look at an individual action, but instead to study their life as a whole. Importantly, these two elements (personal responsibility, sense of context) imply a need to transcend traditional or static notions of what is right and wrong, and instead to approach ethical questions from a critical and ever-questioning standpoint (Burns, 2000a: 45–6). No matter how detailed or explicit moral rules are, a virtue theorist would argue that there is always a need to exercise some judgement to decide how they fit a specific case (Kitson and Campbell, 1996: 16).

For Aristotle, moral judgements are learnt and founded on acquired virtues (Aristotle, 1952: v). Virtues are not rules, but rather personal characteristics, tendencies to behave in one way or another, and influenced by habit. Aristotle suggested that one thing we should try to do is to avoid extremes and aim for moderation or a 'golden mean' between two vices. For example, he suggests that bravery lies between cowardice and recklessness (there is an element of judgement). There are no teachers of virtue, since it is not something that can be transferred. Instead, virtue is something that has to be in part infused from an entire community, in part learnt through direct experience, and in part learnt through reflection of life in works of art. Initially, virtues can be acquired through the process of socialization, but a mature person will learn to adjust his/her behaviour in the light of that person's experiences of the world and the exercise of reason. Whetstone (2001: 101) attempts to translate this framework into the contemporary world of work:

> The excellent manager overcomes pressures to compromise even newly acquired values, at times even opposing and then changing his or her habitual behaviour. Field research in the Southeast U.S. found that those managers most admired by peers and subordinates had successfully rejected values ingrained in them as youths in the period of racial segregation, adopting new habits of language and behavior toward other races.

The emphasis here on learning and sensitivity to changing contexts is one that Aristotle would have approved. Aristotle includes in his catalogue of virtues, among other things – courage, liberality, a sense of self-worth, gentleness, modesty, justice and wisdom. He argued that all of these were required in order to 'live well' (Kitson and Campbell, 1996: 17). Though they differed quite significantly in their moral philosophy (and on many other things), both Plato and Aristotle argued that the cultivation of virtuous traits of character represents the primary function of morality (Beauchamp and Bowie, 1997: 39). Virtue is not something that springs spontaneously from a social environment, but has to be nurtured (Aristotle, 1952: vi).

On the one hand, it could be suggested that, in the world of modern business – as opposed to classical Greece – this list of virtues is somewhat incomplete and requires supplementation. However, that is to ignore the historical context for the development of this form of ethics. Virtue ethics arose during the time of the first city-state, at the birthplace of modern democracy and in a society whose ideas of trade, statecraft and politics have become the cornerstone of Western civilization. Many of the struggles Plato and Aristotle discussed are as relevant today as they were 2,500 years ago. A sad truth is that, while our sophistication in technology and invention has grown exponentially in the intervening years, we appear to be still no further developed in terms of our moral sophistication. One could even argue that if latter-day managers based their conduct on Aristotle's list of virtues, this would solve many of the ethical problems facing modern business. To virtue theorists, 'right' actions are those actions taken by a genuinely virtuous person. All ethical actions, whether they are carried out within or outside the business environment, cannot hinge on absolute rules; at some stage, personal characteristics must take over. An important and ever-present question remains, however: how can virtue be achieved? To proponents of this philosophical tradition, expertise in being virtuous is something to be cultivated over a lifetime, with experience and reflection being necessary (Kitson and Campbell, 1996: 17) – people acquire virtues by acting virtuously and establishing habits that lead to good character. Having a virtuous character is something that is neither natural nor unnatural, but something that has to be cultivated (Beauchamp and Bowie, 1997: 38). Whether there is room for such critical reflection in today's 'runaway' world could be disputed, though one could also argue that such reflection could over time enable more efficient decision-making if it were simply an expression of character. To proponents of virtue theories, firms are only ethical if their actions are prompted by a due process of introspection as to what really is 'virtuous'. So, for example, the marketing of 'green' or 'fair trade' products would not constitute a virtuous act if the firm was motivated solely by wanting to pursue a profit rather than by an innate desire to 'be upstanding' or virtuous.

1.3.5   Rights-based approaches

The rights-based approach holds that individuals have certain basic entitlements. Some famous examples (taken from different contexts) are the right to free speech, to freedom of association, the right to form and join trade unions, the right to liberty, and the right to vote. It is worth noting initially that there is a difference between universal rights and those that are specific to a given community or society. Even within a single society or nation, the rights may not be extended to all members of that society. For example, in almost all nations the right to vote (also known as suffrage) was extended to women only after a political struggle. In Sweden, this happened comparatively early: women could vote in local elections in 1862 (though they had to wait until 1909 for the right to vote in general elections). However, women have only had the right to vote in certain cantons in Switzerland since 1971 (Heater, 2004). In many countries in the developed world, voting was restricted to those from certain classes and races. This echoed the unhappy situation in ancient Greece, where slaves and women were denied the right to be considered citizens. A final problem with the idea of relying on rights as a guide for ethical action is that even where there is a commitment to those basic rights, they may not necessarily be observed. Wherever someone has a right to something (free speech, liberty and so on) this implies that other members of that society – and the state as a whole – have a reciprocal or corresponding obligation. An individual's right to free speech means that others have a duty not to persecute someone for what they say. An individual right to liberty means that others have a duty not to deprive someone of their liberty.

Some readers may be able to see how the contrast between a situation where we have shared and universal rights versus a situation where rights are afforded to an elite or special community, links back to the earlier discussion in the chapter of the difference between ethical relativism and anti-relativism. If you believe that certain rights are inalienable (that is, cannot be transferred or forfeited) and inviolable (cannot be infringed or dishonoured) and furthermore that they are also universal (extend to every person), then you cannot be an ethical relativist. In this vein, some suggest straightforwardly that rights should, wherever possible, be upheld, including life, liberty, and a degree of freedom for people to do as they choose (Beauchamp and Bowie, 1997). To advocates of the rights-based approach, utilitarianism does not properly take rights and their non-violation into account (Nozick, 1984: 101). A classic question on this topic is whether it is acceptable to kill one person if that saves the lives of five (or ten, or a hundred, or a thousand) others? The utilitarian would seem committed to accepting the death of an individual (thereby violating their right to life) if this increased overall utility. Perhaps the most notable theorist on the rights-based approach is John Rawls. Writing at a time of civil unrest in America, Rawls was keen to have an alternative to utilitarianism. He could see a world where utility could be maximized, but some people (minority ethnic groups, women, the poor, the disabled, those with severe learning difficulties, and others) would still be sorely disadvantaged. Rawls was an advocate of the liberties of the individual (Sandel, 1984: 8). However, Rawls argued that inequalities in society are only justifiable if they can be shown to benefit the position of the worst-off (Rawls, 1984). This was in contrast to the more 'red in tooth and claw' liberalism of writers such as Hayek and Nozick: and before them, Bentham, the founder of utilitarianism.

This implies that poverty is not simply a function of inefficiency, incompetence or laziness; it is a social condition that needs to be examined and analysed (Parekh, 1982: 179). Where inequalities are patterned and reproduced, some people are likely to be able to exercise their basic rights more strongly than others. This makes these supposedly basic rights worthless. If there is not the right to equality of opportunity, this compromises the way in which the goods are distributed in society. There will always be some who are unjustly worse off unless there is the right to such equality of opportunity. Rawls advocated various steps designed to bring about a more just society. In *Justice as Fairness*, his final work, Rawls suggested that we could only bring about a just society under the conditions of a form of market socialism, or where a great many members of society owned property (Rawls, 2001). Rawls' approach is a departure from utilitarianism and it is fair to say that it is probably closer to the Kantian notions of enshrining principles or categorical imperatives – where our basic duty is to offer the greatest help to those who are most severely disadvantaged (Lamsa, 1999). What is suggested is that society should be structured so as to minimize violations of rights. In effect, what is suggested is a 'utilitarianism of rights; violations of rights (*to be minimized*) would replace total happiness as the required end state'.

An alternative perspective is as follows. The rights of others determine constraints on actions (because each right implies a reciprocal duty) (Nozick, 1984). In order to have individual liberty it is necessary to reduce to a minimum the interference of the state (Beauchamp and Bowie, 1997). This frame of reference is based on the assumption that individual rights are paramount; the principal function of the state should simply be to ensure that such rights are not infringed. One political conclusion that seems to follow from this position is that we pursue the 'ultraminimalist' state favoured by Friedman and other neoliberal economists. If we pursue liberty above all else, and advocate the barest minimum of intervention by the state, then there will be few constraints on the behaviour of individuals – but also little constraining the behaviour of firms as actors within a market. The same logic that suggests the state should not interfere with individual liberty also seems to imply that the state should impose unnecessary regulation on businesses and instead allow firms to compete in a market that is as free as possible from interference. It is true that there is a distinction between the social, political and economic implications of a commitment to liberty (though, confusingly, they can all be referred to as libertarianism, or liberalism). None the less, in the context of business ethics, those who are strong proponents of libertarian approaches tend to suggest that the ethical duties of the firm are also somewhat minimalist. Shareholders may have a right to a fair return on their investment, and employees may have a right that their employment contract be correctly implemented, and so on – but these rights are only defined minimally. If they were defined at length, there would be a reciprocal duty on firms that would restrict their freedom to compete in the marketplace. As long as one plays by the rules of the game (that is, is legally compliant) then businesses have only one responsibility: to make a profit for their shareholders. The rights-based approach provided much of the philosophical underpinnings

for the policies of the Thatcher (in the UK) and Reagan (in the USA) governments of the 1980s. Reflecting this, legislation protecting social collectives – such
as trade unions – was pared back, though there was an increase in legislation governing the rights of individual employees. None the less, a genuinely rounded,
rights-based ethical approach should call for the protection of the interests of
individuals against the powers of corporations. For example, the discharge of
waste by agricultural enterprises may infringe on the property rights of others downstream (Wetzstein and Centner, 1992). However, the way in which
rights are defined in terms of legislation may result in a formal commitment to
a rights-based approach that amounts to little in practice. One example – again
relating to environmental pollution – is that of recent, ineffectual 'reforms' governing groundwater contamination in the United States (Wetzstein and Centner,
1992).

1.3.6   Postmodern ethics

Critics of postmodernism have argued that this school of thought is fundamentally aethical, representing a fractured and localist rejection of universal standards
governing behaviour (Lash and Friedman, 1992: 8). It may be misleading even
to suggest that there is a coherent body of ideas we can refer to as a 'postmodern'
approach to ethics. Instead, different writers may approach the subject of ethics
from different vantage points, and grouping them together may be inappropriate. Postmodernism is perhaps best understood as a way of thinking about the
world, and the nature of truth and claims by different communities to truth. It
is also a reaction against modernism – an historical period associated with claims
to progress and enlightenment based on reason and the application of science.
The horrors of the twentieth century showed many that these claims were hollow, as instruments developed by science and reason were deployed in ways too
unpleasant to describe. A postmodern perspective involves scrutinizing beliefs as
to what constitutes reality (also known as ontological beliefs), as well as beliefs
about what constitutes knowledge (also known as epistemological beliefs): these
underpin claims to a better world.

It is misleading and a contradiction in terms to call postmodernism a theory,
or to refer to postmodernism as a school. This is because leading writers such as
Lyotard, Baudrillard, Derrida and Foucault (each closely associated with postmodernism) all reject the idea (in different ways) that there are theories or truths
or schools that are independent of history. The belief that what counts as knowledge, certainty, and even reality, is something local and grounded in a particular
community is sometimes expressed as a denial of 'transcendent' truths. For postmodernists, truth is something that is a product of a particular social order
(see Cartoon 1). Lyotard (1984) offers a neat, if somewhat cryptic definition
of postmodernism as incredulity towards metanarratives.

In other words, postmodernism involves suspicion and mistrust of wide-
ranging belief systems (such as Marxism or any religious faith), and scepticism
about the claims produced from within social structures (such as bureaucracies,

People accept as TRUTH themes, which were BUILT up at a CERTAIN MOMENT OF HISTORY ...this can be criticized and DESTROYED

Cartoon 1   Michel Foucault – postmodern guru

or large, multinational corporations). This scepticism – or incredulity towards metanarratives – goes beyond the claims of political philosophies, religions or organizational forms. It means not only that grand systems or structures are suspect, but that what we take to be true anywhere depends on the social and historical setting (Morrell, 2002). Thus any and all truths are partial and local (including presumably any truths about postmodernism?). This would seem to put postmodernists (again, assuming we can refer to them all as one) firmly in the ethical relativist camp. It would certainly be a mistake to suggest that because postmodernism denies transcendent truths, then 'anything goes' for postmodern ethical theorists. Not many people do make such a crass mistake, but relativism remains a problem for postmodernists, as we discuss below. However, it is important to note that some postmodern scholars have provided the most powerful and compelling criticisms of unethical practices.

For example, postmodernism shares with conservative philosophers such as Michael Oakeshott (1983) a fundamental distaste for universal notions of rationality. The rationality metanarrative, to use Lyotard's phrase again, has led to the prioritization of 'development and progress' irrespective of the human costs involved. Some of the worst atrocities in human history have only been realizable because of technological 'progress'; that is, built on the application of reason in science. Moreover, there is often a very narrow interpretation of what rationality means in the context of human behaviour. That narrow interpretation is open to challenge, as we have already discussed, when looking at contemporary economists' explanations of choice. Many of the models used in business to predict both individuals' and firms' behaviour are based on a view of 'rational choice', where rationality is understood as the desire of individual agents to maximize the benefits accruing to themselves. This interpretation is based on an idea of self-interest and it serves to erode the very moral standards that would make other forms of progress (social, philanthropic, ethical) viable and sustainable (Friedman, 1992: 356).

To Baumann (1993), the unprecedented human rights abuses of the twentieth century, coupled with widespread environmental degradation reflects the limitations of modernist ethical theories. He argues that, whether these theories are utilitarian or deontological, rigid notions of reason or general good have been imposed. These notions take little account of diversity and the real needs of the mass of society at a local level. Postmodernists would argue that the modern work organization is one setting where self-serving truths evolve that conceal structures of domination and the interests of those in power. An organization may represent little more than an 'apparatus of capture', a stultifying environment 'overcoding' rationalist norms, repressing individual creativity and expressiveness (Deleuze and Guattari, 1988: 380).

In contrast to the assumption of ultimate social progress that underlies much of the modernist project, postmodernism makes no claims as to the inevitability of a better life. Deleuze and Guattari (1988: 380) assert that it is possible to cast aside the universalistic rationalist codes governing conduct. Individuals or micro-collectives can, and will, continue to seek to escape the oppressive power of the status quo. Instead, they can construct their own, particularistic ethical realities more appropriate to their needs. There are potential problems for postmodernist thinkers that arise from the nature of this approach. Two key ones are *ethical relativism* and *ethical conservatism* (Morrell, 2002). We have discussed the problem of relativism at length in this chapter, but it can be thought of with respect to postmodernism in particular in this way. If we believe that what counts as reality is socially constructed, and that truth is local and partial, then there is no transcendent basis for judgement. How, then, can there be any basis for describing behaviour, an individual or a firm as ethical or unethical? A consequent, related problem is conservatism. Because postmodernism does not offer any scope for transcendent judgements, there is no firm basis for undertaking change. Relatedly, postmodernists may have very little to offer managers seeking guidelines or tools for dealing with ethical dilemmas. Rather, they may argue that contemporary society, and individual work organizations, are inherently repressive environments; none the less, the potential for liberatory action at the grassroots level persists.

1.4   Summary

The field of business ethics seeks to apply the tools of philosophy to understand the day-to-day ethical challenges facing modern work organizations.

After highlighting a number of general ethical quandaries, we have explored and highlighted several distinct philosophical traditions that provide insights of relevance to the modern firm. These included discussion of the following: virtue ethics (with its ties to the traditions of ancient Greece and the emergence of the city-state, where context and individual responsibility are key themes); utilitarian ethics (with its emphasis on the utility principle – a consequentialist doctrine that can be treated somewhat simplistically, but where various refinements to the understanding of the term happiness suggest it can lead to sophisticated debate); deontological ethics (Kant's categorical imperative being the clearest and best-known example); rights-based approaches and the reciprocal obligations that follow from rights (libertarianism in politics and the economy); and postmodernist ethics (incredulity to metanarrative through a critique of contemporary social life rather than by imposing explicit ethical guidelines). We suggest that each of the approaches highlighted has some merit in providing practical analytical tools to help in understanding the nature of contemporary ethical dilemmas, be they in terms of core internal managerial functions or relations with the broader community, or, indeed, the natural environment.

Discussion question

Which ethical perspective, do you think, is most relevant to the world of business? Give reasons for your answer.

References

Aristotle. 1952. *Politics*. London: Everyman.

Arvey, R. D. and Sackett, P. R. 1993. 'Fairness in Selection: Current Developments and Perspectives', in N. Schmitt and W. Borman (eds) *Personnel Selection*. San Francisco: Jossey-Bass.

Barry, A. 2004. 'Ethical Capitalism', in W. Larner and W. Walters (eds) *Global Governmentality*. London: Sage, pp. 195–211.

Bauman, Z. 1993. *Postmodern Ethics*. Oxford: Blackwell.

Baumhart, R. 1961. 'How Ethical Are Businessmen?', *Harvard Business Review*, 38: 6–31.

Beauchamp, T. and Bowie, N. 1997. 'Ethical Theory and Business Practice', in T. Beauchamp and N. Bowie (eds), *Ethical Theory and Business*. Upper Saddle River, NJ: Prentice Hall.

Bowie, N. 1991. 'Business Ethics as a Discipline: The Search for Legitimacy', in R. Freeman (ed.), *Business Ethics: The State of the Art*. Oxford: Oxford University Press.

Bowie, N. 1997. 'New Directions in Corporate Social Responsibility', in T. Beauchamp and N. Bowie (eds), *Ethical Theory and Business*. Upper Saddle River, NJ: Prentice Hall.

Burns, R. 2000a. 'Enlightenment', in R. Burns and H. Raymond-Pickard (eds), *Philosophies of History*. Oxford: Blackwell.

Burns, R. 2000b. 'On Philosophising History', in R. Burns and H. Raymond-Pickard (eds), *Philosophies of History*. Oxford: Blackwell.

Deleuze, G. and Guattari, F. 1988. *A Thousand Plateaus*. Minneapolis, Minn.: University of Minnesota Press.

Daily, C. M., Dalton, D. R. and Cannella, A. A. 2003. 'Introduction to Special Topic Forum Corporate Governance: Decades of Dialogue and Data', *Academy of Management Review*, 28,3: 371–82.

Evensky, J. 2001. 'Adam Smith's Lost Legacy', *Southern Economic Journal*, 67,3: 497–517.

Freeman, R. E. 1991. 'Business Ethics as an Academic Discipline', in R. Freeman (ed.), *Business Ethics: The State of the Art*. Oxford: Oxford University Press.

Friedman, M. 1997. 'The Social Responsibility of Business Is to Increase Its Profits', in T. Beauchamp and N. Bowie (eds), *Ethical Theory and Business*. Upper Saddle River NJ: Prentice Hall.

Ghoshal, S. 2005. 'Bad Management Theories Are Destroying Good Management Practices', *Academy of Management Learning and Education*. 4,1, 75–91.

Gilbert, R. 1991. 'Respect for Persons, Management Theory and Business Ethics', in R. Freeman (ed.), *Business Ethics: The State of the Art*. Oxford: Oxford University Press.

Heater, D. B. 2004. 'Citizenship: The Civic Ideal in World History, Politics and Education', Manchester: Manchester University Press.

Hendrix, L. 1993. 'Illegitimacy and Other Purported Family Universals', *Cross-Cultural Research*, 27,3–4: 212–31.

Jennings, M. M. 2004. 'Incorporating Ethics and Professionalism into Accounting Education and Research: A Discussion of the Voids and Advocacy for Training in Seminal Works in Business Ethics'. *Issues in Accounting Education*, 19,1: 7–26.

Jones, C., Parker, M. and ten Bos, R. 2005. *For Business Ethics*. Kondon: Routledge.

Kant, I. 2000. 'Progress in History', in R. Burns and H. Raymond-Pickard (eds), *Philosophies of History*. Oxford: Blackwell.

Kitson, A. and Campbell, R. 1996. *The Ethical Organization*. London: Macmillan.

Lamsa, A-M. 1999. 'Organizational Downsizing – an Ethical versus Managerial Viewpoint', *Leadership and Organizational Development Journal*, 20,7: 345–53.

Lash, S. and Friedman, J. 1992. 'Subjectivity and Modernity's Other', in S. Lash and J. Friedman (eds), *Modernity and Identity*. Oxford: Blackwell.

Legge, K. 1996. 'Morality Bound', *People Management*, 2,25: 34–7.

Lyotard, J.-F. 1984. *The Postmodern Condition: A Report on Knowledge*, Manchester: Manchester University Press.

Maciver, R. and Page, C. 1961. *Society*. London: Macmillan.

McCall, J. J. 2004. 'Assessing American Executive Compensation: A Cautionary Tale for Europeans', *Business Ethics: A European Review*, 13,4: 243–54.

Menguc, B. 1998. 'Organizational Consequences, Marketing Ethics and Sales-force Supervision: Further Empirical Evidence', *Journal of Business Ethics,* 17,4: 333–52.

Mill, J. S. 1964. *Utilitarianism, Liberty and Representative Government.* London: Everyman.

Morrell, K. 2002. 'Postmodernism/Postmodernity', in T. Redman and A. Wilkinson (eds), *The Informed Student's Guide to Human Resource Management.* London: Thomson, pp. 199–200.

Morrell, K. 2004. 'Socratic Dialogue as a Tool for Teaching Business Ethics', *Journal of Business Ethics,* 53: 325–31.

Morell, K. and Anderson, M. 2006. 'Dialogue and Scrutiny in Organisational Ethics', *Business Ethics,: A European Review,* 15,2: 117–29.

Nozick, R. 1984. 'Moral Constraints and Communicative Justice', in M. Sandel (ed.), *Liberalism and its Critics.* Oxford: Basil Blackwell.

Oakeshott, M. 1983. *On History and Other Essays.* Oxford: Blackwell.

Parekh, B. 1982. *Contemporary Political Thinkers.* Oxford: Martin Robinson.

Rawls, J. 1984. 'The Right and Good Contrasted', in M. Sandel (ed.), *Liberalism and its Critics.* Oxford: Basil Blackwell.

Rawls, J. 2001. *Justice as Fairness: A Restatement.* Cambridge, Mass.: Harvard University Press.

Ridley, M. 1996. *The Origins of Virtue: Human Instincts and the Evolution of Cooperation.* London: Penguin.

Sandel, M. 1984. 'Introduction', in M. Sandel (ed.), *Liberalism and Its Critics.* Oxford: Basil Blackwell.

Singer, P. 1995. *Practical Ethics.* Cambridge: Cambridge University Press.

Solomon, R. 1992. *Ethics and Excellence: Co-operation and Integrity in Business.* Oxford: Oxford University Press.

Vinten, G. 2000. 'Corporate Governance: The Need to Know', *Industrial and Commercial Training,* 32,5: 173–8.

Whetstone, T. 2001. 'How Virtue Fits within Business Ethics', *Journal of Business Ethics,* 33,2: 101–14.

Wetzstein, M. and Centner, T. 1992. 'Regulating Agricultural Contamination of Groundwater through Strict Liability and Negligence Legislation', *Journal of Environmental Economics and Management,* 22,1: 1–11.

The ethical business and the business of ethics

Chapter objectives

- To understand the approach to studying ethics taken in this book.
- To be able to discuss the account in this chapter of ethics as 'science of the good'.
- To be able to identify some of the advantages and disadvantages of:

    (i) a theory-based approach to business ethics;
    (ii) a case-based approach; and
    (iii) a situated approach (that is, the approach taken here).

- To discuss the problem of assigning responsibility in the context of complex social problems.

2.1 Introduction

In the previous chapter we introduced some of the most influential ideas in ethical theory. Having done so, it is important to say where we feel that this book stands in relation to those ideas. Although the previous chapter offers some powerful conceptual tools that can be used to study the cases we present, it is not enough by itself. This is because we need to suggest ways in which readers of the rest of the chapters in the book can apply these conceptual tools. In our experience, too many text books on business ethics assume there is a seamless connection between the kinds of ethical theory we have discussed, and the world of business. This implies there is a straightforward connection between the sort of fundamental moral philosophy we introduced in the Chapter 1 (virtue ethics, utilitarianism, rights-based approaches, deontology and postmodern ethics); and some cases from the business world. What we suggest in this chapter is that this connection is not really straightforward at all. Instead, there needs to be some kind of conceptual bridge from the abstract world of ethical theory to the more concrete world of ethics in particular settings. In trying to provide such a bridge, we also need to provide a justification for our approach to studying business ethics. In the subsequent chapters, we begin with introductory case studies that set the scene for that chapter. Here we want to begin with a really interesting extract from an influential philosopher whom we have not yet discussed. This extract takes the place of an opening case study, and it forms the basis for this chapter. It is our conceptual bridge between the abstract world of ethical theory, and the concrete world of ethics in business.

Case study

Introductory extract

What makes one regard philosophers half mistrustfully and half mockingly is not that one again and again detects how innocent they are – how often and how easily they fall into error and go astray, in short their childishness and childlikeness – but that they display altogether insufficient honesty, while making a mighty and virtuous noise as soon as the problem of truthfulness is even remotely touched on. They pose as having discovered and attained their real opinions through the self-evolution of a cold, pure, divinely unperturbed dialectic [dialectic here means argument]...while what happens at bottom is that a prejudice, a notion, an 'inspiration', generally a desire of the heart sifted and made abstract, is defended by them with reasons sought after the event – they are one and all advocates who do not want to be regarded as such, and for the most part no better than cunning pleaders for their prejudices, which they baptize 'truths'. (Nietzsche, 1886, Book 1, ch.5)

This passage is taken from Nietzsche's *Beyond Good and Evil*, first published in 1886, but despite being over 120 years old, the implications of what Nietzsche says in this passage are still dynamite. He is scornful of, and abusive about, an entire community that has shaped all our ideas of ethics. He suggests that moral philosophers are people whom we regard 'half mistrustfully and half mockingly' for their naïve clumsiness – the ease with which they fall into error and their 'childishness and childlikeness'. Nietzsche doesn't even suggest that we *should* be scornful of these theorists – for him it is something that is inevitable and that has already happened: he begins with 'what *makes* one regard philosophers'. This scorn is an inevitable response not simply because of these philosophers' stupidity, but because they are hypocrites who display 'insufficient honesty' themselves while sounding off about honesty to others. They 'pose' as rational and above self-interest when underlying their view of moral philosophy is basic prejudice, 'a desire of the heart sifted and made abstract', and then defended 'with reasons sought after the event'. Damningly, he describes them as 'cunning pleaders for their prejudices, which they baptize "truths" '. What are we to make of this, and how is it relevant to *The Ethical Business*?

Some readers may recognize that Nietzsche's hostile scepticism towards truth claims has very strong connections with ideas that we described towards the end of the previous, introductory chapter as being common to postmodern ethics. Nietzsche is sometimes regarded as the originator of postmodern thought. What is striking in his moral philosophy is that (with some exceptions) he displays such contempt for those philosophers who had gone before him (see Cartoon 2).

Cartoon 2   Friedrich Nietzsche – scepticism personified

We shall show how Nietzsche has a particularly hostile fascination with the ancient Greek philosopher Socrates, but he also dismissed utilitarianism with sneering sarcasm as a 'profoundly erroneous moral doctrine that is celebrated especially in England' (Nietzsche, 1882/1974: 1(4)). He said of the categorical imperative (Kant's idea that we also discussed in the previous chapter), 'this term tickles my ear and makes me laugh' (4(335)). These extracts suggest that what Nietzsche offers us is less a basis for a conceptual bridge joining moral philosophy to practice, but rather something that is like an impenetrable barrier of scorn and derision. However, his derision and scepticism can be cause for hope.

There is one benefit of a denial of absolute standards and authority figures, which is that it imposes a personal responsibility on us when it comes to making ethical choices. This applies when reading the cases in this book, but also to us in advocating a particular approach in *The Ethical Business*. There are a number of ways of providing an introduction to ethical theory. In this chapter we shall outline the two most popular traditions for doing this, and describe why the approach we take in this book is different. Importantly too, we shall try to argue that our approach has some advantages in comparison with these two traditions. In a way that is consistent with the first edition of *The Ethical Business* (Mellahi and Wood, 2003), this introductory chapter illustrates how we understand ethics not as a separate activity or specialism, but as something that is of immediate relevance in different 'arenas of action': marketing, human resource management, accounting and finance, supply chain management and so on. We refer to the business of ethics in this chapter, but by that we do not mean that ethics is a commercial enterprise; instead, we are trying to signal that ethics is an applied activity. For us, as pleaders for our own prejudices, ethics is fundamentally a practical endeavour and one that is rooted in human experience. To respond to the challenge that Nietzsche lays down, we wish to tackle the problem of truthfulness as we see it, since that is what underpins our understanding of ethics and ethical theory. This struggle is at the heart of the theoretical foundation for this book. It should result in our offering students and other readers a clear place to stand in relation to ethics and business. As a first step, we want to offer another definition of ethics. This definition is consistent with the broader discussion of ethics in the previous chapter. Importantly, though, we see it as one that is relevant to our purposes and that allows us to build a conceptual bridge from the world of ethical theory to the world of business. So, we would suggest that – with some important qualifications – ethics can be understood as the 'science of the good'. In *The Ethical Business* we try to explore what that means in a number of the different arenas of action. Chapter 1 offered an introduction to some of the most influential philosophical frames of reference that we typically take to make up 'ethics'. This chapter says more about how we propose to link these to the cases and contexts discussed in this book.

2.2   The science of the good?

Like any brief definition of such a rich and complicated topic as ethics, the phrase 'science of the good' does need some unpacking. For a start, the word 'science' is what we might call a 'loaded' term. In colloquial English, science is associated with the disinterested search for truth, and with certainty. Indeed, the Latin origin of the term is 'to know' (scire). The idealized picture of the scientist as a humble seeker after truth draws on notions of innocence and impartiality for its power, but in the physical and social sciences, and also in moral philosophy – just as Nietzsche suggests – this picture conceals self interest and other sorts of bias. Scientific research, like any social practice, is influenced by, indeed at times totally governed by, issues of politics and power. The very claim to science – as an objective standard is an ideological one (that is, one that is based on a particular set of beliefs about what should be done). Another way of expressing this is that, rather than being in any sense independent or objective or value-free, the claim to be pursuing science is based on particular values (Thorpe, 2001). To illustrate this, and to show how the simple term science (and our definition) is 'loaded', consider the following two questions: (i) Who says what counts as science?; and (ii) Who says what counts as good? These each highlight some of the baggage with which the term science (and by extension, our definition 'science of the good') comes loaded. In different ways, they point to underlying issues of power and authority. These simple questions not only suggest there are potential problems with our brief definition – of ethics as science of the good – they trace fault lines between different justifications for people's behaviour.

Each atrocity from the twentieth century had its advocates, with their own justifications and claims to truth. These and the ongoing horrors of the twenty-first century should teach us to be sceptical about any claims to truth or certainty when it comes to justifying people's behaviour. Nietzsche's call to recognize the 'problem of truthfulness' can be seen as a fundamental scepticism that is a powerful rejection of any claims to certainty. Claims to certainty often sanction the use and abuse of political power. We know from past examples of genocide that some groups have relied on what were presented as scientific explanations for why different races should be treated differently – these kinds of explanations were what Lyotard referred to as metanarratives (grand stories about how the world is and should be, as discussed in the previous chapter). Similar claims to certainty may be based on what some people identify as religious truth. More sweepingly, any one group's 'truth' may be unpalatable to others if it is used to justify behaviour that can be thought of as unethical. Slavery was justified on both religious and scientific grounds, for example. Some atheistic (rejecting belief in God or gods) regimes have tried to justify horrendous acts by appealing to the very philosophers we refer to most in this chapter (Socrates, Plato, Aristotle and Nietzsche). For example, in Nazi Germany, elements of Nietzsche's work were bastardized in support of a virulent strain of racist nationalism that he himself as an anti-nationalist would have found repugnant.

However, Aristotle (5th century BCE) condoned slavery, and for himself, Socrates and Plato it would have seemed part of the natural order of society (Kraut, 2002). We should be careful, then, that we may be only a step away from trying to claim certainty or superior knowledge by using the label science, or by invoking authorities whom we want to use in support of our definition and the project in this book. The extract from Nietzsche suggests that even the apparently cold logic that underpins frameworks of moral philosophy is influenced by visceral (gut) prejudice, 'a desire of the heart sifted and made abstract'. This charge of prejudice also applies to us as the authors of this book. This means it should encourage critical engagement from our readers with our approach. Part of this should include scepticism with the way that we have 'recruited' authoritative figures from ethical theory to our cause.

We are certainly aware that some of our academic colleagues will balk at us including the term science in a definition of ethics. Why, then, despite all these concerns and problems, do we want to stick with science of the good as our definition for ethics? Well, if we want to overcome the initial prejudice which that definition could arouse, then to explain this we need to go back to the original author of the phrase 'science of the good'. For Aristotle, who first used the phrase in a book called the *Nicomachean Ethics*, science consisted in looking at how the natural world and the social world are organized. Aristotle believed that all our knowledge ultimately came from direct experience of the world, but that it was possible to develop systematic and logical accounts of that knowledge. In that sense, science was the systematization and rigorous development of the lessons from that direct experience. It was a pursuit and a practical activity. These basic aspects of Aristotle's account of science are still very close to our contemporary understanding of science and the scientific method. However, when considering what Aristotle meant in relation to the 'science' of ethics he goes a little further than this sense of the scientific method that we still hold on to today. To develop the basis for a science of the good, he believed we had to start by looking at what makes people unique (for example, in seeing how we are different from animals) and then try to develop an account of excellent character, or *virtue*. This had to be rooted in accounts of behaviour or practical activity. In addition, when it comes to understanding what Aristotle means by 'the good' (the second half of our definition), he believed that behaviour needed to be studied in a given context to assess whether it was ethical. This was more than a matter of applying pure reason, but it required judgement in the face of experience, or what is typically translated as perception. So, while Aristotle believed that in principle there was one perfect way of attaining virtue, in what he called the pursuit of the good life, he felt that it was impossible in practice to have definitive rules for what were good (virtuous) or bad (vicious or un-virtuous) actions. Using the example of when it is appropriate to be angry, in the *Nicomachean Ethics*, Aristotle acknowledges that a definitive rule is not possible and that we cannot say in the abstract whether being angry is a good or a bad thing:

> this is no doubt difficult, and especially in individual cases; for it is not easy to determine both how and with whom and on what provocation and how long one should be angry; for we too sometimes praise those who fall short [that is, stay calm] and call them good-tempered, but sometimes we praise those who get angry ... up to what point and to what extent a man must deviate [from a normal mood] before he becomes blameworthy it is not easy to determine by reasoning, any more than anything else that is perceived by the senses; such things depend on particular facts, and the decision rests with perception. (*Nicomachean Ethics*, II, 9)

So, it may well be appropriate to get angry if someone steals your car or attacks you in the street, but if you deviate too much from a normal mood of calmness in response to minor annoyances – for example, your pen runs out of ink, or somebody pronounces your name wrongly – then you are not demonstrating an excellent character. Feelings of anger are likely to influence your behaviour towards others and to prevent you acting reasonably. Since ethical behaviour is a combination of intellect (what truly makes us human) and the emotions (what we share with other animals), both of these need to be in harmony to act virtuously.

2.3   Business ethics, and the business of ethics

Aristotle also believed that ethics should not be treated as something that was a separate discipline, but instead as something that was integrated with his theories of how society should be governed. So, for example, it features strongly in his book *Politics*, and in his account of the role of art in human experience in his essay, *Poetics*. One problem with the phrase 'business ethics' is that it tends to imply 'a very narrow definition of what counts as "the ethical"' (Jones *et al.*, 2005: 5). In this book, we do not and cannot claim any sort of ownership of business ethics, nor do we claim definitive knowledge of what counts as the ethical. Instead, we examine specific contexts, or what we have called arenas of action, where we look at ethical issues. Rather than think about business ethics – the subject – we are interested in the business of ethics – the activity. Playing with the word 'business' in this way is helpful because it is provocative, and also perhaps because it helps to shake off some of the prejudices and assumptions that Nietzsche suggests we all struggle with when thinking of baptized 'truths'. In addition, it also moves us further away from the established and narrow senses of 'business' that can lead to a narrow or shrunken account of the ethical. At the same time, in considering the business of ethics, we want to mark a move away from the most popular ways of discussing business ethics and redirect attention to problems in practice and in particular domains. This approach is informed by Aristotle's account of science, just as our definition was of ethics as the 'science of the good'.

Aristotle's emphasis on human activity and experience was a marked point of departure from his contemporary Plato (5th century BCE) (Plato, 1956, 1974, 1993). Plato believed that the good (the ethical) was an abstract, divine and perfect ideal; a universal truth that we could access through argument and logical reasoning. Nietzsche, the philosopher with whom we chose to introduce this chapter, had a peculiar attitude towards Socrates – the inspiration behind Plato's ethical theory. In the opening passages of *Twilight of the Idols* (1888/1990), Nietzsche describes Socrates as decadent, as a buffoon, a criminal, a monster and even as 'a misunderstanding' (he doesn't say that Socrates misunderstood something, he says he *was* a misunderstanding!). It is very likely that Nietzsche had Socrates in mind when describing those who 'pose as having discovered and attained their real opinions through the self-evolution of a cold, pure, divinely unperturbed dialectic' (in the extract from *Beyond Good and Evil* that we used to begin this chapter). The alternative title Nietzsche gave to *Twilight of the Idols*, was 'or How to Philosophize with a Hammer'. Nietzsche certainly seems to want to wield that hammer at Socrates and at Socrates' idea that the good can be reached through reason. Though it is dangerous and simplistic to ascribe a single position to Nietzsche (his relationship with Socrates is rather complicated and often apparently inconsistent, for example), these extracts and sentiments are helpful in contrasting the Platonic ethical theory with an Aristotelian one. Aristotle's science of the good was rooted in experience and the lived world – the sense of 'business' we want to draw on in the phrase the 'business of ethics'. Plato and Socrates are more associated with the pursuit of knowledge and truth through reason alone (see Cartoon 3).

I am quite conscious of my ignorance

Cartoon 3   Socrates – wise because he knew his limitations

In contrast to the Socratic search for truth – which is associated with a struggle from first principles using abstract reasoning – it is clear that Aristotle is very keen to undermine any abstract account of the ethical, which he calls the 'good itself', when it comes to everyday activity:

> It is hard, too, to see how a weaver or a carpenter will be benefited in regard to his own craft by knowing this 'good itself', or how the man who has viewed the Idea itself will be a better doctor...a doctor seems not even to study health in this way [that is, in the abstract], but the health of man, or perhaps rather the health of a particular man; it is individuals that he is healing. (*Nicomachean Ethics*, I, 6)

Though he ultimately felt that there was a good towards which we should work, his emphasis on particular cases, individuals and examples is what genuinely marked out Aristotle's view of science. It is this that underpins our definition, and so if we are to unpack what we mean by 'science of the good', we would say that it is the study of what it means to behave ethically, where this is informed by analysing activity in a given context.

2.4   Theory-based and case-based approaches to business ethics

Let us consider now two ways in which people could be given an introduction to the field of business ethics. We introduce this in part as a stereotype (for the sake of simplification), and in part as a 'conceptual inventory' or kind of mental catalogue (to encourage further reflection and thought). In truth, though, another benefit of doing this is because it is a useful way to differentiate *The Ethical Business* from other text books in the field. This is the kind of exercise that Michael Porter (1980), might describe as 'product differentiation'. Most texts on business ethics (even the more abstract ones) will typically include some concrete examples of ethical dilemmas alongside discussions of philosophical theory. Similarly, even the most concrete and specific collections of ethical problems will typically include references to theory (if only at the level of the unquestioned baptized truths' that Nietzsche mocks in the abstract at the beginning of this chapter). Assuming that these texts don't hit on the perfect blend of theory and cases, it is fair to say that some of them will tend to prioritize a theory-based approach to ethics, and that others of them will tend to prioritize a case-based approach.

Though this is something of a simplification, it is useful in considering the approach of different 'pleaders for their prejudices' (Nietzsche, 1886/1973: 1(5)) (and please remember, we include ourselves in this category). So, one way of providing an introduction to business ethics would be to summarize some of the main ethical theories: virtue ethics, Kantian ethics, utilitarianism, rights-based approaches, contemporary ethical theories and so on, and then, taking these as a starting point, provide illustrations of how these could be applied in practice. Indeed, in the first chapter of this book we offered a similar summary. While we would not wish to stereotype or oversimplify, it appears to us that the fashion in several contemporary and leading textbooks on business ethics is perhaps closer to this approach: Crane and Matten (2004), Chryssides and Kaler (1993), Fisher and Lovell (2006), Jones *et al.* (2005). It is important to note that we are not claiming these authors are of one mind, merely that their approach to introducing ethical theory can be characterized (one hopes, not caricatured) as predominantly theory-based rather than case-based. To try to substantiate this, our reading of some of these texts is that their respective main contributions to the field of business ethics are in terms of helping their readers to revisit accounts of *theory*. So Crane and Matten make a notable contribution to ethical philosophy in their discussion of corporate citizenship; Chryssides and Kaler bring together some influential texts in ethical theory and encourage readers to reflect on their implications; Fisher and Lovell incorporate aspects of applied psychology and decision theory in their discussion of ethical behaviour; and Jones *et al.* make a notable contribution in encouraging a more careful, critical and contemporary reading of ethical theory and theorists.

Another way of providing an introduction to business ethics would be to place greater emphasis on some practical problems and then see what it would mean to think about these 'ethically' (thereby introducing some of the ethical theories in the process). Though less common or fashionable nowadays, perhaps the best example of this approach can be found in a contemporary text that is explicitly case-based (Velasquez, 2001) and which incidentally has its roots in the early beginnings of business ethics as a discipline (De George, 2007). There are also case-based elements in Gibson's (2007) text *Ethics and Business*, and in Murray's (1997) topic-based introduction for MBA students. The case- or problem-based approach is also a feature of more populist texts (for example, Dobrin, 2002). This case-based approach has a rich historical tradition. It can be traced back to the narrative mode of stories and parables used in Christian and Zen teachings, for example. Using cases and stories also has its roots in ancient philosophy, where examples form the basis for theorizing in both Aristotelian thought and in the Socratic dialogues (particularly the early dialogues) (Morrell, 2004a; Morrell and Anderson, 2006). In other spheres of human activity (science and technology, engineering) it might seem that historical heritage is no guarantee of validity or reliability. However, we should not forget that beliefs about what is ethical and appropriate stem from, and are founded in, humanity's earliest experiences. An additional factor in the longevity of a case-based approach is that stories are powerful vehicles for conveying sense and meaning (Barry and Elmes, 1997; Boje, 1991; Weick, 1995).

Both theory-based and case-based approaches have advantages and disadvantages. We naturally advocate the approach taken in this book, where, rather than being based predominantly on theory or on cases, we think of business ethics in terms of several arenas of action: marketing, the environment, accounting and finance, human resource management and so on. This also has advantages and disadvantages, but before explaining in more detail why we see this as a useful way to introduce ethical theory, let us examine the two most popular approaches as we have described them.

In the theory-based approach (placing greater emphasis on the role of theory and then seeing how it can be applied) there is a sense of a definite starting point and this can provide a feeling of comfort or security when grappling with ethical problems. A corresponding disadvantage can be that originating frameworks or theories are also constraining, so they can close off the possibility for a rich and sophisticated account of an ethical problem. In the passage immediately preceding the quote at the beginning of this chapter, Nietzsche advocates that we should, 'recognize untruths as a condition of life: that, to be sure, means to resist customary value sentiments in a dangerous fashion; and a philosophy which ventures to do so places itself, by that fact alone, beyond good and evil' (Nietzsche, 1886/1973). His vision was one in which the sacred tablets of Western morality were shattered and our very concepts of good and evil were reinvented. A more modest interpretation of this sentiment could be that the business of ethics is one where we, 'recognize untruths as a condition of life'. In other words, it is where we show some scepticism towards, and at the very least scrutinize, the notion of truths and certainty. This is especially important when these notions have been distilled into basic frameworks of morality. Any given framework might open up one possible way of looking at an ethical issue, but it will also simultaneously close off other ways of looking at it. This is a problem, because no matter what similarities there are among some of the main ethical theories, there are also points of tension between them. This means that it is not possible to reach a consensus about what is the best way of looking at an ethical issue. One implication of this is that, when faced with an ethical problem or set of related ethical problems, we can be confused about which theory or theories to use. Consequently, we may spend a disproportionate amount of time focusing on that rather than on dealing with the practical detail of the business of ethics: the study of what it means to behave ethically, informed by analysing activity in a given context. Admittedly, being confused and having to struggle with a problem is far preferable to blithely assuming one knows the answer: ethical problems typically do not have any one answer or solution, even if whatever action is taken may be thought of retrospectively as the solution (Morrell, 2004b). However, the struggles involved in the business of ethics are not fundamentally about the limitations or advantages of different theories. Instead, we believe they are about being focused on the issue at hand.

Even so, it is easy to see why the theory-based approach is popular and has merit. There is a long line of philosophers advocating their particular approach to ethics, and it is certainly understandable for contemporary authors to work their way along this line before reaching their own version – which they in turn (implicitly) advocate as the definitive endpoint. This theory-based approach also sits well with a stereotypical account of academic research. In what is again admittedly a simplification, academic research can be reduced to three steps: (i) study 'the literature'; (ii) study a 'real-world' problem; and (iii) explore how well the literature can explain the real-world problem and in doing so contribute to some more of 'the literature'. Of course, we could ask the same kinds of questions about academic research (as we have simplified it), as we did of the loaded term science: Who is to say what the real world is? Who is to say what a genuine contribution to the literature is? Even so, the important point to remember is that academics are very comfortable in starting with theory, looking at practical problems and then reflecting on how well the theory stands up to the test of explaining what happens in the real world. This is all well and good, but we think that text books in ethics, perhaps particularly 'business ethics', should be designed to help students think about ethical problems, and not really to think about whether or not a particular theory is in itself of merit. Having considered what we think of as the theory-based approach, let us now look at the other approach.

In the case-based approach, we could start with a problem or context and by studying that see what it tells us about other problems. So, for example (taking Oxfam's data – see below), European citizens support the European dairy industry with €16 billion-worth of subsidies every year. This works out at approximately 1.32 euros per cow, per day. More than half of the world's population has less than this daily amount to survive on. This level of subsidy means that European dairy farmers can dump their products on the world markets at prices that undercut farmers in developing countries, which undermines the opportunities for farmers in developing countries to make a decent living and reinforces the cycle of poverty (see www.oxfam.org.uk/what_we_do/issues/trade/bp34_cap.htm). Rather than thinking about whether this problem is best understood in terms of utilitarian or Kantian ethics or whatever theory (where we could refer to the previous chapter), it could be more interesting to think about this as an ethical issue that is set in a particular historical, economic and political context. If we start from the assumption that this is unfair, then we could identify and analyse the structures that support such inequity: the way the European Union is governed, the political power bases of the respective member states, 'globalization', even the complicity of European citizens, such as the authors of this book. Learning about this problem in all its depth and complexity could be a more appropriate grounding for looking at other issues to do with trade or global justice than studying whatever philosopher or bundle of theories and concepts is currently fashionable.

One advantage of a case-based approach (beginning with examples from practice and trying to think about the ethical issues they raise) can be that we get a richer sense of the complexity and intractability of a problem. We often describe ethical problems as intractable because there does not seem to be a perfect solution to them. We might be able to solve an equation in maths or engineering, or even to achieve what we think are the best possible sales figures, the different avenues open to us when facing an ethical problem cannot really be thought of in this way. Looking in detail at a case means we are confronted with complexity and deprived of the false comfort of a particular theory – 'we recognize untruths as a condition of life', as Nietzsche expresses it. It has its disadvantages too, however. No two cases are exactly alike. They will have some similarities and some differences. Studying our Oxfam case, a 'macro' issue may mean that we are completely unprepared to look at a different but potentially related 'micro' issue – for example, what to do in the case of an individual who is getting paid less than a colleague who is doing exactly the same kind of work. Equally, though the Oxfam case may tell us about unfair levels of subsidy for one constituency (farmers), it may not tell us enough of what we need to know to address another 'macro' issue relating to the fair distribution of goods in society – for example, the gap in pay between men and women who do identical jobs. Though in some senses all these cases are about fairness and justice, differences in scale or what we might call the 'level of analysis' may mean that comparisons will be difficult to find. This in turn means that whatever lessons we learn in one case may not be applicable to another. It might be more sensible to think of the first case about the EU subsidy as being about 'global trade', the second case could be about 'fairness at work', while the third could be about the interplay between patriarchy (a system where power is largely in the hands of men) and capitalism: 'a sociological problem'. In contrast, an advantage of the theory-based approach would be that if we have a well-formulated system or ethical theory, it could provide us with a language to discuss a great variety of ethical problems.

Another disadvantage of the case-based approach is that explanations and discussions that start with examples can be shiftless and rooted in sand. What we mean by this is that, rather than beginning with something that everybody agrees on to at least some degree (for example, a basic account of the main ethical theories – such as utilitarianism), if we use a case study then we are immediately beginning with someone's representation of a particular scenario at a particular point in time. As the authors of this book, that representation will be ours, and it comes filtered through our own sets of prejudices. Others may disagree with our interpretation and the way in which we choose to present the issues in a given case. To continue with our examples, we did not even try to make the case for why EU farm subsidies (or differential pay, or the gender pay gap) might be justifiable, for example. In a sense, it could be argued that all that we are doing if we prefer the case-based over the theory-based approach is substituting one set of untruths (the various ethical theories) with another (a set of inevitably biased accounts of various cases). In defence of the approach taken here, we do not claim that accounts of the cases are definitive, and we have largely used independent (from us) sources to describe the cases. The context within which we present each case is to suggest it as a useful vehicle for prompting ethical thinking. The cases help us, and more importantly our readers, to work on the business of ethics.

2.5   A domain-based, situated approach to the business of ethics

Having looked at the advantages and disadvantages of both the theory-based and case-based approaches we move on to discuss the approach taken in this book. As we outlined at the beginning of the chapter, we want to describe our understanding of ethics as the science of the good (the study of what it means to behave ethically, where this is informed by analysing activity in a given context). To do this, we suggest that it is important to look at different arenas of action. These become the places within which we locate different case studies. In this sense, we are closer to what we have labelled a case-based approach than to a theory-based one, but while we study cases in each of the chapters, we also offer a frame for all of these. For each of the cases, we situate it in terms of an underlying issue (in Part 2 of the book) or practice (in Part 3): an arena of action. We hope that this attempt to specify a broad context for the problems can overcome one of the disadvantages of a purely case-based approach. Simply looking at cases can leave one feeling adrift, but studying them in the context of a particular arena of action offers the opportunity for greater coherence. Rather than beginning with the security or comfort of a particular ethical theory, we advocate understanding the contextual backdrop that throws ethical problems into relief. So, for example, the (potentially quite different) case studies of global logging and war, and the role of businesses in combating global warming are understood in terms of a broader issue, that of environmental ethics (see Chapter 5). Analogously, the case studies of indoctrination and training at work, and the phenomenally high levels of executive pay are understood in terms of the field of organizational behaviour and an associated area of practice – human resource management (HRM) (see Chapter 8). In each of these chapters, we locate the cases in a given arena of action. We shall describe this approach as domain-based, or situated, in order to differentiate it from what we have called the theory-based and case-based approaches. When we use the term situated we want to emphasize the importance of considering the domain for a problem – rather than suggesting that the situation dictates the solution (confusingly, there is a branch of ethical theory called situation ethics; without going into unnecessarily distracting detail about that, it is enough to say that that is not what we mean here). There are limitations with this approach as well, of course, which it is only appropriate to examine (even if we are only doing this to shore up our own prejudices).

In what will be a limitation for some, apart from this chapter and the opening chapter, which gave a general introduction to ethical theories, we do not have extensive sections dedicated to purely theoretical or philosophical topics such as virtue ethics, utilitarian ethics, Kant, feminist ethics, justice, the ethics of care, and postmodern ethics. Since this approach seems to be pursued by so many other authors, we felt there was little we could add in this area and instead, in combination with the brief overview given in Chapter 1, we try to offer appropriate references and guidance where appropriate. In line with the previous edition of *The Ethical Business*, we have decided to retain the brief discussion of some of these major themes in the opening chapter. Fundamentally, though, what we hope to do is to use problems from different domains as a basis for prompting ethical thought among our readers. We are not attempting to provide a one-stop shop because we don't think that is possible with questions about ethics and morality. None the less, we recognize that there is a danger (with this potentially being used as an undergraduate text book) that *The Ethical Business* will be the only text on its respective topic – ethics – that some students will read. That places an uncomfortable degree of responsibility on us as the authors, but in our case we felt that that responsibility was best discharged by trying to pursue a simple goal in a coherent fashion. Having said all that, it is still true that our basic approach is just as open to question as any other. For example, it is certainly legitimate to ask whether it is even sensible to break up the social world into the kinds of categories we use in our book. We could also have chosen different categories/domains, and other people will be able to think of arenas of action that we have omitted. Another, and related, problem is that it is also difficult to demarcate (draw boundaries) between some of the activities we discuss. For example, one could blur the lines between accounting and finance, and corporate governance – even though we treat them here as two separate domains. In addition, it is certainly true that there are generic ethical problems that would feature in each arena – for example, what to do when people lie, cheat or steal. A partial defence for this (in Part 3) is that most organizations are structured using a similar logic; there is typically a head of marketing, a head of human resources, a head of accounting, and a function responsible for supply chain management. So, in that sense, our categories at least reflect business to a degree (and we do have other categories in Part 2 as well). Even in these organizations, however, no matter how neatly the lines and boxes of an organization chart are drawn, some problems (and admittedly perhaps ethical problems in particular) will fall between the lines or outside the boxes. Perhaps a more persuasive justification is that, just as in the first edition of *The Ethical Business*, we remain interested in looking at sets of relations: between the firm and its contexts – the theories and issues facing 'management'; as well as looking within the firm in terms of core business activities – ethics and management in practice. However, rather than pretend there is a solution or perfect response to these challenges, we simply encourage readers to be aware of the limitations of our approach and also, we hope, to benefit from the advantages: an attention to context, an emphasis on human activity and experience, and an opportunity for coherence within a given arena for action. With this in mind, let us introduce the first extended case in this book.

2.6   The case of Jean Charles de Menezes' death

Despite this chapter being largely theoretical, it will help to illustrate some of the ideas in it by looking at a case. The following case is perhaps not one that would typically be associated with a book on business ethics; however, because it illustrates some of the important themes discussed in this chapter it forms an appropriate introduction to the rest of this book. To try to illustrate our approach in action, let us consider the following example where there was an evident and stark failure by an organization, and where the consequence for an innocent bystander was fatal. This case also concerns that most basic of questions: how the liberty of the individual can be balanced with the need for security in society as a whole. This extract was posted on the BBC's news website (http://news.bbc.co.uk/1/hi/uk/6927140.stm) on Thursday 2 August 2007, at 15:58 Greenwich Mean Time:

Anti-terror chief 'misled' public

There were 'serious weaknesses' in the Metropolitan Police's handling of information after the shooting of Jean Charles de Menezes, a report has found. Assistant Commissioner Andy Hayman 'misled' the public, the Independent Police Complaints Commission ruled. The IPCC has examined statements issued by police after the 27-year-old was mistakenly shot dead by officers at Stockwell Tube station on 22 July 2005. Met [Metropolitan] Commissioner Sir Ian Blair said Mr Hayman 'retains my full support'.

'Inconsistent statements'

Mr Menezes was shot dead after police launched a massive manhunt for four suspects following a series of attempted bombings across London's transport network. The Brazilian was mistaken for a suicide bomber. After the shooting, there were reports about Mr Menezes in the media which turned out not to be true – such as that he was wearing a bulky jacket – and the IPCC considered whether the Met was responsible. The report highlighted inconsistencies between what Mr Hayman had told a crime reporters' briefing and a

Metropolitan police authority management meeting on the day of the shooting. It said Mr Hayman – the UK's most senior counter-terrorist officer – had advised the reporters that the dead man had not been one of four attempted bombers.

However, he had also allowed a Metropolitan Police press release to be issued later on the same afternoon, saying that it had not been clear whether he had been one of the four. 'He could not have believed both inconsistent statements were true,' the IPCC said. Sir Ian did not announce that an innocent man had been killed until the following morning, but a complaint against the commissioner was not substantiated. IPCC Commissioner Naseem Malik told a news conference information had been 'deliberately withheld' from Sir Ian. She said: 'What the commissioner could, and should, have been told was the emergence of evidence throughout the day that pointed increasingly strongly to a terrible mistake having been made.'

'Important job'

Sir Ian later said officers did not inform him on 22 July that an innocent man had been shot, because of the time it took to establish that Mr Menezes's identity was not an alias. He added: 'I neither believe that my senior colleagues let me down nor that my position on that night was unreasonable.' Sir Ian said he could not comment on the allegations against Mr Hayman, but said he retained his support in a 'crucially important job'. In a statement, the Metropolitan Police apologized for 'errors in both internal and external communication'. It said its approach to information-handling had changed since 2005. The Met had 'previously apologised to the de Menezes family for their loss and we apologise again,' it added.

BBC home affairs correspondent Andy Tighe said the ball had now entered the court of the Metropolitan Police Authority, which will decide whether Mr Hayman should be disciplined. After the IPCC's Stockwell One report into the events surrounding the shooting, the Crown Prosecution Service decided last year that no individual would be prosecuted in connection with the case. However, the Metropolitan Police is facing trial under health and safety legislation in October. Allesandro Pareira, a cousin of Mr Menezes, told a press conference through an interpreter that 'this report shows that the police were a shambolic mess and that senior officers lied'. Liberal Democrat party president Simon Hughes said Mr Hayman should resign, but [then] London Mayor Ken Livingstone earlier gave the officer his backing.

It is difficult to see how the complexities involved in such a case could be addressed adequately by starting with an ethical theory and then seeking to apply it. Naturally, there are ways in which one could bring to bear a number of different theories, but each of these would only offer a partial take on this scenario. The shocking facts are that, in a liberal democracy, in broad daylight, an innocent and unarmed man was shot dead on public transport. Gruesome and alarming though it is, the events leading up to Jean Charles de Menezes' death and his death itself are eclipsed in a grotesque way by the bombings of 7 July in London (only fifteen days earlier). Fifty-two innocent commuters and four suicide bombers were killed as bombs were detonated on the Tube and a London bus. The climate of fear and terror in the UK, and London in particular, is absolutely crucial for our understanding of the events leading up to de Menezes' death. Just the day before the fatal shooting, on 21 July, an attempt to bomb three more Underground trains and a bus had failed: none of the bombs had exploded fully. Three of the 21 July bombers were arrested later that month, one of them having fled as far as Rome. All three were still at large on 22 July. In the immediate aftermath of the failed 21 July bombings, police officers were posted at every train station in London, and according to *The Guardian*, over 1,000 detectives were assigned to the job of preventing further terrorist attacks (www.guardian.co.uk/flash/0,5860,1544853,00.html). The almost impossible challenge these officers and the Metropolitan police had to face was in confronting an enemy who not only was willing to risk his or her life in an act of terrorism, but who was actually expecting to die.

There is, inescapably, a political context to these events and their aftermath; not simply the way in which political parties and party politicians respond and position themselves in relation to these events, but also in terms of the internal politics of the police force and the macro politics governing the relationship between the state and the executive (that is, the police force). If we try to view this event dispassionately – and this is typically what we try to do when we approach something as a case rather than simply as a tragic event – we can see how it prompts questions about the balance between individual liberties and the security of society as a whole. There are a number of operational and organizational questions here too, about individual competence, communication and leadership. There are wider questions about the nature of society and the relationships between the media, the state, and the machinery of the state. The quotation from de Menezes' cousin (above in the first extract) is likely to provoke sympathy and questions such as 'How would I feel if this happened to a member of my family?' We could ask other uncomfortable questions that would prompt examination of our own prejudices, such as: Would de Menezes have been shot if he were white, or old, or a woman?

2.7   The problem of assigning responsibility

These sorts of questions resonate with debates in ethical theory that are as old as the subject itself. In the case studies we use in this book, we offer questions at the end of each case to prompt discussion and deliberation. Here, though, we want to use just one question that we feel illustrates why our 'situated' approach has advantages over the case-based and theory-based approaches to introducing ethical theory and the business of ethics. That question is, 'Who is responsible for de Menezes' death?' It is a very simple and obvious question, but at the same time it is deeply problematic and complicated. Holding on to the complexity and problematic nature of this question means that we shall be bound inexorably to the particular context for this event. While we may reflect on moral theories during our attempts to address that question, we shall inevitably be drawn back to the considerations about individual liberty, the security of society, the political context, individual competence, leadership and so on. Consider, for example, some possible responses to these statements: 'Sir Ian Blair as Metropolitan police Commissioner is responsible for the actions of the police in London'; 'senior officers within the police are collectively responsible'; 'the officer with operational responsibility for that incident is responsible'; 'the police were institutionally racist, and responsible for shooting a Brazilian on the basis that they thought he was an Asian'; 'the officers who shot him are responsible'; 'the 7 July bombers are responsible not only for the deaths of fifty-two innocent citizens, but also for this death because their actions created the climate of fear within which these acts took place'; 'terrorists who encourage acts such as the 7 July bombings are responsible'; 'the state is responsible for allowing an environment in which officers have a shoot-to-kill policy in such cases'; 'terrorism is a response to geopolitical failures and the leaders of the most powerful nations are responsible for their inadequate foreign policies and their ultimate consequences'; 'it was a horrible accident and no one person is truly responsible'.

Addressing such statements seriously involves a struggle. To try to hold on to the very real and terrible events in this case and at the same time to come up with a satisfactory answer to the question 'Who is responsible?' may not even be possible. When faced with such an obvious and compelling injustice, our gut response is to find a solution, to find someone who is culpable and – simply – to discover an answer that allows us to carry on with our comfortable beliefs about the way our particular society works. Even where horrendous injustices are immediate and pushed in our faces by television, newspapers, the radio and the internet, there is a tendency to seek simple 'truths' that allow us to carry on with our life as normal. Some of us experience and live out this tendency to seek comfortable 'truths' in compassion fatigue, where the sight of starving children being brought via TV into our living rooms no longer appals us, or even diverts our attention. Some of us live out this tendency when we enjoy wearing clothes produced by people working in conditions that we would ourselves think of as slavery. It may be lived out in the engagement ring sporting a diamond, the sale of which may have contributed to financing a war, or in our basket of goods from the supermarket with its huge carbon footprint. For each of these occasions, and in each of these places, we can find questions that become for us 'truths' and that excuse us from responsibility: how can I make a difference, I'm only one person; these injustices would happen anyway; I'll do something about it later; I can't be expected to live like a saint; if I stopped to analyse everything that had ethical implications, I would never get anything done; or – in what incidentally was the title of an excellent album by the rock band, The Cranberries– 'everyone else is doing it so why can't we?'.

All of these banal truths boil down to a simple sentiment: 'I am not responsible'. Businesses, governments and organizations of all forms can adopt the same perspective in their own search for banal 'truths': our competitors are doing this and by trying to do something different we put ourselves at a competitive disadvantage; we are in business to make money for our shareholders and that is all; we're not a charity; this is something the state should do (the state might argue that this is something industry should 'take a lead' in); if we don't do it, someone else will. In other words, 'this business (government, organization) is not responsible'. Stopping at these banal truths is what we want readers to avoid in this book. The business of ethics and the science of the good is a struggle in which we question such truths, and where we explore who is responsible: where we, in Nietzsche's words, 'recognize untruths as a condition of life'.

2.8   The way forward

In the following four chapters, in Part 2 of this book, we address a series of themes and issues that we feel are confronting business. These are Corporate Governance (Chapter 3); Social Partnerships (Chapter 4); Green Issues (Chapter 5) and 'Ethics in a Globalizing World' (Chapter 6). In Part 3 of the book, our situated approach leads us to consider particular areas of practice: Accounting and Finance (Chapter 7); Organizational Behaviour and Human Resource Management (Chapter 8); Marketing (Chapter 9); and Supply Chain and Operations Management (Chapter 10). In each of these chapters, we try to provide readers with a summary of some of the most pressing issues in these domains, by developing both introductory, and then more extended, case studies to encourage reflection and analysis. In this way we offer a means of exploring the 'science of the good' as it relates to topics and issues in the field of business ethics.

 Case study

Closing case study

Try to think for a moment about a time when you were treated very badly by someone acting on behalf of a 'business'. The business could be selling goods or services (a garage, a shop or restaurant, your mobile phone company or internet provider, public transport and so on), or it could be somewhere where you actually worked. We use business in its widest sense in this book so it could also refer to a not-for-profit organization such as a school or university; or a public sector organization such as the NHS, the police or social services.

Question

Who do you think was ultimately responsible for your being treated badly?

References

Aristotle 1980. *The Nicomachean Ethics* (trans. D. Ross). Aylesbury: Hazell Books.

Aristotle 1997. *Poetics* (Dover Thrift edn). New York: Dover.

Barry, D. and Elmes, M. 1997. 'Strategy Retold: Toward a Narrative View of Strategic Discourse', *Academy of Management Review*, 22,2: 429–52.

Bentham, J. 1781/2006. *An Introduction to the Principles of Morals and Legislation*. Full text available at: www.utilitarianism.com; accessed 25 September 2006.

Boje, D. M. 1991. 'The Storytelling Organization: A Study of Story Performance'. *Administrative Science Quarterly*, 36,1: 106–26.

Chryssides, G. D. and Kaler, J. H. 1993. *An Introduction to Business Ethics*. London: Thomson.

Crane, A. and Matten, D. 2004. *Business Ethics: A European Perspective – Managing Corporate Citizenship and Sustainability in the Age of Globalization*. Oxford: Oxford University Press.

De George, R. T. 2007. 'A History of Business Ethics'. Available at: http://www.scu.edu/ethics/practicing/focusareas/business/conference/presentations/business-ethics-history.html; accessed 8 October 2007.

Dobrin, A. 2002. *Ethics for Everyone: How to Increase Your Moral Intelligence*. London: Wiley.

Fisher, C. and Lovell, A. 2006. *Business Ethics and Values: Individual, Corporate and International Perspectives*. London: Prentice Hall.

Gibson, K. 2007. *Ethics and Business: An Introduction*. Cambridge: Cambridge University Press.

Jones, C., Parker, M. and ten Bos, R. 2005. *For Business Ethics*. London: Routledge.

Kraut, R. (2002) *Aristotle: Political Philosophy*. Oxford: Oxford University Press.

Mellahi, K. and Wood, G. 2003. *The Ethical Business: Challenges and Controversies*. Basingstoke: Palgrave.

Morrell, K. 2004a. 'Enhancing Effective Careers Thinking: Scripts and Socrates', *British Journal of Guidance and Counselling*, 32: 547–58.

Morrell, K. 2004b. 'Socratic Dialogue as a Tool for Teaching Business Ethics', *Journal of Business Ethics*, 53: 325–31.

Morrell, K. and Anderson, M. 2006. 'Dialogue and Scrutiny in Organizational Ethics', *Business Ethics: A European Review*, 15,2: 117–29.

Murray, D. 1997. *Ethics in Organizations*. London: Kogan Page.

Nietzsche, F. 1886/1973. *Beyond Good and Evil* (trans. R. Hollingdale). London: Penguin.

Nietzsche, F. 1887/1974. *The Gay Science* (trans. W. Kaufmann – based on the 2nd edn). New York: Random House.

Nietzsche, F. 1888/1990. *Twilight of the Idols, or, How to Philosophize with a Hammer* (trans. R. Hollingdale). London: Penguin.

Oxfam (2005) Data available at: www.oxfam.org.uk/what_we_do/issues/trade/ bp34_cap.htm.

Plato 1956. *Protagoras and Meno* (trans. W. K. C. Guthrie). London: Penguin.

Plato 1974. *Republic* (trans. D. Lee). London: Penguin.

Plato 1993. *The Last Days of Socrates* (*Euthyphro; The Apology; Crito; Phaedo*) (trans. H. Tredennick). London: Penguin.

Porter, M. E. 1980. *Competitive Strategy: Techniques for Analyzing Industries and Competitors.* New York: Free Press.

Thorpe, C. 2001. 'Science against Modernism: The Relevance of the Social Theory of Michael Polanyi', *British Journal of Sociology*, 52,1: 19–35.

Velasquez, M. G. 2001. *Business Ethics: Concepts and Cases*, 5th edn. London: Prentice Hall.

Weick, K. E. 1995. *Sensemaking in Organizations.* London: Sage.

Part 2
Issues facing management

Corporate governance

Chapter objectives

- To understand what constitutes corporate governance.
- To discuss the role of the board of directors.
- To examine why questions relating to corporate governance have become increasingly important.
- To gain an insight into the problems of sound corporate governance in practice.
- To understand what constitutes a stakeholder.
- To outline the basic principles of stakeholder management.

3.1 Introduction

In August 2002, one month after becoming chairman and CEO of Tyco, Ed Breen undertook an extreme corporate governance action. He chose to replace the entire board of directors who served under former Tyco CEO Dennis Kozlowski and former CEO Mark Swartz who were accused, and found guilty, of corporate misconduct and stealing more than $150 million. Tyco's new management team argued that directors 'were duped for years as millions were allegedly looted from the firm' (Strauss, 2002). The aim of this radical corporate governance action was to restore Tyco's credibility with investors, customers, government leaders and employees. Ed Breen noted that when he arrived at Tyco in July 2002, his biggest challenge was to begin the process of restoring genuine trust in the leadership of this company (Tyco.com). Since 2002, Tyco has developed a number of leading ethical governance practices, increasing

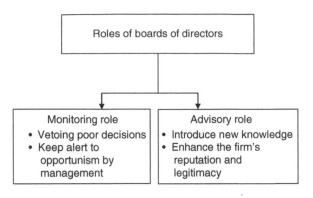

Figure 3.1   The roles of boards of directors

accountability and responsibility of the board and becoming an exemplar of best practice in corporate governance. This chapter discusses the ethics of corporate governance and shows the relevance of corporate governance and stakeholder concepts to business ethics.

Broadly, corporate governance is about the mechanisms by which firms should be directed and controlled so that they are run effectively and efficiently, and ensure that they act in a manner that is fair, responsible, accountable and transparent. The governance of ethics refers to the processes by which firms govern their ethical performance – that is, boards of directors and management oversee and monitor the firm's actions to ensure that the firm adheres to its ethical standards and acts fairly and responsibility towards its stakeholders.

While Friedman (1982) argues that the only 'ethical' role of the firm is to take care of its shareholders, more recent thinking provides insights into the inappropriateness of this viewpoint. The roots of both corporate governance and the concept of 'stakeholder' are central issues in contemporary debates on business ethics. As shown in Figure 3.1, the term 'stakeholder' commonly includes all who are affected by, or can affect, the firm's activities, including not just managers, shareholders and employees, but also representatives of the broader community. Understanding these concepts and the current debates around them should enhance our understanding of the ethical challenges facing businesses nowadays. The chapter is in two parts: the first looks at corporate governance, while the second examines different stakeholder theories and their relevance to business ethics.

3.2   Corporate governance and business ethics

3.2.1   What is corporate governance?

The question as to what constitutes corporate governance is still a topic of debate. The term 'corporate governance' was rarely encountered before the 1990s (Keasey *et al.*, 1997). However, its rapid and wide adoption resulted

Table 3.1   Summary of theories affecting corporate governance development

Theory name	Summary
Agency	Agency theory identifies the agency relationship where one party, the principal, delegates work to another party, the agent. In the context of a corporation, the owners are the principal and the directors are the agent.
Transaction cost economics	Transaction cost economics views the firm itself as a governance structure. The choice of an appropriate structure can help align the interests of directors and shareholders.
Stakeholder	Stakeholder theory takes account of a wider group of constituents rather than focusing on shareholders. Where there is an emphasis on stakeholders, then the governance structure of the company may provide for some direct representation of the stakeholder group.
Stewardship	Directors are regarded as the stewards of the company's assets and will be predisposed to act in the best interest of the shareholders.
Class hegemony	Directors view themselves as an elite at the top of the company and will recruit/promote to new appointments taking into account how well new appointments might fit into that elite.
Managerial hegemony	Management of a company, with its knowledge of day to day operations, may effectively dominate the directors and hence weaken the influence of directors

Source: Mallin, 2006. *Corporate Governance*, 2nd edn, Oxford: Oxford University Press, p. 12.

in inconsistent usage of the term. In its narrowest sense, corporate governance can be viewed as a system, made up of a set of arrangements by which business corporations are directed and controlled. A narrow definition of corporate governance refers to efforts to make top executives more accountable and responsive to shareholders, and to enhance value in the investment process of the company they manage. A broader, and more inclusive, definition encompasses accountability towards not only shareholders, but also the company's relevant stakeholders (see Table 3.1 for a summary of main corporate governance theories).

The Organisation for Economic Co-operation and Development (OECD) defined the role of corporate governance as the structure that 'specifies the distribution of rights and responsibilities among different participants in the corporation, such as the board, managers, shareholders and other stakeholders, and spells out the rules and procedures for making decisions on corporate affairs' (OECD, 1999). This definition fits well with the agency and stakeholder theories of corporate governance that are the focus of this chapter.

3.2.2   Why corporate governance now?

A number of factors have pushed corporate governance to the forefront of business ethics. Brown (1994) noted that:

evolving regulatory requirements, increased media attention and mounting public scrutiny have pried open boardroom doors to challenge directors with expanding responsibilities amid concerns that go far beyond the bottom line . . . 'corporate governance' was an arcane, somewhat esoteric term known only to boardroom lawyers and business school academics. But now, corporate governance is a topic that dances through the business pages and sometimes stomps gracelessly over the front pages of newspapers with threats of lawsuits against directors and officers, public concern over corporate ethics . . .

At least three factors are behind the recent increase in the importance of corporate governance in academic and professional business circles.

3.2.2.1   Separation between ownership and control

In the past, most companies were managed by their owners or closely monitored by a small number of shareholders. Today, however, many people in Western countries own shares. Koehn (2001) reported that studies in the USA have shown that the business section of newspapers is now the first page read by more than 25 per cent of readers. As a result, the way companies govern themselves has come to the forefront of public scrutiny, because the latter has a stake in the way that companies are managed.

3.2.2.2   The birth of the supranational corporations

Recent changes in the global business environment have resulted in a shift of power towards large global corporations. These changes include the end of the Cold War, global economic liberalism, the economic conglomeration of Western Europe, the rapid advancement in technology, and the explosion of e-commerce. Chang and Ha (2001) note that 'as the supranational corporation becomes an increasingly large factor in the world, the question arises as to how far it has a responsibility to maintain the framework of the society in which it operates and how far it should reflect society's priorities in addition to its own commercial priorities'. Many transnational corporations (TNCs) are richer and more powerful than some states and regions. For example, Chang and Ha (2001: 33) note that the total revenue of Mitsubishi, a giant corporate '*keiretsu*' (alliance of related organizations) in Japan, exceeds the gross domestic product (GDP) of South Korea. Also, the American financial services company Citigroup has revenue that exceeds the total output of India. In this sense, Microsoft is 'bigger' than the Netherlands, General Motors (GM) is 'bigger' than Turkey, Philip Morris is 'bigger' than New Zealand, and Wal-Mart is bigger than Israel. The combined revenues of GM and Ford exceed the combined GDP for the whole of sub-Saharan Africa. In fact, 51 of the 100 largest economies in the world are corporations. The Top 500 corporations account for nearly 30 per cent of the world's total economic output and 70 per cent of worldwide trade (Chang and Ha, 2001). Notwithstanding their power and influence, these corporations, and more precisely their managers, are not chosen by the people who work for them or by the communities that are affected by them. If these companies are managed badly or act irresponsibly, the results go beyond the boundaries of these companies and affect shareholders, employees, suppliers and whole communities, and sometimes the political stability of the country. In simple terms, we cannot leave the management of these global corporations solely to the consciences of their managers and the influence of their shareholders.

3.2.2.3   Increase in reported corporate failure and crisis

The recent spectacular collapses of high-profile organizations have wreaked havoc on the management profession and brought the role of boards of directors to the forefront of management research. Articles in the business media and academic journals criticized boards of directors for remaining inactive during such failures. They also blamed directors and senior executive boards for keeping silent about chief executive officers'(CEO) and management's actions which they knew (or ought to have known) were likely to lead to failure (Mellahi, 2005).

3.3   Corporate governance and boards of directors

At the centre of a firm's governance is the board of directors. Its overriding responsibilities are to balance diverging interests and ensure the long-term viability of the firm. As it will be seen later in the discussion of stakeholders, often the interests of those who have control over a firm – that is, those in management – have different interests from those who supply the firm with its external resources, its legitimacy and other critical success factors. Felo (2001) notes that 'corporate governance structures can sometimes lead to conflict between the interests of directors and shareholders'. Take, for example, the diverging interests of those in control with those who supply the firm with external resources. The latter own the company, while the former manage it. Put simply, there is a separation between ownership and control. As discussed below, those in control are often perceived to be responsible for failure, and sometimes abuse their power (Mellahi, 2005). The media is full of stories of managers who misuse their position to misappropriate economic and social benefits, often at the expense of the long-term performance, or even the survival, of the company. As a result, outsiders want a mechanism with which they can protect their interests from opportunistic behaviour or from the incompetence of managers or controlling shareholders. This is done through boards of directors, who have a fiduciary duty to shareholders and other stakeholders. They can fulfil this duty by carrying out different roles. These include a monitoring role and an advisory role.

3.3.1   Monitoring role

This is carried out by overseeing and monitoring the actions of CEOs and management, and by vetoing poor decisions to protect the interest of the shareholders. This role is very important, because the board of directors is perhaps the last line of defence against management misbehaviour and poor management decisions (Mellahi, 2005). Boards of directors are supposed to draw on their collective wisdom to spot some of the bad decisions made, or to be made, by the management (Chatterjee, 2003). Williamson (1985) stresses the importance of boards in guarding against opportunism by management. Opportunist behaviour by management includes 'blatant forms, such as lying, stealing, and cheating', but also often involves a more 'subtle form of deceit'. Williamson argues that opportunism may be prevented or discouraged by monitoring and governance. Similarly, Berle and Means' (1932), seminal work on the separation of ownership and control suggests that managers do not have sufficient equity (ownership) in the firms they manage to give them the incentive to turn their full attention to profit maximization. Instead, some managers may pursue self-interested initiatives at the expense of shareholders (Mellahi, 2005).

3.3.2   Advisory role

This role is undertaken by assisting and advising management in their effort to increase shareholders' wealth (Mellahi, 2005). Board members are expected to bring knowledge and experience from their past managerial experiences and membership on other boards. The diverse experiences of the board of directors, it is hoped, would help firms to run more effectively and efficiently. Further, their high social and professional status may enhance the firms' reputation and legitimacy. This can in turn be used to obtain external political and social resources that the organization depends upon.

3.4   Potential barriers to the involvement of the board of directors

The case of Tyco, discussed in the introduction to this chapter, is more of an exception than a rule. In 2006, the *Financial Times* reported that only a third of the largest UK companies claim full compliance with the country's code. Further, non-executive directors were failing to challenge their boards when they depart from agreed best-practice corporate governance (*Financial Times*, 28 December 2006). *Business Week* caricatured board members as follows:

> They sit in a corporation's inner sanctum. They settle into high-backed chairs around burnished mahogany conference tables. And what they say and do is often an enigma to anyone outside those closed doors. They are the directors in the boardroom, a collection of names, egos, and experience that serves as the critical link between a public company's owners – its shareholders – and management. That, at least, is the theory. In practice, too many boards have been mere 'ornaments on a corporate Christmas tree', ... decorative and decorous baubles, with no real purpose. Little more than a claque of the CEO's cronies, they would quietly nod and smile at their buddy's flip charts and rubber-stamp his agenda for the corporation ... Somehow, directors forgot – if they ever knew – that they were in the boardroom to act on

behalf of shareholders and oversee that collection of hired hands known as management (*Business Week*, 25 November 1996).

Mellahi (2005) asked why supposedly talented, ethical and experienced boards of directors often fail to carry out their fiduciary role effectively in failing firms. When they do detect warning signals, why do they, often with the best of intentions, decide to remain silent about their concerns over management incompetence, unethical behaviour, or both? Here we revisit these important questions and suggest that there are two key barriers to boards' involvement in the management of the firm: lack of time; and board atmosphere.

3.4.1   Lack of time

One of the contributory factors to limited board involvement in the management of organizations is lack of time. For effective monitoring to take place, a greater devotion to the firm is needed from board members. It is time-consuming, and board members must be available at short notice to attend urgent meetings (Mellahi, 2005). Also, board members must study their firm's strategies carefully and diligently to gain an adequate degree of mastery and confidence. However, typically, board members lack the necessary time to do this well for the boards on which they serve (Harris and Shimizu, 2004). This is mainly because most board members are over-stretched by several directorships – a phenomenon that is referred to in the business press as their being 'over-boarded directors'. Serving on multiple boards increases the likelihood of board members missing crucial meetings because of clashes with other board's meetings, and not having the necessary time to examine materials distributed in advance of meetings (Mellahi, 2005). This compromises the advice and decision-making quality of board members (Harris and Shimizu, 2004). Indeed, most recent board effectiveness 'best practice' manuals recommend that directors should limit the number of directorships and budget the necessary time for each board on which they serve. For example, the National Association of Corporate Directors (NACD) recommends that directors should allocate a minimum of four full 40-hour weeks of service to each board on which they serve (Harris and Shimizu, 2004: 776).

3.4.2   Board atmosphere

Atmosphere is different from culture. We use the term 'board atmosphere' to refer to the degree of consensus held by board members in a governance situation, and the states of conflict or co-operation between board members and the CEO and management. Generally, directors tend to serve for a long period of time on the board. On the one hand, directors who stay too long on the board have a good knowledge of both day-to-day operations and strategy of the firm, hence are able to provide internal monitoring. But on the other hand, these directors are more likely to befriend or sympathize with managers, and as a result they are perhaps less likely to monitor them (Mellahi, 2005). It is reasonable to expect that an overly collegial boardroom atmosphere may compromise board members' valuable contribution to the governance process. Research on the dynamic relationship between group conflict and performance suggests that 'groups that experience moderate task conflict tend to make better decisions than those that do not' (Peterson and Behfar, 2003: 102). This is because conflict encourages greater understanding of the issue being discussed.

Furthermore, having a dominance of long-tenured board members can create what Janis (1982) termed 'groupthink'. In applying Janis's principles, we could see how in a situation where there are pressures for unanimity, periods of long tenure can result in a group forming where members avoid conflict (Janis, 1982: 243). He suggests that once a groupthink mentality sets in, a host of pathologies (damaging behaviour and habits) can become prevalent. These may not be obvious to the group, observers of the group or its members, because it can include self-censorship of any misgivings an individual may have – as they don't want to disturb the status quo. Other features of groupthink may be collective rationalization, an illusion of invulnerability, poor search for alternatives, ignorance of outside information, overestimation of the group's chances of success, and biased information processing. In the context of corporate governance, because of the tight social network between board members and the top management team, board members may value the camaraderie of the CEO and top management team more than they respect their fiduciary duties to the shareholders. Consequently, board members, quite unconsciously and unintentionally, can miscalculate events and make decisions that could lead to failure (Peterson *et al.*, 1998).

Mellahi (2005) argued that constant vigilance is key to an effective board. Boards should foster a culture that is mindful of mistakes and keeps board members constantly looking for signs of unethical or illegal conduct. As Bibeault (1982) notes, 'for the most part, business warning signals don't jump up and demand to be noticed; they have to be sought out'. Mellahi (2005: 276) noted that constant vigilance requires directors to be aware of potential groupthink culture in the board, to have a thorough knowledge of how the organization operates, and to have a clear understanding of the strategic direction the organization is taking. Other antidotes to groupthink culture, where it is present, include practices that encourage board members to voice their concerns about management proposals. During meetings, the board should embrace rather than suppress annoying and contrary views. By so doing, the board is more able to spot unexpected and unintended outcomes in the making, and halt their development. Organizations may also reduce the risk of groupthink by putting a limit on the number of years a board member serves on the board, since research shows that longer-tenured board members often become too close to top management and as a result lose their objectivity. Morrell and Anderson (2006) argue that the Greek philosopher Socrates can be a useful role model to draw on in this context. Socrates used a powerful technique of scrutiny to examine people's beliefs and assumptions. Through a sustained and rigorous process of cross-examination, his questioning would reveal, 'inconsistencies that would normally go unnoticed and hence unchallenged' (Morell and Anderson, 2006: 123). In this sense, Socrates was a 'problem-finder' – a capacity that boards suffering from groupthink lack, because they do not want to cause friction. Socrates was also a radical, and in referring to Janis's work, Morrell and Anderson identify the dangers of a comfortable consensus in the boardroom, 'there is a danger in any community where there is a monoculture...lack of diversity can result in diminution of creativity, or damage the ability to respond effectively to changes in the context. Legitimizing the role of a radical is one way to safeguard against this' (2006: 122).

In addition to vigilance, boards of directors should be engaged and they should intervene periodically (Mellahi, 2005). Nadler (2004) suggests that, for the board to be engaged, it should overcome 'knowledge malnutrition' and find ways to stay engaged with the organization's issues outside formal meetings because, as he put it, board meetings are often 'too packed with must-accomplish items to allow an in-depth examination' of key issues. Knowledge malnutrition may be addressed by frequent workshops and visits to the organization to help board members gain first-hand knowledge about the business. Montgomery and Kaufman (2003) suggest that, when dealing with technical and/or important issues such as merger decisions, boards should be able to consult external experts to gain an independent perspective. This will give boards much needed 'independent' information to help them make the decision. Staying engaged with what goes on and what should go on in the organization may be achieved by regular off-site meetings and 'away days' focusing on specific issues, such as the strategic direction of the organization (Mellahi, 2005). Such meetings are vital for acquiring and digesting the necessary information with which board members need to be engaged. Furthermore, board members should have an influence over board agendas. As Nadler (2004) has put it: 'to control the agenda is to control the board'. Nadler suggests that, at the end of each board meeting, board members identify some of the key issues they want to deal with and place them at the top of the agenda for the following board meeting.

3.5 A framework for ethical corporate governance

There is no one best governance model. The governance arrangements depend on the ownership structure, corporate sector and, when dealing internationally, national corporate governance systems, and cultural values and norms. For example, for a publicly traded company with a widely dispersed shareholding, the challenge is for outsider stakeholders to control the performance of managers. In this case, managers have strong control because shareholders are widely dispersed, and therefore it is hard, if not impossible, for the latter to control or influence the former's activities. In this case, outsiders can influence governance indirectly by setting rules for selecting directors, and provide them with enough power to ensure that they will monitor managers' activities, behaviour and performance effectively. By contrast, consider the case of a closely held company with a controlling shareholder and a minority of outside shareholders. In this scenario, the manager is constantly under the control and scrutiny of the controlling shareholders. The challenge here is preventing the controlling shareholders from extracting excess self-benefits from the company and controlling it as it as their personal property by denying minority shareholders their rights. In the latter instance, the company should develop governance mechanisms to protect minority shareholder rights and limit the controlling shareholders' power.

Researchers have long been interested in the best structure, composition and decision-making process of boards of directors to help managers run their firms effectively and efficiently. Overall, the state-of-the-art literature calls for smaller boards, a balance of outside and inside directors, the separation of the roles of CEO and chairman, and significant equity holdings by directors. The US-based National Association of Corporate Directors (NADC) issues a number of guidelines for enhancing the professionalism of board members (*Business Week*, 25 November 1996; http://www.businessweek.com/1996/48/b350310.htm). They recommended that directors should:

- Become active participants and decision-makers in the boardroom, not merely passive advisers.
- Budget at least four full 40-hour weeks of service for every board on which they serve.
- Limit board memberships. Senior executives should sit on no more than three boards, including their own. Retired executives or professional directors should serve on no more than six.
- Consider limits on length of service on a board to ten to fifteen years to allow room for new directors with fresh ideas.
- Immerse themselves in both the company's business and its industry while staying in touch with senior management.
- Know how to read a balance sheet and an income statement, and understand the use of financial ratios.
- Own a significant equity position in the company.
- Submit a resignation on retirement, a change in employer, or a change in professional responsibilities.

These recommendations were guided by a code of ethics for boards of directors that embodies the following commitments:

- To honesty, transparency and integrity.
- To acting responsibly.
- To maintaining the public trust through full accountability.
- To complying with the spirit and the letter of all applicable laws, regulations and rules.
- To avoiding conflicts of interest, whether actual or apparent.
- To responsible stewardship of resources.

- To treating directors, officers, employees, members, faculty and individuals served by NADC with respect and fairness.
- To report violation of this code of ethics to the designated third party and or the chairman of the Audit Committee.

3.6 Corporate governance and different institutional frameworks

Although globalization is bringing some degree of harmonization to the global corporate governance systems, there is still a strong divergence between the systems. For example, the UK and USA corporate governance models focus on dispersed controls, whereas the Japanese and German models reflect a more concentrated ownership structure (we shall return to this point later). The OECD (1999) conducted a number of reviews of corporate governance regimes in specific countries. As a result, it proposed principles of corporate governance (listed below). Nevertheless, the OECD states clearly that these principles are 'non-binding and do not aim at detailed prescriptions for national legislation. They can be used by policy makers, as they examine and develop their legal and regulatory frameworks for corporate governance that reflect their own economic, social, legal and cultural circumstances and by market participants as they develop their own practices' (OECD, 1999). The principles, the OECD suggests, can be a useful point of reference both for member countries as well as many emerging markets and economies in transition. The report noted that not only do the principles provide a benchmark for internationally accepted standards, they also offer a solid platform for analysis and practices in individual countries, taking into account country-specific circumstances, such as legal and cultural traditions. Below is a summary of the OECD principles:

- *The rights of shareholders.* The corporate governance framework should protect shareholders' rights. These rights include the right to participate in the management of the company disproportionate to equity ownership (in other words, even one share allows one a voice); the right to have relevant information about the company's state of affairs; the right to information about decisions concerning fundamental corporate changes; the opportunity to participate effectively and vote at general shareholder meetings; and finally that they should be informed of the rules, including voting procedures, that govern general shareholder meetings.
- *The equitable treatment of shareholders.* The corporate governance framework should ensure the equitable treatment of all shareholders, including minority and foreign shareholders. All shareholders should have the opportunity to obtain effective redress for violation of their rights. More specifically, all shareholders of the same class should be treated equally, and insider trading and abusive self-dealing should be prohibited.
- *The role of stakeholders in corporate governance.* The corporate governance framework should recognize the rights of stakeholders as established by law and encourage active co-operation between corporations and stakeholders in

creating wealth, jobs and the sustainability of financially sound enterprises. The corporate governance framework should assure that the rights of stakeholders that are protected by law are respected, stakeholders should have the opportunity to obtain effective redress for violation of their rights, and the corporate governance framework should permit performance-enhancing mechanisms for stakeholder participation.

- *Disclosure and transparency.* The corporate governance framework should ensure that timely and accurate disclosure is made on all material matters regarding the corporation, including the financial situation, performance, ownership and governance of the company.
- *The responsibilities of the board.* The corporate governance framework should ensure the strategic guidance of the company, the effective monitoring of management by the board, and the board's accountability to the company and the shareholders. Board members should act on a fully informed basis, in good faith, with due diligence and care, and in the best interest of the company and the shareholders. In cases where board decisions may affect different shareholder groups differently, the board should treat all shareholders fairly.
- *The board should be able to exercise objective judgement on corporate affairs independent, in particular, from management.* Boards should consider assigning a sufficient number of non-executive board members capable of exercising independent judgement to tasks where there is a potential for conflict of interest. Examples of such key responsibilities are tasks involving financial reporting, consideration of nominations to the board, and any questions concerning executive and board remuneration.

In the UK, the publication of the 'Cadbury Report' in 1992 drew attention to the concern about the 'proper' governance of organizations; and in particular the governance of public, quoted companies. The stated objective of the Committee was: 'To help to raise the standards of corporate governance and the level of confidence in financial reporting and auditing by setting out clearly what it sees as the respective responsibilities of those involved and what it believes is expected of them.'

The Committee concluded that the recommendations in the final report 'will involve a sharper sense of accountability and responsibility all round' (Report of the Committee on the Financial Aspects of Corporate Governance, 1992). The report argued for a clearly accepted division of responsibilities at the head of a company, which would ensure a balance of power and authority, such that no individual will have unfettered powers of decision. This reflects UK practice historically, where the chief executive's and chairman's position are held by two people. The chairman chairs the board and oversees external communications with large investors and government, presenting the corporation's public face. The CEO attends to executive and operational aspects – co-ordinating the work of other executive directors and running the company internally. This separation is a common UK model, whereas the North American model tends to position one person in a combined role. In Japan, where the concept of the company as a community dominates, the system puts trust in the management, who traditionally seek profit for pluralist-orientated stakeholders rather than the traditional Western approach of maximizing profit for shareholders. Generally, the Japanese corporate governance system consists of a dual structure: the board of directors, which carries out the functions of strategic decision-making; and the board of editors, which audits management's execution of business activities. It is worth mentioning that the latter body does only *ex post facto* auditing (that is, scrutinizes company accounts after decisions have been made and recorded), and tends to distance itself from the strategic and day-to-day management process. Even the board of directors does not have the power to make strategic decisions. Instead, these are reserved for the management board who includes the board and directors as well as independent, non-executive directors who have no direct (financial) interest in the company and who should comprise a majority on the board.

3.7   Corporate governance and stakeholder theory

So far, we have focused on the agency theory of corporate governance by discussing the fiduciary role of boards of directors towards shareholders. In this section we discuss the stakeholder theory of corporate governance by looking at firms' responsibility towards a broad range of stakeholders. The stakeholder view of the firm contrasts with the traditional (shareholder or stockholder) view. The shareholder or stockholder view asserts that the primary function of the firm is to maximize the return on investments to the owners of the business. This was memorably expressed in the title of a still much-discussed article by Milton Friedman, 'The Social Responsibility of Business Is to Increase Its Profits' (Friedman, 1970). From a stakeholder theory perspective, the social responsibility of the firm means more than this. Instead, the firm (principals and agents of the firm) needs to consider the interests of 'all' groups affected by the firm. Stakeholder theory is an important and commonly used framework for business ethics (Gibson, 2000; Carroll and Buchholtz, 1993; Weiss, 1994). Freeman (1984) asserts that stakeholder theory is a promising framework for business ethics because it acknowledges a 'plurality of values'.

Since Freeman's (1984) landmark book, *Strategic Management: A Stakeholder Approach*, the topic has been the subject of a lively debate in the literature. Several special journal issues and books have been published on the topic, and numerous conferences and academic seminars have taken place. Much of the debate centres on the definition of stakeholders, and whether or not management's ability to satisfy one group of stakeholders is at the expense of their ability to satisfy another (Strong *et al.*, 2001). Another fundamental question is the issue of how to reconcile competing stakeholders.

Defining such a broad concept as stakeholder is somewhat problematic. Over the years, several definitions have been proposed, most encompassing the general definition provided earlier in this chapter. The academic literature separates stakeholders into groups: primary and secondary. Primary stakeholders are those who have a formal, often official, or contractual relationship with the firm, such as suppliers, employees, shareholders, managers and so on. All others are classified as secondary stakeholders, having a looser contract with the firm (Carroll and Buchholtz, 1993). A widely quoted classic definition of stakeholders is that proposed by Freeman (1984: 46): 'A stakeholder in an organization is any group or individual who can affect or is affected by the achievement of the organization's objectives'.

Several authors have contested Freeman's definition; it has been criticized for being either too broad (does it include trees and animals, for example) or too narrow (does it exclude invisible stakeholders – future generations, perhaps – who are affected by the firms indirectly). None the less, most researchers have used a variation of Freeman's definition (see Clarkson, 1995; Frooman, 1999). Clarkson (1995) grouped stakeholders into primary stakeholders, which includes investors, employees, customers; and public stakeholders, which includes the government, communities and regulatory bodies. To this list, Donaldson and Preston (1995) add trade associations and environmental groups.

As will be seen later, the power and influence of secondary stakeholders can dictate the type of relationship the firm wishes to establish with them. Donaldson and Preston (1995) draw a careful distinction between influencers and stakeholders. They noted that 'some actors in the enterprise (e.g. large investors) may be both, but some recognizable stakeholders (e.g. the job applicants) have no influence, and some influencers (e.g. the media) have no stake'.

The absence of any real consensus on the definition of stakeholders in the burgeoning literature on the subject is symptomatic of the whole debate on the stakeholder concept. Freeman and Gilbert (1988) argue that the stakeholder theory or concept is strongly linked to business ethics and specifically to moral principles. Stakeholder theory proposes that firms go beyond the traditional narrow focus on shareholders' interests, and often short-term profits, and consider the wider impact of their activities on all affected parties – that is, their stakeholders. According to one variant of stakeholder theory, in the long term, firms benefit more from a non-adversarial relationship with stakeholders than they do by focusing on short-term shareholder interest. Clarkson (1995) argues that a firm's survival and continuing success depends on the ability of its management to create sufficient wealth, value or satisfaction for all primary stakeholder groups.

The foundations of the concept of stakeholder are the relationships and interactions within the firm, and between it and others (Lampe, 2001). These interactions may produce a win–lose outcome, in that improved managerial performance in one stakeholder group could be achieved at the expense of the performance of another group. De Castro et al. (1996), for example, found that wealth creation strategies in the privatization of state-owned enterprises resulted in losses for the employee stakeholders and gains to the ownership group (quoted in Strong et al., 2001). In similar vein, Laban and Wolf (1993) argue that outside investors are less likely to provide capital to firms that have powerful employees. Similarly, McDonald (1993) notes that, when employee groups become powerful, labour peace is valued above all else, leading to a decline in customer service and a disregard for profitability. Jawahar and McLaughlin (2001) argue that: 'Organizations are unlikely to fulfil all their responsibilities they have toward each primary stakeholder group. Instead, they are likely to fulfil economic and all non-economic responsibilities of some primary stakeholders but not others and, over time, to fulfil responsibilities relative to each stakeholder to varying extents'.

The above literature seems to indicate that conflict between an organization and its stakeholders is inevitable. Several scholars argue that the company should balance the interests of all stakeholders. For example, Clarkson (1995) noted that 'the primary economic and social purpose of the corporation is to create and distribute increased wealth and values to all its primary stakeholder groups, without favouring one group at the expense of others'. Similarly, Jones and Wicks (1999) argue that 'the interests of all (legitimate) stakeholders have intrinsic value and no set of interests is assumed to dominate the others'.

3.8   The different perspectives of stakeholder theory[1]

Ethics and stakeholder concept have been examined from three different perspectives: descriptive, instrumental and normative (Donaldson and Preston, 1995).

3.8.1   The descriptive perspective

By and large, much of the literature on stakeholders adopts a descriptive perspective and focuses on the *management* of them. This perspective focuses on describing how organizations interact with stakeholders (Brenner and Cochran, 1991). Brenner and Cochran argue that '[t]he stakeholder theory of the firm posits that the nature of an organization's stakeholders, their values, their relative influence on decisions and the nature of the situation are all relevant information for predicting organizational behavior'. Freeman argues that the management of stakeholders should focus on 'the principle of who or what really counts'. Similarly, Mitchell *et al.* (1997) offered a theory of stakeholder identification that suggests that *managers' perceptions* of three key stakeholder attributes – power, legitimacy of the claim, and urgency of the claim – affect stakeholder salience and subsequently the degree to which managers give priority to competing stakeholder claims.

The descriptive perspective is largely underpinned by the resource dependence theory proposed by Pfeffer and Salancik (1978), which states that 'organizations must attend to the demands of those in its environment that provide resources necessary and important for its continued survival ... organizations will (and should) respond more to the demands of those organizations or groups in the environment that control critical resources' (Pfeffer, 1982). Post *et al.* (2002) argue that corporate success is underpinned by 'managing relationships with stakeholders for mutual benefit' because, they argue, organizational wealth 'can be created (or destroyed) through relationships with stakeholders of all

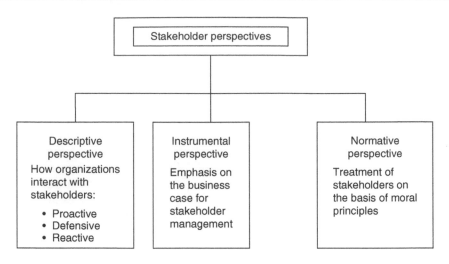

Figure 3.2   Different perspectives in the management of stakeholders

kinds – resource providers, customers and suppliers, social and political actors'. Thus resources dictate the relative importance of primary stakeholder groups to an organization. In other words, the extent to which an organization is dependent on stakeholders depends on the importance of a particular resource to the organization, the degree to which those who control the resource have monopoly over the resource, and the discretion they have over its allocation (Frooman, 1999). Extending the resource dependency theory to stakeholders seems to suggest that organizations will pay more attention to, and be more concerned with, issues of stakeholder groups who control resources critical to the survival of an organization (Agle *et al.*, 1999) This dependence of firms on stakeholders for resources translates into power for the stakeholder groups involved (Mitchell *et al.*, 1997) and gives those stakeholders leverage over firms (Frooman, 1999). The basic argument here is that, for the firm to achieve its strategic objectives, stakeholders need to be considered because they have the potential to help or harm the firm in its quest to achieve its corporate objectives.

Mellahi and Wood (2003) argued that the descriptive perspective looks for the best way to deal with primary stakeholders and powerful secondary stakeholders, while minimizing damage to shareholder value. It advocates the adoption of different approaches to deal with each primary stakeholder group according to certain attributes such as a degree of 'perceived' influence. Generally, the literature suggests a limited number of strategies including proaction, defence and reaction (Clarkson, 1988, 1991, 1995) (see Figure 3.2).

- The *proactive* strategy implies doing a great deal to address stakeholder issues, including 'anticipating and actively addressing specific concerns or leading an industry effort to do so' (Carroll, 1979; Watrick and Cochran, 1985). That is, being proactive is to anticipate and fully accept one's responsibilities.

In contrast, being defensive is to admit responsibility but to fight it, or simply deny responsibility (Jawahar and McLaughlin, 2001). An example of being proactive could be an organization involving the community or other primary stakeholder in the early discussion of a management plan such as (re)location, job cuts or expansion.

- The *defence* strategy involves doing only the minimum legally required by law to address a stakeholder issue. This strategy involves a company preparing a defensive strategy for not going beyond what is legally required. An example of a defensive strategy would be the Ford Motor Company's refusal to recall the Pinto model, which had a number of safety problems that caused explosions and fires after rear-end collisions,claiming that each explosion was an isolated incident (*AutoWeek*, quoted in Jawahar and McLaughlin, 2001; also discussed in Velasquez, 2001).
- The *reactive* strategy advises firms to involve either fighting against addressing a stakeholder issue or completely withdrawing and ignoring the stakeholder (Jawahar and McLaughlin, 2001).

According to the descriptive perspective, if the defensive strategy is cheaper and less damaging to the firm (albeit damaging to a primary stakeholder) than a proactive strategy, then the firm should opt for the defensive. The fundamental assumption here is that organizations operate in a highly competitive environment and have finite resources in terms of time and money, organizations are unlikely to (and they should not) proactively address and accommodate the issues and concerns of all stakeholders all the time. Put differently, according to the strategic approach of stakeholder management, companies should only be proactive with stakeholders who hold power and have control over critical resources (Mellahi and Wood, 2003).

3.8.2   The instrumental perspective

This perspective was put forward by Jones (1995). It differs from the descriptive perspective by focusing on the financial effects if the managers approach and manage stakeholders in particular ways. This focus on financial effects is in contrast to the descriptive approach, which focuses on how managers should acts towards their stakeholders (Mellahi and Wood, 2003). Donaldson and Preston (1995) noted that an instrumental stakeholder perspective is a 'framework for examining the connections, if any, between the practice of stakeholder management and the achievement of various financial performance goals' (p. 67). That is, the key tenet of this perspective is that the ultimate objective of corporate decisions is marketplace success, and stakeholder management is a means to that end. For example, Jones and Wicks (1999) sought to synthesize ethics and economics, and propose that if firms contract with their stakeholders primarily through their managers on the basis of mutual trust and co-operation, they will have a competitive advantage over firms that do not (Jawahar and McLaughlin, 2001).

3.8.3 The normative perspective

The normative perspective literature prescribes how all stakeholders should be treated on the basis of some underlying moral or philosophical principles (Jawahar and McLaughlin, 2001). This perspective rests on the moral viewpoint that firms' responsibilities towards their stakeholders ought to go beyond what is prescribed by the descriptive and instrumental approaches. That is, the implication is that moral principles should drive stakeholder relations. One of the key pillars of the normative stakeholder theory is that firms should attend to the interests of all their stakeholders – not just their stockholders (Jawahar and McLaughlin, 2001). A common theme among these scholars is that firms should treat stakeholders as 'ends' rather than as means to an end. There is a further point of contrast in comparison to the descriptive and instrumental approaches. These prioritize their stakeholders according to levels of resource dependency, power, legitimacy and urgency. However, according to Phillips (2003), from the normative perspective, stakeholders are 'those to whom the organization has a moral obligation, an obligation of stakeholder fairness, over and above that due other social actors simply by virtue of them being human' (Phillips, 2003, p. 31).

3.9   Principles of stakeholder management

The Clarkson Centre for Business Ethics outlines the following core principles for stakeholder management:

- Principle 1   Management should acknowledge and actively monitor the concerns of all legitimate stakeholders and should take their interests appropriately into account in decision-making and operations.
- Principle 2   Managers should listen to and openly communicate with stakeholders about their respective concerns and contributions, and about the risks that they assume because of their involvement with the corporation.
- Principle 3   Managers should adopt processes and modes of behaviour that are sensitive to the concerns and capabilities of each stakeholder consistency.
- Principle 4   Managers should recognize the interdependence of efforts and rewards among stakeholders, and should attempt to achieve a fair distribution of the benefits and burdens of corporate activity among them, taking into account their respective risks and vulnerabilities.
- Principle 5   Managers should work cooperatively with other entities, both public and private, to ensure that risks and harms arising from corporate activities are minimized and, where they cannot be avoided, appropriately compensated.
- Principle 6   Managers should avoid altogether activities that might jeopardize inalienable human rights (e.g., the right to life) or give rise to risks which, if clearly understood, would be patently unacceptable to relevant stakeholders.
- Principle 7   Managers should acknowledge the potential conflicts between (a) their own role as corporate stakeholders, and (b) their legal and moral

responsibilities for the interests of stakeholders, and should address such conflicts through open communication, appropriate reporting and incentive systems and, where necessary, third party review.

(*Source*: Clarkson Centre for Business Ethics, 2000)

3.10   Summary

It appears that ethical behaviour, in the long run, may reduce the cost of social and economic partnership with different stakeholders. Corporate governance has become an increasingly pressing issue because of the increasing separation between ownership and control, the sheer power of TNCs, and a recent rash of high-profile corporate failures. However, the practice of sound corporate governance is a complex business, needing considerable thought as to the most appropriate manner for reconciling divergent interests. Managers should consider the rights of different groupgs of shareholders, and pay attention to issues relating to disclosure and transparency. Also, they should take into account the needs and interests of other groups with an interest in the affairs of the firm, and seek to exercise objective judgement on corporate affairs. In this chapter we argued that, regardless of the primary intention of the company, good corporate governance and stakeholder management could enhance the company's long-term profit.

Discussion questions

- Can board members be responsible for firms' unethical behaviour?
- Identify an organization with sound and ethical corporate governance standards. Describe its corporate governance structures and processes.

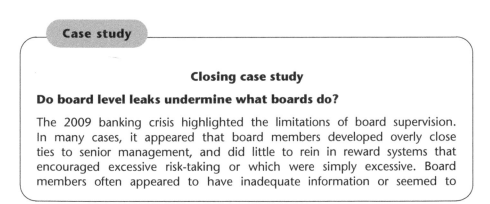

Case study

Closing case study

Do board level leaks undermine what boards do?

The 2009 banking crisis highlighted the limitations of board supervision. In many cases, it appeared that board members developed overly close ties to senior management, and did little to rein in reward systems that encouraged excessive risk-taking or which were simply excessive. Board members often appeared to have inadequate information or seemed to

Case study

Continued

simply be incapable of either understanding or reining-in the complex and risky financial practices engaged in or tolerated by senior managers. This reflects problems in selecting board members and their over-dependence on senior management. But if the board system fails in its task, what should the individual board member do? 'Awkward' board members who challenge senior managers may risk their position on the board, or find themselves relegated to be a lone – and unheard – voice in the wilderness. Perhaps, in such instances, board members should be encouraged to go public with their concerns? Defenders of the status quo have argued that this would deter genuine debate at board level, encourage divisions and/or force boards to reach premature decisions.

Questions

- Do you think that the leaking of information by board members about a firm's suspected unethical behaviour is itself ethical?
- What, if anything, should board members do if they suspect that a CEO is behaving unethically?

Note

1. This section draws extensively on an earlier article published by Mellahi and Wood (2003), pp. 202–22.

References

Agle, B. R., Mitchell, R .K. and Sonnenfeld, J. A. 1999. 'Who Matters to CEOs? An Investigation of Stakeholder Attributes and Salience, Corporate Performance, and CEO Values', *Academy of Management Journal* 42,5: 479–87.

Berle, A. A. and Means, C.G. 1932. *The Modern Corporation and Private Property.* New York: Harcourt, Brace and World.

Bibeault, G. D. 1982. *Corporate Turnaround: How Managers Turn Losers into Winners.* New York: McGraw-Hill.

Brenner, S. N. and Cochran, P. L. 1991. 'The Stakeholder Theory of the Firm: Implications for Business and Society Theory and Research', *International Association for Business and Society Proceedings*, 449–67.

Brown, R. D. 1994. 'Corporate Governance: The Director as Watchdog, Juggler or Fall Guy', *Canadian Business Review*, 21,1: 39–45.

Business Week. 1996. 'New Expectations for Directors', 25 November.

Carroll, A. B. 1979. 'A Three-Dimensional Conceptual Model of Corporate Social Performance', *Academy of Management Review*, 4: 497–505.

Carroll, A. B. and Buchholtz, A. K. 1993. *Business and Society: Ethics and Stakeholder Management*. Cincinnati, Ohio: South-Western Publishing.

Chang, S. J. and Ha, D. 2001. 'Corporate Governance in the Twenty-First Century: New Managerial Concepts for Supranational Corporations', *American Business Review*, 19,2: 32–44.

Chatterjee, S. 2003. 'Enron's Incremental Descent into Bankruptcy: A Strategic and Organizational Analysis', *Long Range Planning*, 36 :133–49.

Clarkson, M. B. E. 1988. 'Corporate Social Performance in Canada, 1976–1986', *Research in Corporate Social Performance and Polic*, 10: 241–65.

Clarkson, M. B. E. 1991. 'Ethics Education: How To Do It', *Canadian Public Administration*, 34 (Spring), 192–5.

Clarkson, M. B. E. 1995. 'A Stakeholder Framework for Analyzing and Evaluating Corporate Social Performance', *Academy of Management Review*, 20: 92–117.

Clarkson Centre for Business Ethics. 2000. *Principles of Stakeholder Management*. Toronto: CCBE.

Cohen, S. 1995. 'Stakeholders and Consent', *Business and Professional Ethics*, 14,1: 3–16.

De Castro, J. O., Meyer, G. D., Strong, K. C. and Uhlenbruck, N. 1996. 'Government Objectives and Organizational Characteristics: A Stakeholder View of Privatization Effectiveness', *International Journal of Organizational Analysis*, 4,4: 373–92.

Donaldson, T. and Preston, L. E. 1995. 'The Stakeholder Theory of the Corporation: Concepts, Evidence and Implications', *Academy of Management Review*, 20: 65–91.

Driscoll, D. and Hoffman, M. 1998. 'HR Plays a Central Role in Ethics Programs', *Workforce*, April.

Felo, A. 2001. 'Ethics Programs, Board Involvement, and Potential Conflicts of Interest in Corporate Governance, *Journal of Business Ethics*, 32,3: 205–18.

Financial Times. 28 December 2006.

Freeman, R. E. 1984. *Strategic Management: A Stakeholder Approach*. Boston, Mass.: Pitman.

Freeman R. and Gilbert, D. R. 1988. *Strategy and the Search for Ethics*. Englewood Cliffs, NJ: Prentice Hall.

Friedman, M. 1970. 'The Social Responsibility of Business Is to Increase Its Profits', *New York Times Magazine*, 32–3: 122–6.

Friedman, M. 1982. *Capitalism and Freedom*. Chicago/London: University of Chicago Press.

Frooman, J. 1999. 'Stakeholder Influence Strategies', *Academy of Management Review*, 24: 191–205.

Gibson, K. 2000. 'The Moral Basis of Stakeholder Theory', *Journal of Business Ethics*, 26,3: 245–57.

Harris, I. C. and Shimizu, K. 2004. 'Too Busy to Serve? An Examination of the Influence of Overboarded Directors', *Journal of Management Studies*, 41,5: 775–98.

Janis, I. L. 1982. *Groupthink: Psychological Studies of Policy Decisions and Fiascos.* Boston, Mass.: Houghton Mifflin.

Jawahar, I. and McLaughlin, G. 2001. 'Toward a Descriptive Stakeholder Theory: An Organizational Life Cycle Approach', *Academy of Management Review*, 26: 397–414.

Jones, T. M. 1995. 'Instrumental Stakeholder Theory: A Synthesis of Ethics and Economics', *Academy of Management Review*, 20: 404–37.

Jones, T. M. and Wicks, A. C. 1999. 'Convergent Stakeholder Theory', *Academy of Management Review*, 24: 206–21.

Keasey, K., Thompson, S. and Wright, K. 1997. *Corporate Governance.* Oxford: Oxford University Press.

Koehn, D. 2001. 'Ethical Issues Connected with Multi-Level Marketing Schemes', *Journal of Business Ethics*, 29,1/2: 153–60.

Laban, R. and Wolf, H. 1993. 'Large-Scale Privatisation in Transition Economies', *American Economic Review*, 83,5: 1199–210.

Lampe, M. 2001. 'Mediation as an Ethical Adjunct of Stakeholder Theory', *Journal of Business Ethics*, 31,2: 165–73.

Mallin, C. A. 2006. *Corporate Governance*, 2nd edn, Oxford: Oxford University Press.

McDonald, K. R. 1993. 'Why Privatization Is Not Enough', *Harvard Business Review*, 71,3: 49–59.

Mellahi, K. 2005. 'The Dynamics of Boards of Directors in Failing Organizations', *Long Range Planning*, 38,3: 261–79.

Mellahi, K. and Wood, G. 2003. 'The Role and Potential of Stakeholders in "Hollow Democracies"', *Business and Society Review*, 108,2: 183–202.

Mitchell, R. K, Agle, B. R and Wood, D. J. 1997. 'Toward a Theory of Stakeholder Identification and Salience: Defining the Principle of Who and What Really Counts', *Academy of Management Review*, 22,4: 853–86.

Montgomery, C. A. and Kaufman, R. 2003. 'The Board's Missing Link', *Harvard Business Review*, March, 81,3: 86–93.

Morrell, K. and Anderson, M. 2006. 'Dialogue and Scrutiny in Organizational Ethics', *Business Ethics: A European Review*, 15,2: 117–29.

Nadler, D. A. 2004. 'Building Better Boards', *Harvard Business Review*, May: 1–10.

OECD. 1999. *OECD Principles of Corporate Governance.* Paris: OECD.

Peterson, R. S. and Behfar, K. J. 2003. The Dynamic Relationship between Performance Feedback, Trust, and Conflict in Groups: A Longitudinal Study, *Organizational Behaviour and Human Decision Processes*, 92: 102–12.

Peterson, S. R., Owens, D. P., Tetlock, E. P., Fan, T. E. and Martorana, P. (1998). 'Group Dynamics in Top Management Teams: Groupthink, Vigilance, and Alternative Models of Organizational Failure and Success', *Organizational Behavior and Human Decision Processes*, 73,2/3: 272–305.

Pfeffer, J. 1982. *Organizations and Organization Theories*, Marshfield, Mass.: Pitman.

Pfeffer, J. and Salancik, G. R. 1978. *The External Control of Organizations: A Resource Dependence Perspective*, New York: Harper &Row.

Phillips, R. 2003. 'Stakeholder Legitimacy', *Business Ethics Quarterly*, 13: 25–41.

Post, J. E., Preston, L. E. and Sachs, S. 2002. *Redefining the Corporation: Stakeholder Management and Organizational Wealth* (Stanford, Calif.: Stanford University Press).

Report of the Committee on the Financial Aspects of Corporate Governance (The Cadbury Report). 1992.

Strauss, G. 2002. 'Tyco Events Put Spotlight on Directors' Role, *US Today*, 9–15.

Strong, K. C., Ringer, R. C. and Taylor, S. A. 2001. 'The Rules of Stakeholder Satisfaction (Timeliness, Honesty, Empathy)', *Journal of Business Ethics*, 32: 219–30.

Velasquez, M. G. 2001. *Business Ethics: Concepts and Cases*, 5th edn. London: Prentice Hall.

Watrick, S. L. and Cochran, P. L. 1985. 'The Evolution of the Corporate Social Performance Model', *Academy of Management Review*, 10: 758–69.

Weiss, J. W. 1994. *Business Ethics: A Managerial, Stakeholder Approach*. Belmont, Calif.: Wadsworth.

Williamson, O. E. 1985. *The Economic Institutions of Capitalism*. New York: Free Press.

Social partnerships*

Chapter objectives

- To understand what constitutes a social partnership.
- To explore the differing conceptualizations of social partnerships in different national contexts.
- To gain insight into the benefits and the costs of social partnerships.
- To locate the importance of social partnerships within the philosophical tradition.

Case study

Introductory case study

Autocom Ltd. is a supplier for a Japanese automobile manufacturing plant based in the UK. Autocom itself is situated at a 'greenfields' industrial site in Bedfordshire, to which it relocated from a 'brownfields' industrial site in the mid-1980s. Historically speaking, the firm had relied on a very stable workforce of long-serving workers. They were unionized, with a long tradition of militancy. In part, the relocation was driven by a desire to break with the past, and to develop new HR policies. Management sought to 'regain their prerogative', above all on the right to increase and reduce the workforce without having to risk a dispute with the then union. In addition, since the relocation, management has frequently stated its commitment to develop greater task flexibility, though in practice this has amounted to little more than a limited job rotation among the workforce.

In order to 'make a fresh start', the firm has adopted a policy of employing younger workers since its relocation, as these are 'less likely to have the wrong ideas'. Training is done on an informal, 'on the job' basis. While the workforce is, on average, a relatively productive one, the firm has been dogged by a high staff turnover, and the firm is beset by high levels of absenteeism, especially on Fridays. In the end, both these problems have driven the limited job rotation that takes place, rather than particular innovations in work organization. This has made it particularly difficult to meet orders for the principal customer, which operates on a strict just-in-time system. As a result, Autocom has recently considered reviewing its staffing policy.

Moreover, it seems that workers derive little satisfaction from the work. Indeed, their sole interest in the job seems to be in terms of the pay received. As HR manager, you have often overheard workers voicing sentiments such as: 'Well, it's just another job'; 'I don't want to do this for the rest of my life, but it pays the rent'; and 'The firm is OK, but the work is fairly boring'.

Questions

- Could Autocom's decision to relocate to a Greenfields site be considered unethical? If so, why?
- Could some of the problems experienced at Autocom be resolved through a formally agreed partnership with employees?

4.1   Introduction

Over the past decade, there has been increasing interest in possibilities for social partnerships, especially ones that are characterized by deals between employers and employee representatives within a particular firm, or between the firm and community organizations. On the one hand, proponents of social partnerships have suggested that they represent the epitome of ethical management; firms are compromising their interests and making real concessions in order to improve the lot of the less endowed, be they individual employees or a disadvantaged community. On the other hand, critics of social partnerships have argued that their contemporary manifestations tend to be devoid of any moral worth; firms are motivated to enter into partnerships largely by the exigencies of profitability and to promote employee consent. In this chapter, we outline the changing nature and role of social partnerships, assess the relationship between classic corporate social responsibility and more recent partnership initiatives, outline current trends, and locate social partnerships within classical ethical theories.

4.2   What is a social partnership?

As Guest (2001: 101) notes, partnership 'is one of those warm words, that can mean all things to all people'. Above all, social partnerships represent attempts

to balance the needs of individuals (and communities) with those of the organization. As Prechel (1999) notes, 'successful social partnerships begin with
acknowledging that there are legitimate partners within the workplace that
have contrasting but legitimate interests: the firm and the economy'. Traditionally, social partnerships have been associated with what is referred to as the
'Rhineland model', implying long-term state support for representative trade
unions, 'an affiliation to collective bargaining, and the establishment of long
term strategies between government, business and organized labour' (Beardwell
and Holden, 2001: 489; Iankova, 1996). More recently, social partnerships have
been taken to entail a recognition that, as members of an economic community,
key stakeholders have a legitimate interest in an enterprise (see Chapter 3 for a
fuller discussion of the concept of 'stakeholder').

Social responsibility represents 'the obligation a business assumes toward
society . . . to be socially responsible is to maximize positive effects and minimize negative effects on society' (Ferrell *et al.*, 2000: 6). Classic corporate social
responsibility represents an attempt by the firm to divert a proportion of revenues to 'good to worthy causes, as well as finding creative ways to improve the
quality of life of the firm's employees and the local community' (Ferrell *et al.*,
2000: 278). However, any outreach is very much on the firm's terms; assistance
is seen as a 'free gift' to be extended or revoked at will; the firm does what it
sees as socially desirable, taking only limited account of the views and interests
of the subject. Community-linked social partnerships are based on a recognition
of the limits of classical corporate social responsibility initiatives; here, the views
of key stakeholders are considered andused to inform policy, making for more
sustainable and, ultimately successful outreach initiatives.

As Rao and Sita (1993: 566) note, 'the interactive relationship leading to
mutual problem solving and benefits has been variably referred as a collabo-
rative or participative strategy', becoming a social partnership when issues and
efforts of a broader scope are encompassed. While much of the literature on
social partnerships focuses on possible long-term relations between unions and
management (see Beardwell and Holden, 2001; Guest, 2001), social partnerships can also encompass deals reached between governments at central and local
level, employers and communities (Rao and Sita, 1993). For example, a social
partnership arrangement may develop between a multinational company and a
host community to, say, reduce levels of environmental pollution. Similarly, a
broadly-based social partnership could provide community-based development
organizations with the necessary resources and backing to 'undo the damage
of business flight and racial animosity that plague poor communities' (Rubin,
1993: 428). In short, social partnerships may be focused on the two central
groupings within the firm, employers and employees – but with some degree
of state involvement as well, or have a broader social focus, also involving one
or more community groupings (Waddock and Post, 1991). In Britain, much
of the emphasis in the contemporary literature has been on the former; that is,
primarily in terms of a partnership between employees and management to promote 'better work' and better corporate performance. In contrast, in the United

States, social partnerships have been rather more wide-ranging in scope, in some cases seeking to involve entire communities.

Social partnerships can only be realized through stakeholders making appropriate contributions for mutual benefit, which, in turn, is only possible in a situation where partners can take a basic degree of fairness for granted. In short, what is sought is a situation of 'mutual advantage' (Huxham and Vangen, 2000). Underpinning contemporary notions of a social partnership are a desire to provide some protection for individual employees and their collectives, but within a context that retains many of the key manifestations of the neo-liberal orthodoxy, including flexibility, general regulation and an emphasis on ensuring competitiveness (Huxham and Vangen, 2000).

Social partnerships are not necessarily characterized by an absence of conflict; rather, conflict becomes institutionalized, with established mechanisms for conflict resolution that do not endanger the existing social order (Kirichenko and Koudyukin, 1993: 43). In other words, the emphasis in social partnerships is on fairness, inclusivity, economic growth and social progress rather than order at all costs.

To Waddock (1988), partnerships will only succeed if a degree of flexibility is incorporated. In implementing a partnership, key issues include the anticipated fragility of any deal made, the time needed to develop a partnership, the degree of co-operation present, staff support, and the expectations of the various partners.

4.3 Social partnerships as an ethical principle

It will be apparent from the above discussion that there are three principle drivers of social partnerships: ethical concerns; the desire for peace and stability and/or better relations with stakeholders; and/or better performance outcomes. In practice, these three are often conflated: to proponents of partnerships – whatever the form – any costs could be justified as being offsettable against long-term organizational performance gains. Indeed, an optimistic strand of the human resource management (HRM) literature in the 1990s suggested that it was possible through partnership or partnership-like arrangements to place the firm on a mutual gains footing, with the best possible organizational performance being secured through granting staff a greater degree of co-determination in the running of the firm (see, for example, Kochan and Osterman, 2000).

From the Kantian tradition, good behaviour simply prompted by the desire to make more money would be devoid of any moral worth; in contrast, writers in the utilitarian tradition, such as Singer (1995) would argue that such debates are meaningless: what counts is if the outcomes are generally better for the main parties. However, whatever the rationale, this debate has been rather overtaken by events. Whether it is the provision of low-cost fast food in the developed world, or the operation of a sweatshop in rural China, it has become palpably obvious that it is possible to make a great deal of money in the short term (whatever the long-term sustainability of a particular business model) through demonstrably unethical behaviour; there is no evidence that enlightened action is driving out bad behaviour in the interests of making profits, and, in fact, the converse may be true. Hence, the ethical case for social partnerships needs to be made in its own right – that social partnership represents a 'positive good' whatever the profitability outcomes.

It can be argued that partnerships may provide the basis for a more democratic work experience, through infusing new forms of participation (Burnell, 2003: 14). It may similarly give surrounding communities a say in how an organization that has a central impact on their lives operates (Burnell, 2003). However, partnerships may limit existing participation, through broadening the scope of consultation (Beardwell and Holden, 2001: 490): in other words, social partnerships may undermine existing forums for granting employees a say – such as collective bargaining – with much business being shifted to consultatative forums, where employers can pick and choose which recommendations of the 'partners' they wish to take on board.

4.4   Types of social partnership

While the term 'social partnership' is widely deployed, it can in fact refer to three very distinct phenomena: community partnerships also referred to as community outreach philanthropy; neo-corporatism; and firm-level partnerships with employees.

4.4.1   Community partnerships

4.4.1.1   The emergence of community philanthropy

Community philanthropy has its origins in the United States. Relatively early democratization relieved many of the revolutionary pressures that emerged elsewhere in the developed world in the nineteenth century (Davis, 2001: 145). Hence, indigenous socialist movements or working-class parties never gained much strength, and there were fewer pressures to regulate the activities of emerging industrialists (Davis, 2001). Quite simply, access to the vote allowed more disadvantaged groups in society at least some redress – or the appearance of it – in the polls, relieving pressure to democratize the workplace, or to make firms more accountable to society. Hence the American state in the nineteenth century focused primarily on issues such as the absorption of newly-gained territories and the provision of a physical infrastructure, rather than a perceived need to promote social solidarity (Davis, 2001). This gave firms a relatively free hand to organize work as they saw fit. However, this relative freedom came at a price: the state's 'hands-off' approach meant that firms had to develop and secure their own relations with surrounding communities, rather than relying on the state to bankroll a supportive social infrastructure. Quite simply, firms needed at least workable relations with surrounding communities as suppliers of labour and consumers of products. In other words, a hands-off approach by government still required firms to build a basic degree of trust to make commercial exchange relations possible.

This led in the late nineteenth century to some enlightened managers promoting an early form of social partnership, which has sometimes been referred to as 'community philanthropy'. In essence, emerging industrialists sought to legitimize their new power and wealth – and, perhaps, to salve their consciences – through building relations with surrounding communities through 'good works'. The latter could encompass the provision of housing, the payment of reasonable wages and/or the provision of some basic social services. Of course, there was always a tension between this and the continued desire to generate profits. On the one hand, this led to many 'community philanthropy' programmes failing in their objectives of ensuring labour quiescence, an example being the great struggles within the Ford Motor Company in the 1920s and 1930s. On the other hand, the rationale of many industrialists was not simply to secure peace: others were genuinely concerned with 'putting something back into society'. However, in either case, such initiatives were a voluntary 'gift' that presupposed no ongoing obligation. Moreover, the nature and extent of any philanthropy was purely up to the choice of the givers: by implication, they know what was best for the recipient. Again, 'good work' initiatives were often prompted by a desire to fend off government intervention (Currie and Skolnick, 1988).

However, community partnerships could help to improve employment relations, and provide the firm with more ideas as to the needs of its customers and workers (Sagawa and Segal, 2000). Again, the nature of a federal system meant that there were strong political reasons for firms to have some support from local and regional communities (Currie and Skolnick, 1988: 38).

4.4.1.2   *The emergence and rise of community outreach philanthropy*

The economic crisis of the early 1970s prompted far-reaching structural changes in the economies of the advanced societies. Rising energy costs and intensifying overseas competition forced many manufacturing firms to cut back greatly on employment, contributing to increasing income inequality. In practice, this had the effect of weakening ties between firms and surrounding communities; traditional relations between firms and employees, and the areas they came from, were undermined.

Partially in reaction to the excesses of the 1980s, this in turn stimulated a new variation on a philanthropic theme: 'community outreach philanthropy' or 'community outreach social partnership' (Mellahi and Wood, 2004). Such schemes centre on the firm engaging in formal dialogue with bodies operating in surrounding communities, in order to deal with issues of mutual concern, often focusing on social problems and regeneration.

It was hoped that this could allow firms to deepen their geographical reach, make better use of relevant local skills, and be more in tune with the needs and concerns of immediate customers (Sagawa and Segal, 2000). Indeed, such was the appeal of community outreach social partnerships, that, to proponents, it could be argued that they were rapidly becoming the norm in the US business world (Sagawa and Segal, 2000).

Contemporary community social partnerships are, in many respects, the natural development of traditional corporate philanthropy: in its more recent manifestations, the firm forges partnerships with community organizations, in order to ensure that its activities have the maximum impact. Examples of such partnerships would include those between several firms, local authorities and voluntary associations to revitalize central Cleveland in the late 1980s (Austin, 1998). While to proponents, such partnerships represent a 'win–win' situation, often such arrangements are relatively fragile, and depend on both mutual respect and co-operation, and delivery (Waddock, 1988).

4.4.1.3   Limits of community outreach partnerships

On the one hand, community-based social partnerships can prove beneficial to all parties: hence, they may be justifiable on utilitarian grounds. On the other hand, from a Kantian perspective, if prompted purely by the desire to promoted legitimacy or competitiveness, such initiatives are devoid of moral worth. Indeed, such initiatives may be even criticized from a utilitarian perspective, if they fail to prove beneficial to the wider community, and weaken pressure for more meaningful reforms.

It could further be argued that many community-linked partnerships represent little more than a form of marketing by other means. Corporate assistance for community development may result in favourable exposure for the firm, through both formal and informal mechanisms. However, many utilitarians would have little problem with such developments, as long as they result in a general bettering of the social condition, or, indeed, of the biosphere.

An alternative, and somewhat bleaker, view of corporate social responsibility – particularly in its more holistic partnership manifestations – is provided by David Korten. Korten asserts that, given the predatory nature of contemporary capitalism, with its emphasis on short-term profits, any company that acts in a socially responsible fashion is automatically placed at a disadvantage: 'corporate managers live and work in a system that is virtually feeding on the socially responsible' (quoted in Ferrell et al., 2000: 279).

Critics of the more recent manifestations of community partnerships have charged that such initiatives are little better than their Victorian precursors: the firm engages in limited and tightly budgeted good works to improve its image, while continuing with the untrammelled pursuit of profit. For example, 'green initiatives' may represent little more than 'feel good stunts' to promote over-priced products, rather than genuine attempts to do something about a real global crisis (Ferrell et al., 2000: 280). Again, partnerships with community organizations may be difficult to manage, and often fail to live up to expectations (Huxham and Vangen, 2000). In part, this reflects a tendency for such developments to be top-down, involving local 'experts' and 'leaders', rather than grassroots individuals (Huxham and Vangen, 2000).

Finally, as is the case with traditional community philanthropy, modern community partnerships represent a 'good works' gift of the firm, that may be withdrawn. In contrast to government spending, communities have less room to debate the desirability or scope of any social provision provided by firms (Chomsky, 1996). Indeed, the political pressures to rein-in corporate excesses in the USA remain slight, while the limited and fragile nature of corporate philanthropy is unlikely to serve as an effective mechanism for resolving underlying crises of legitimacy (Brenner, 2002).

4.5   Social accords: neo-corporatism

Much of interwar Europe was beset with ruinous social conflicts, contributing to the rise of fascism and war. Postwar reconstruction led to a strong emphasis on a rather different form of social partnership, 'neo-corporatism', characterized by consensual decision-making by key interest groups, most notably employers, unions and the state (Wood and Harcourt, 2001). The latter would encompass basic wage rates and working conditions, regulated through a sequential series of deals and agreements (Kuhlmann, 2000). Neo-corporatist deals contributed to unprecedented social equality, low unemployment and strong economic performance across much of Western Europe in the 1950s and 1960s (Teague, 1995: 255–6). Of course, for a deal to work, participating negotiating parties need to be representative of their relevant constituency, and able to sell any deal made back to their constituents, even if it is ostensibly against their short-term interests (Olson, 1982).

Again, economic crises in the 1970s and 1980s placed the neo-corporatist model under strain. First, the rise of non-standard work – insecure, temporary and part-time – and unemployment placed a growing proportion of society outside the neo-corporatist tent (Casey and Gold, 2000). Moreover, the rising power of employers during periods of recession (Kelly, 1999: 107) led to growing pressures for earlier trade-offs to be revisited.

While there is no doubt that neo-corporatism may be beneficial to all parties, such deals may be criticized on a number of grounds. First, parties to any deal need to ensure their supporters adhere to any deal: this reining-in of constituents may mean that legitimate grassroots concerns and interests may be ignored (Olson, 1982). Second, those interest groups not party to any negotiations may similarly be ignored: this may in the end result in a relatively small group of privileged insiders pursuing their own interests, to the detriment of wider society. However, such deals do recognize the legitimacy of employee concerns, and indeed via government, of the electorate, and hence also the wider society. Therefore, they may represent an ethical good, on utilitarian grounds, or indeed, even from certain strands of the rights-based tradition – most notably the later works of Rawls (Rawls, 2001).

4.6   Workplace-based social partnerships

The nature of contemporary workplace-based social partnerships – that is, partnerships between employees and managers *within* the firm – represents a response to the economic crisis of the 1970s. To optimistic writers, the crisis of the traditional paradigm of mass production – Fordism – led to the adoption of new manufacturing techniques and organizational forms (Hirst and Zeitlin, 2001: 516), reflecting a need to produce high quality and varied products to meet increasingly sophisticated consumer demand. This use of new techniques necessitated new, more highly skilled and more empowered workforces; work became reskilled and 'debureaucratized' (that is, with a lesser role for formal rules and procedures, and a more human-centred and less confrontational employment relations system); however, such predictions have proved to be premature (Belussi and Garibaldo, 2001: 466). None the less, it could be argued that a new reliance on a firm's human attributes has paved the way for fairer and more partnership orientated ways of working that are mutually beneficial (Waddock, 1988).

Typically, such partnerships take the form of a negotiated deal between the employer and the union to work together for the common good of the firm – and, hence, for core stakeholders – through greater consultation and co-determination. Workplace-based partnerships stress the mutual responsibility of unions and managers to work together in a way that is non-confrontational and conciliatory, 'to introduce change, improve productivity and resolve disputes' (Beardwell and Holden, 2001: 490).

Companies can benefit from flatter organizations, as employers take more responsibility for their own management. Co-operation would make employees more willing to embrace change, and hence enable the firm to respond more rapidly to external challenges. Indeed, there is little doubt that employees place a high premium on quality of work (including a stake in how it is organized) and job fulfilment (Beardwell and Holden, 2001: 490). This has led to workplace-based social partnerships gaining strong support from unions in Britain (Bacon and Storey, 2000; Undy, 1999; Beardwell and Holden, 2001: 490).

Critics of workplace-based social partnerships have suggested, that, as with community outreach initiatives, they are really more about securing profitability than ensuring fairness (Breitenfellner, 1997). Moreover, workplace-based partnerships have tended to be nationally specific, with firms often marrying 'good practice' at home with extreme labour repression – most commonly through the use of subcontractors – in subsidiaries in the developing world (Breitenfellner, 1997).

Workplace-based social partnerships give unions a formal role in the workplace, though one that is firmly subordinated to overall organizational strategic objectives: hence, critics have charged that participation in such partnerships represents little more than a device for incorporation into management that unions have to acquiesce to because of their growing weakness (Guest, 2001: 101). In contrast to industry-level (or national-level) collective bargaining, partnerships place heavy demands on union resources, which have to service many workplace-level deals on an ongoing basis (Turner, 2000). Once they have formally bought into partnerships, unions may face relegation to a largely consultative role, with diminishing recourse to collective bargaining (Beardwell and Holden, 2001: 490).

Hence, the costs 'can be high (to unions), and the benefits may be sufficient to warrant these costs in only a limited number of workplaces' (Godard, 1997). Employers promoting partnerships may lack commitment, using them as a means of extracting concessions from unions, before switching to more hard-line, top-down HRM policies: examples would include General Motors (GM), Caterpillar and Boeing (Moody, 1998). Indeed, it can be argued that 'what employees can do for the firm' is the primary agenda of partnerships, not what the firm can do for its people, the members of the organizational community (Beardwell and Holden, 2001: 101). Moreover, Godard (1997) suggests that the introduction of partnership deals at workplace level and job shedding are closely connected (Godard, 1997).

4.7   Social partnerships and European integration

As Hyman (1997) notes, important by-products of social partnership debates have been efforts to introduce a social dialogue dimension into the process of European integration. It is argued that, in an age of increasingly mobile capital, it is desirable to strengthen transnational institutions, underpinned by international partnership agreements (Oberman, 2000). Indeed, it can be argued that transnational partnership deals represent the best chance for preserving the classical 'Rhineland model' of social partnerships (Apeldoorn, 2000). In the European Community (EC), social partnership has been promoted through a new article in the treaty, Article 118b, which prescribes that 'the Commission shall endeavour to develop the dialogue between management and labour at European level which could, if the two sides consider it desirable, lead to relations based on agreement', amplified in the Maastricht protocol (Hyman, 1997). These agreements aim to promote agreement between management and labour on an EU-wide level, agreements that could possibly become encoded in legislation. Critics have argued that, to date, this process has yielded little, other than placing considerable demands on trade union resources (Hyman, 1997).

4.8   Social partnerships and the philosophical tradition

A central theme of this volume has been whether, if solely motivated by the exigencies of profit, managerial decisions that ameliorate or enhance social conditions within or outside the workplace, are devoid of any moral worth. A deontologist would argue that ethical decisions are only ethical if made for the right reasons; in contrast, a utilitarian would see any act that improves overall social happiness as being essentially 'good'. This debate is of particular importance when social partnerships are considered; in most cases, viable social partnerships have only been established or reconstituted when there is a lack of a viable policy alternative and/or when managers see clear gains in terms of the 'bottom line'.

4.9   Summary

Social partnerships are founded on the notion that the interests of management and labour are essentially heterogeneous; however, they may be reconciled through a series of deals and trade-offs (Gebert and Boerner, 1999). To proponents of such arrangements, the outcome of a successful social partnership is a 'win–win' situation, whereby the firm trades-off genuine concessions calculated to improve the material circumstances of other parties in return for their support. To critics, in their contemporary manifestations, they represent little more than a crude attempt to build consent while firms seek ruthlessly to maximize profits, and, as such, are devoid of any moral worth. The social partnership debate underscores the complexity of the ethical dilemmas facing the modern firm; above all, the question of why firms should act ethically in the first place. In other words, firms should consider whether ethical conduct is worth pursuing in its own right, or should simply be subordinated to the quest for profits.

Discussion questions

- How do the different forms of social partnership differ?
- Does the fact that many social partnerships are prompted by profitability rather than ethical reasons make them devoid of moral worth?

Case study

Closing case study

Rebuilding the social contract at work: Saturn

The Saturn Corporation is a wholly-owned subsidiary of General Motors that manufactures and sells small cars. From its initial planning process, conducted in 1983 by a 'Committee of 99' consisting of GM and UAW representatives, Saturn was conceived of as a full partnership between the union and the company. The decision to create Saturn was motivated by company and union desire to build and sell a small model in the United States that would compete well against imports and to create jobs for UAW members. The decision to create an entirely new company at a greenfield site was made after management concluded that GM could not competitively manufacture a small car in the U.S. under the existing labor contract and management policies.

Key events

Several key events have shaped the GM–UAW labor–management experiment taking place at Saturn: equal partnership between union and management in the design of the organization; the emergence of co-management; the importance of performance *and* image; the introduction of conflicts and controversies about Saturn's future within the union and GM after its original champions retired; and concerns over Saturn's long-term viability as expressed during 1998 contract negotiations.

Joint approach to organizational design: the Committee of 99

The Committee of 99 developed an organizational design that makes the UAW an institutional 'partner,' participating in consensus-based decision-making from the shop floor to the levels of senior management. This structure is overseen by a series of 'decision rings' at the department, plant or business unit, manufacturing policy, and strategic policy levels of the organization. Through the partnership's arrangements, the UAW becomes an important part of strategic decisions made regarding supplier and retailer selection, choice of technology, and product development. An initial 28-page collective bargaining agreement outlines the basic principles governing the relationship and the team-based system of work organization.

The partnership process is complemented by employment practices designed to ensure that employees have the knowledge, skills, and motivation to contribute to the performance of the enterprise. Saturn requires all employees to take a minimum of 92 hours of training each year. In 1995, 20 per cent of compensation at Saturn was contingent on the completion of this minimal amount. In addition, more than 80 per cent of the workforce is guaranteed employment security for life. Work organization at Saturn is based on self-directed work teams of 10 to 15 members, who are cross-trained and rotate responsibility across the tasks in their unit. Teams have collective responsibility for hiring new members and electing their own team leaders. The next level of organization, called modules, cover an average of five to seven teams and conduct weekly governance meetings in which teams are represented by their leaders. Teams also have responsibility for quality assurance, job assignments, record keeping, safety and health, material and inventory control, training, supplies, and housekeeping.

Emergence of co-management

As the organization took shape, local union officials and management added another unique feature. At the department or module level, management responsibilities became shared by two 'module advisors', who are partnered. Each 'partnership' at the department level consists of union module advisors who are partnered with non-represented management module advisors. This feature of the partnership makes Saturn the boldest experiment in co-management found in the U.S. today.

Until 1994, jointly-selected UAW crew co-ordinators maintained responsibility, along with their non-represented partners, for managing crews across

Case study

Continued

several departments, which is the responsibility of superintendents in GM's more traditional plants. However, in 1994 – as a result of a negotiated agreement and in response to considerable pressure from rank and file workers – the 14UAW crew coordinators became elected officials with the authority to file grievances.

Performance and image

Saturn uses as its marketing slogan and logo the following phrase: 'A Different Kind of Company. A Different Kind of Car'. Thus, it builds on its partnership with the UAW and several other distinctive features of the company's practices – such as its fixed price, no-haggle, retail sales and service strategy – in positioning the company and its products in the minds of consumers. To date, this approach has been very well received by the market. According to the J.D. Power Customer Satisfaction Index, within two years of its first production run in 1990 and in every year since, Saturn achieved higher ratings in initial vehicle quality, in satisfaction after one year of ownership, and in service than any car in its class. Only Lexus and Infiniti, two upscale models costing three times as much as Saturn, received higher customer satisfaction ratings.

Saturn's productivity and profitability, however, are not as high as its quality ratings. Yet, its productivity levels still remain near the top of those at GM's other plants. In evaluating profitability, a question arises: Should Saturn amortize this investment alone, or should the rest of GM's enterprise – which was supposed to learn from this experiment – share in their costs? Regardless, Saturn generated its first operating profit in 1993 after mobilizing its third crew and being pressured by its GM parent to cut costs and move up the date targeted for achieving a profit. Bonuses based on financial, productivity, and quality goals have been paid to Saturn employees each year since 1993. The 1995 and 1996 bonuses totaled $10,000 for each member, which is the maximum allowable under the contract. Bonuses declined in 1997 and 1998, as Saturn's sales declined.

Conflicts and controversies

Despite its successes, Saturn is a controversial topic within both the UAW International Union and GM. Several years after Saturn was created, its original champions within both the UAW and GM retired. Their successors were not as committed to Saturn's principles and partnership structure. Meanwhile, over the course of the 1990s, GM and the UAW experienced an intermittent set of strikes, largely over questions about outsourcing. These conflicts peaked during a seven-week strike in the summer of 1998, which shut down nearly all of GM's production operations. At the end of this strike, both GM and UAW leaders pledged to find a better way of dealing with these issues – yet what, exactly, this promise means remains uncertain. GM continues to feel intense pressure to outsource more of its component production to outside vendors. In fact, it announced shortly after the end of the strike its intention to group component operations into a separate division (Delphi), as well as to continue exploring options for divesting component operations that are not competitive with outside alternatives.

UAW leadership and the leaders of the Saturn local have been experiencing considerable internal conflict over the past decade on a host of issues ranging from the adequacy of representation on traditional issues to shift schedules, overtime and shift premiums, and other administrative matters. Political factions have also arisen wi thin thelocal (similar to the dynamics at other UAW local unions). For example, each election of union officers since 1992 has been hotly contested.

GM management has also been ambivalent about Saturn. On the one hand, the corporation relishes the positive image that Saturn has achieved, and urges other divisions to learn from Saturn's experiences. On the other hand, while some technical and marketing innovations have been adopted, there is little evidence that significant learning from or diffusion of Saturn's organizational principles has occurred within GM. Moreover, in 1996, GM decided to accede to the International UAW's preference to build the second-generation Saturn model in GM's Wilmington, Delaware plant – not in Spring Hill, as requested by the local union and management. The labour agreement negotiated at Wilmington calls for some use of teams and employee involvement, but does not include the full partnership model found in Spring Hill; it remains a part of the national UAW–GM contract.

In 1998, GM announced that Saturn's engineering, design, and parts sourcing decisions would be integrated into the GM small car division as part of its overall re-centralization of these functions.

Finally, Saturn has somewhat of a schizophrenic identity. On the one hand, it receives many accolades for innovative organizational design and employee relations, as well as for favorable customer satisfaction performance. On the other hand, many of the provisions of the partnership are of questionable legality under American labor and employment laws; the co-management and shared governance structures have been criticized by some business leaders as rescinding important managerial prerogatives; and some union leaders are critical of the many long-standing work rules that the union abandoned in return for this type role in the governance and management process.

1998 negotiations

Concerns over these developments came to a head in Spring Hill in 1998. In April of that year, the union – in response to rank and file concerns over the long-term viability of Saturn – held a referendum over whether to continue the partnership as specified under the local agreement or to return to the national contract. Sixty-eight per cent of the membership voted in favor of continuing the partnership as specified in the Saturn agreement. Then, in the summer of 1998, the union took a strike authorization vote and issued a 30-day strike letter in an effort to resolve an ongoing dispute over both the formula for the

Case study

Continued

risk–reward plan and the broader issue of the future product stream planned for Spring Hill. These negotiations produced an agreement that included the following provisions: GM would build a Saturn Sport Utility Vehicle at Spring Hill; the union would be included in the sourcing decisions affecting Saturn products; moreover, four factors (cost, quality, brand image, and job security) would be considered in making sourcing decisions; and a compromise resolution to the parties' different interpretations of the risk–reward formula would be enacted.

These negotiations served to force a decision on Saturn's future, which had been either delayed or allowed to drift for several years. GM was forced to decide how Saturn would fit into its larger centralization effort, as well as its common engineering, purchasing and platform strategies, and structural realignment. It also had to choose which – if any – future products would be produced at Spring Hill. The result was that GM stated its continuing commitment to the Saturn Partnership and reinforced this commitment by agreeing to build the Sport Utility Vehicle in Spring Hill, as well as to give the union a voice in sourcing decisions. Yet, despite these major compromises and commitments, GM continues to follow its recentralization and outsourcing strategies. GM's strategy remains rather ambivalent – trying to accommodate the principles of the Saturn partnership while simultaneously integrating Saturn into the corporation.

The negotiations involved considerable use of traditional bargaining tactics by the union, including severe criticism of the commitment and competence of Saturn's senior management. A strike vote was held, the pace of production slowed, union leaders went around Saturn management to pressure GM executives, and the union used the leverage created by bad publicity. These strategies, in turn, irritated Saturn management officials and fostered bad feelings.

Summary and implications

In a recent paper, Kochan and Rubinstein (1998) argue that Saturn represents not only the most comprehensive labor–management partnership model found in the U.S. but also an organization that embodies many of the principles of what is meant by a 'stakeholder' corporation:

1. Saturn was designed to achieve both GM's shareholders' goal of making a small car profitably, and the workforce and union's goal of building small cars in the U.S. with U.S. workers and UAW members; this fact implies that the success of the firm should be measured against these multiple objectives.
2. Workers and union representatives were to be full and legitimate partners in the governance and management processes of the firm, and
3. Workers share the risks and rewards of the firm's performance with shareholders.

Thus, more than any other U.S. case, Saturn illustrates a type of organizational partnership and employment system that can be created when a union with a vision of its own participates in the design, governance, and management of the enterprise. Workers have a strong voice on both traditional labor–management and broader managerial or strategic issues. Principles of teamwork, continuous improvement, quality, safety, ergonomics and customer satisfaction are given high priorities. Conflicts occur both within and across traditional labor and management boundaries, but are managed and resolved differently through the reliance on traditional contract negotiations or grievance arbitration processes.

Whether Saturn's limited profitability to date implies that this organizational model inevitably redistributes some of the financial rewards across the different stakeholders at the expense of shareholders is still an open question – one that is likely to be the subject of considerable debate in the future. Thus, despite the positive publicity that the UAW–Saturn partnership has received and its success on the quality and marketing fronts, the ambivalent support from both parents (UAW International and GM), leave the future of Saturn somewhat uncertain.

At the same time, GM and the UAW both realize that the traditional approaches they have taken to their relationship in general have not addressed the underlying competitiveness and job security challenges they face. Both parties are examining future options. Whether any of the principles, practices, and lessons from a decade of Saturn experience will be brought to bear on this larger relationship remains to be seen.

Over the past several years – and particularly over the past year – the parties have been caught in a downward, reinforcing spiral. The union was frustrated with a lack of leadership and decision-making power within Saturn management and the lack of support from UAW national leaders. Its renewed militancy has left some managers feeling they have been betrayed. At the workplace, the partnership was put on hold. Workers, in turn, became demoralized, as they saw sales and production fall; as the relationship deteriorated, they began falling into traditional patterns. Therefore, performance declined, adding further to costs and the frustration of management.

GM agreed to a settlement that is inconsistent with its larger strategy of centralizing design, purchasing, and outsourcing components. It gave the union a role in purchasing/sourcing decisions, using the criteria of cost, quality, brand equity (image) and job security. They did so in this instance because the UAW threatened a strike that would have imposed big economic and public relations costs on the company – and might have signalled the death of the partnership principles. How the new arrangement will be implemented and made to work in the context of GM's broader centralization and outsourcing decisions remains to be seen.

Saturn represents the most far-reaching example of a labor–management partnership model, one that embodies more of the features of a stakeholder model of the corporation than any other example discussed here. As such, it suggests both some strengths and limitations.

On the one hand, it shows that multiple objectives of firms and employees can be achieved and balanced if both labor and employer representatives share

---

Case study

Continued

a commitment to building and sustaining a partnership – that is, a legacy of mutual commitment fostered by the first generation of leaders who built Saturn. Second, it demonstrates that this type of employment relationship and the commitment to quality and customer service resonates positively with consumers and has a positive market value.

But the case also illustrates the significant resistance that exists to sharing power fully and redefining the basic mission, goals, and governance structures of the American corporation – and, therefore, the difficulty Saturn has experienced in sustaining support from leaders both within its parent labor and corporate organizations. It also suggests that significant changes in labor and employment laws, as well as perhaps in corporate law, would be needed to allow this full type of stakeholder firm to emerge and survive in the United States.

A further limitation of the Saturn model is the fact that – like the other examples discussed here – 'non-represented' managers and professionals were not formally included in the governance process. How to treat these employees remains an open question.

(*Source*: Kochan, 1999)

Questions

- Why do you think the union management partnership at Saturn ran into difficulties?
- How sustainable, in your opinion, is the partnership model at Saturn?

Note

*Some of the points made in this chapter are developed more fully in Mellahi and Wood (2004), pp. 667–83.

References

Apeldoorn, B. 2000. 'Transnational Class Agency and European Governance: The Case of the European Round Table of Industrialists', *New Political Economy*, 5,2:157–81.

Austin, J. 1998. 'Business Leadership Lessons from the Cleveland Turnaround', *California Management Review*, 41,1: 86–106.

Bacon, N. and Storey, J. 2000. 'New Employment Strategies in Britain: Towards Individualism or Partnership?', *British Journal of Industrial Relations*, 38,3: 407–27.

Beardwell, I. and Holden, L. 2001. *Human Resource Management: A Contemporary Approach.* London: Prentice Hall.

Belussi, F. and Garibaldo, F. 2001, 'Variety of Pattern of the Post-Fordist Economy', in B. Jessop (ed.), *Regulationist Perspectives on Fordism.* Cheltenham: Edward Elgar.

Breitenfellner, A. 1997. 'Global Unionism: A Potential Player', *International Labour Review,* 136,4: 531–55.

Brenner, R. 2002. *The Boom and the Bubble: The US in the World Economy.* London: Verso.

Burnell, P. 2001. 'Perspectives', in P. Burnell (ed.), *Democracy Through the Looking Glass.* Manchester: Manchester University Press.

Burnell, P. 2003. *Democracy through the Looking Glass.* Manchester: Manchester University Press.

Casey, B. and Gold, M. 2000. *Social Partnerships and Economic Performance.* Cheltenham: Edward Elgar.

Chomsky, N. 1996. 'New Wine in Old Bottles: A Bitter Taste', *Electronic Journal of Radical Organizational Theory,* 2,1: 1–9.

Crouch, C. 1979. 'The State, Capital and Liberal Democracy', in C. Crouch (ed.), *State and Economy in Contemporary Capitalism.* London: Croom Helm.

Croucher, R. and Brewster, C. 1998. 'Flexible Working Practices and the Trade Unions', *Employee Relations,* 20,5.

Currie, E. and Skolnick, J. 1988. *America's Problems: Social Issues and Public Policy.* Glenview, Ill.: Scott Foresman and Co.

Davis, M. 2001. 'Fordism in Crisis', in B. Jessop (ed.), *The Parisian Regulation School – Regulation Theory and the Crisis of Capitalism 1.* Cheltenham: Edward Elgar.

Ferrell, O., Fraedrich, J. and Ferrell, L. 2000. *Business Ethics: Ethical Decision Making and Cases.* Boston, Mass.: Houghton Mifflin.

Gebert, D. and Boerner, S. 1999. 'The Open and Closed Corporation as Distinctive Forms of Organization, *The Journal of Applied Behavioral Science,* 35,3: 341–59.

Godard, J. 1997. 'Review: New Forms of Work Organization – Can Europe Realize Its Potential?', *Relations Industrielles,* 54,1: 203–5.

Guest, D. 2001. 'Industrial Relations and Human Resource Management', in J. Storey (ed.), *Human Resource Management.* London: Thomson Learning.

Hirst, P. and Zeitlin, J. 2001. 'Flexible Specializaton Versus Post-Fordism', in B. Jessop (ed,), *Regulationist Perspectives on Fordism.* Cheltenham: Edward Elgar.

Huxham, C. and Vangen, S. 2000. 'Ambiguity, Complexity and Dynamics in the Membership of Collaboration', *Human Relations,* 53,6: 771–814.

Hyman, R. 1997. 'Trade Unions and European Integration', *Work and Occupations,* 24,3: 309–31.

Iankova, E. 1996. 'Labour Relations and Political Change in Eastern Europe', *Industrial and Labor Relations Review,* 50,1:177–86.

Kelly, J. 1999. *Rethinking Industrial Relations: Mobilization, Collectivism and Long Waves*. London: Routledge.

Kirichenko, O. and Koudyukin, P. 1993. 'Social Partnerships in Russia: The First Steps', *Economic and Industrial Democracy*, 14: 43–55.

Kochan, T. 1999. 'Rebuilding the Social Contract at Work: Saturn', Institute for Work and Employment Research, Sloan School of Management, MIT. Caseplace.org – available at: http://www.caseplace.org/collections/collections_show.htm?doc_id=226102.

Kochan, T. and Osterman, P. 2000. 'The Mutual Gains Enterprise', in C. Mabey, G. Salaman and J. Storey (eds), *Strategic Human Resource Management*. London: Sage.

Kochan, T. and Rubinstein, S. 1998. *Toward a Stakeholder View of the Firm*. Boston, Mass.: MIT.

Kuhlmann, R. 2000. 'Coordination of Collective Bargaining Policy in the European Metalworking Sector: A Response to the Challenges Posed by the Euro', in R. Hoffman, , O. Jacobi, B. Keller and M. Weiss (eds), *Transnational Industrial Relations in Europe*. Dusseldorf: Hans Böckler Stiftung.

Mellahi, K. and Wood, G. 2004. 'Variances in Social Partnership: Towards a Sustainable Model?', *International Journal of Social Economics*, 31,7: 667–83.

Moody, K. 1998. 'Up Against the Polyester Ceiling: The "New" AFL–CIO Organizes – Itself!', *New Politics*, 6,4.

Oberman, W. 2000. 'Review: The Conspicuous Corporation: Business, Public Policy, and Representive Democracy', *Business and Society*, 39,2: 239–44.

Olson, M. 1982. *The Rise and Decline of Nations: Economic Growth, Stagflation and Social Rigidities*. New Haven, Conn.: Yale University Press.

Prechel, H. 1999. 'Fighting for Partnership', *Work and Occupations*, 26,4: 539–40.

Rao, A. and Sita, C. 1993. 'Multi-national Corporate Social Responsibility', *Journal of Business Ethics*, 12,7: 553.

Rawls, J. 2001. *Justice as Fairness: A Restatement*. Cambridge, Mass.: Harvard University Press.

Rubin, H. 1993. 'Understanding the Ethos of Community-Based Development', *Public Administration Review*, 53,5: 428–48.

Sagawa, S. and Segal, E. 2000. 'Common Interest, Common Good: Creating Value Through Business and Social Sector Partnerships', *California Management Review*, 42,2: 105–22.

Singer, P. 1995. *Practical Ethics*. Cambridge: Cambridge University Press.

Sisson, K. 1999. ' The 'New' European Social Model: The End of the Search for an Orthodoxy or Another False Dawn?', *Employee Relations*, 21,5.

Teague, P. 1995. 'Pay Determination in the Republic of Ireland: Towards Societal Corporatism?', *British Journal of Industrial Relations*, 33,2, 253–73.

Teague, P. 2001. 'Converging Divergences and European Employment Relations', *Industrial & Labour Relations Review*, 54,3.

Turner, L. 2000. 'Review: The Brave New World of European Labor: European Trade Unions at the Millennium', *Industrial & Labor Relations Review*, 54,1: 186–8.

Undy, R. 1999. 'Annual Review Article: New Labour's "Industrial Relations Settlement": The Third Way', *British Journal of Industrial Relations*, 37: 315–36.

Waddock, S. 1988. 'Building Successful Social Partnerships', *Sloane Management Review*, 29,4: 17–24.

Waddock, S. A., and Post, J. E. 1991. 'Social Entrepreneurs and Catalytic Change', *Public Administration Review*, 51,5: 393–401.

Wood, G. and Harcourt, M. 2001. 'The Consequences of Neo-Corporatism: A Syncretic Analysis', *International Journal of Sociology and Social Policy*, 20,8: 1–22.

Green issues

Chapter objectives

- To explore what is meant by environmental ethics.
- To understand why environmental issues have become increasingly pressing.
- To locate current environmental debates within the philosophical tradition.
- To introduce contemporary approaches to conservation.
- To examine current legal trends with regard to the environment.

 Case study

Introductory case study

Global logging, war and business

Timber fuels some of the world's most brutal wars, sustains the illegal arms trade and those mercenaries and militias who have tortured, detained, sexually exploited, intimidated and enforced the displacement of populations. Poorly enforced arms laws and trade laws and an almost unregulated shipping industry open to abuses bind together timber, weapons smuggling and war, and keep the business open to criminals. Timber, as an easily exploitable, valuable commodity, has become a resource of choice for warring factions, criminal networks and arms dealers, providing finances and logistics. Host governments or rebel groups sometimes allocate timber concessions to reward supporters. This has gone relatively unchecked and timber fuels conflicts in Cambodia, Sierra Leone, Ivory Coast, Democratic Republic of Congo (DRC), Burma and Liberia.

Sierra Leone's civil war, which by 2001 had reduced average local life expectancy to 25.9 years, was partly financed by elements of the Liberian timber industry. In April 2003, the former Liberian president, Charles Taylor, indicted for war crimes and crimes against humanity by a United Nations special court, admitted to using timber funds to buy weapons in contravention of a UN arms embargo. Investigations revealed that the Liberian government also armed and supported rebels in western Ivory Coast, using a Liberian timber company's warehouse to store weapons and its bush camp to house rebel fighters. Even in countries at peace, such as Cameroon, illegal logging has led to corruption and loss of revenue to the state.

Elsewhere in Africa a few people coordinate the supply of arms in return for natural resources, including diamonds and timber. Leonid Minin, a Ukrainian-born international arms dealer, was awarded a logging concession in Liberia and brokered arms deals with connections that he brought with him, according to the UN. In 2000 he arranged the import of 10,500 AK47 rifles, 8m rounds of ammunition, RPG-26 rocket launchers and sniper rifles. The shipments were transported via Ivory Coast and sent by the Aviatrend Company based in Moscow.

There are two problems: conflict timber and illegal timber. Conflict timber is defined by the NGO Global Witness as 'traded in a way that drives violent armed conflict and threatens national or regional security'. Illegal timber has been logged in contravention of national or international laws. In both cases, funds are siphoned from national budgets, mostly unnoticed by the international community. Due to lack of transparency, legislation needs to be targeted against the strong ties between conflict timber and the arms trade, and against the shipping industry.

The timber trade is often abused by unscrupulous logging companies, governments and rebel groups to facilitate weapons imports and fuel conflict. It is estimated that 40–50% of world trade in small arms is illegal, but the figure is probably much higher as a significant number of legally traded arms end up in the illegal arena. Without proper controls, this trade will remain attractive and lucrative, and international agreements that have made unregulated cross-border trade easier will continue to be exploited. In 2002 only six countries had specific measures in place.

Arms are transported by air and, increasingly, imported by sea. As the world is discovering after the 11 September 2001 attacks, the shipping industry, especially when operating under flags of convenience, provides a dangerously secretive environment with minimal regulation. Goods are shipped inside containers, while exporters create the cargo manifests and individual containers are rarely screened. So shippers seldom know exactly what is being transported. Many ships can hold 5–7,000 containers and it is alarmingly easy to smuggle weapons in them.

The term conflict timber was first coined in 2001 by a UN panel of experts investigating the illegal exploitation of natural resources in the DRC. Since 1998

Case study

Continued

timber there has helped fund a conflict that has killed 3.3–4.7 million people – the greatest loss of life since the Second World War. The volume of wood removed by rebel factions, companies and government-armed forces of neighbouring countries is significant, so great that in neighbouring Uganda the market price halved. The panel found that the conflict was self-perpetuating, as each party had financial interests in its continuation. It uncovered extensive networks established and maintained by Uganda, Rwanda and Zimbabwe, and listed some 50 Congolese and foreign nationals who should be sanctioned and another 85 companies judged in violation of OECD guidelines for multinational enterprises.

Cross-border timber sales in the 1990s provided the Khmer Rouge in Cambodia with a monthly $10–20m during the dry season to fund its fighting. The trade not only sustained the Khmer Rouge's activities, but control of timber resources became a cause for conflict. In 1991 the Khmer Rouge leader, Pol Pot, said: 'Our state does not have sufficient capital to expand its strength or enlarge the army. Resources [in liberated and semi- liberated zones] must be utilized as assets.'

In Burma [Myanmar], a country with a poor human rights record, the government relies heavily on its forests, its second most valuable export, accounting for approximately $280m in 2001. This figure does not take into account significant quantities of timber clandestinely exported by sea.

While all governments have the sovereign right to use natural resources within their borders, they must follow their own laws and international regulations, extracting resources sustainably and for the benefit of all. Often, where timber has been used to fund conflict, governments, rebel groups or individuals have used war to loot natural resources, financing political goals or personal fortunes. Funds are taken from an already impoverished population and given to a small elite.

Each logging company's circumstances are different, where they assist government forces and government-supported rebels, and their engagement varies in degree: some may have been directly complicit, while others might have been coerced. But either way the results for local people – abuses, corruption and destabilization – are the same. In Liberia, according to the UN, offenders have included Minin, of the Exotic Tropical Timber Enterprise (ETTE); Gus Kouwenhoven, of the Oriental Timber Company (OTC); and arms dealers Victor Bout and Sanjivan Ruprah. All four are on the UN travel ban list for providing financial and military support to the Revolutionary United Front (RUF) in Sierra Leone's civil war.

Companies that import conflict timber have claimed that if there is a problem it is within the supplier country; traders continued to buy from companies known to have been involved in arms imports. Several importing companies have launched extensive public relations campaigns: they proclaim their concern for human rights and the environment and give their buyers a false sense that their products have no link with environmental destruction and human calamity. This sells timber but hides the truth.

The UN expert panel report on Sierra Leone in 2000 outlined the role of elements of the Liberian timber industry in sustaining the RUF; subsequent reports on Liberia have mentioned the role of some logging companies in arms purchases and imports. Global Witness and other NGOs have for years provided information to importers about the abuses and unsustainable practices of many in the Liberian logging industry. However, despite claims to import only from responsible, sustainable providers, many importers continued to purchase from Liberia; the Danish company DLH-Nordisk, which had halted imports from Liberian companies ILC and MGC, purchased Liberian products up to February 2003. It seems that only the recent UN ban on all Liberian timber products will stop importers.

While companies along the chain of custody deny responsibility, the effects of the conflict timber industry on civilians are immediate. The people that governments, logging companies and importers claim to be concerned about rarely see the revenue improve their lives; the industry worsens conditions by facilitating arms imports, and there are human rights abuses committed by government and logging company militias, long-term destruction of forests and an infrastructure of violence and plunder. People who live in or near logging concessions have their way of life destroyed and lose access to forests. Because of deforestation and because they are often forcibly removed from their land, local non-timber resources such as medicines and vegetables, become scarce. Changes to local ecologies often lead to floods and droughts. The argument that the timber industry betters lives is wrong and usually only made by those who have a vested interest in the trade.

The effects of conflict timber are long-term, since it destroys what could be a sustainable source of revenue for impoverished people; much of the revenue in the short term goes directly to an elite. The uncontrolled exploitation of the resource funds further conflict; the conflict creates a demand for timber, which worsens the conflict, and which then creates further demand for timber.

The criminalization of the timber trade has not been checked much by the international community. Shipping laws have not changed significantly and lack of transparency continues. The international community has also not taken proper action over trade laws, especially those covering the arms trade and conflict commodities, so trade in conflict timber appeals to corrupt governments, rebels, international criminal networks, small arms traders and unscrupulous companies.

There have been some positive developments. In May 2003 the UN Security Council imposed a ban on all Liberian timber, which came into effect on 7 July 2003. The latest expert panel report on Liberia is highly critical of the logging industry, including the lack of benefits for local populations and the potential for exploitation by armed outsiders. Reports by the UN expert panel on the DRC forced companies mentioned to rethink business policies, while many assets were frozen and several people in government positions were suspended. In Cambodia, Global Witness was introduced as an independent forest monitor to decrease the level of corruption and illegality of the timber trade.

Case study

Continued

However, a lot of the expert panel's recommendations for the DRC were not heeded by the international community. In the case of Cambodia, the independent monitor has been dismissed despite doing the job properly, while the international donor community has sat back and watched a small hope for transparency there dwindle.

The progress from the imposition of timber sanctions on Liberia is possibly threatened by a proposed wood-for-food programme, which would allow logging to resume to pay for humanitarian supplies, in contradiction of the most recent expert panel report that not only recommended that a moratorium on all extractive industries 'should remain in place until such time as peace and stability are restored and good governance is established' but that 'the Security Council must accept its responsibility for the negative impact of the timber sanctions and ensure that emergency relief aid is provided'. Moves to lift timber sanctions ignore the links between the Liberian logging industry and the arms trade, the abuses of company militia members, and the fact that both government and rebel groups have access to, and would profit from, logging concessions. It would be almost impossible to regulate the trade in a country so torn by conflict. Such a programme could further push Liberia's people towards catastrophe by enriching warring parties, mortgaging an important economic resource, and benefiting only a small elite.

The international community, trade organizations and importers must take greater responsibility in fighting the trade instead of dismissing it so readily. Not taking action licenses some of world's worst violence and human rights abuses. This inaction is unacceptable, as citizens and consumers of importing states, as well as their trading partners, have a right to expect that the goods they buy are not a cause of conflict.

(*Source*: Blondel, 2004)

Questions

- What role can business play in 'cleaning up' the timber industry? And, what prevents companies from playing such a role?
- What ethical responsibility should the consumer bear for bad practice by large sections of the global timber industry?

5.1 Introduction

The environment is often not cast as an ethical issue at all, but rather something that firms should take into account to secure their long-term profitability. None the less, there is little doubt that environmental debates are also fundamentally ethical ones. In this chapter, we explore the relationship between business and the environment, both in terms of theoretical debates and contemporary issues.

5.2   What is environmental ethics?

The environment can be defined as 'a dynamic and evolving system of natural and human factors in which all living organisms operate or human activities take place, and what has an direct or indirect... effect or influence on human actions at a given time in a circumscribed area' (Vaillancourt in Kulkarni, 2000). Environmental ethics aims to provide ethical guidelines governing humanity's relationship with nature. A green firm will adopt 'resource conservation and environmentally friendly strategies at all stages of the value chain' (Oyewole, 2001).

A number of writers in the fields of business and environmental ethics have argued that the firm needs to meet the concerns of all relevant stakeholders regarding the environment (Kulkarni, 2000). However, particularly if different stakeholder groupings have different agendas, disputes may arise, with the exigencies of short-term wealth creation overriding long-term environmental concerns, leading to calls for a fairer negotiating framework founded on trust (Kulkarni, 2000). There is little doubt that trust matters – not just with regard to the environment, but also with a wide range of other ethical issues. The importance of firms being able to operate in an environment of trust is underscored by the proliferation of ethical codes of conduct, aimed at setting yardsticks to be adhered to, and rules governing disclosure of information (Kulkarni, 2000).

5.3   Why does the environment matter?

There are a range of reasons why firms should take the environment seriously. First, it has been argued that, quite simply, wilful environmental devastation is ruining the planet; it is becoming increasingly obvious that 'what goes around comes around' (Graybill, 2000; see Welford, 1995). An increasingly visible example of the latter would be global warming. It has now been widely recognized that excessive emissions of carbon dioxide and other greenhouse gases from industry and intensive farming have already had adverse consequences for the global climate, and that a 60 per cent reduction in carbon dioxide emissions will be necessary to stabilize atmospheric concentration (Roberts and Sheail, 1993). This has led to a number of major industrial countries, most notably Germany, taking concrete steps to control the scale of atmospheric pollution. Unfortunately, the world's largest producer of greenhouse gases, the United States under the Bush II administration, has remained reluctant to take serious measures in this regard: while in December 2007 it agreed at the Bali Climate Conference to further intensive talks to reduce carbon admissions, this was only once so many concessions had been made as to, arguably, make this commitment meaningless.

Second, there is the legal dimension. There has been a great proliferation of environmental legislation (Rezaee, 2000). Quite simply, environmental issues are increasingly popular with both politicians and the wider community (Anonymous, 2000). There is always an incentive for firms to resort to free-riding, to try and opt out from any limiting ground rules, no matter how ethically desirable. However, the proliferation of environmental legislation has greatly constrained the ability of firms to do so (Welford, 1995: 10).

Moreover, looking after the environment increasingly makes economic sense. There is a strong demand for green products. While this is especially the case in Western Europe (for example, opinion surveys have indicated that 80 per cent of consumers in Germany, Italy and Spain would switch to greener products if given the opportunity), this demand is rapidly spreading worldwide (Oyewole, 2001). People are inherently risk-adverse; they will choose greener products if there is a fear of the personal health costs of 'ungreen' goods (Oyewole, 2001). However, it should be noted that this risk aversion varies greatly between social contexts. For example, consumers in the United States have been far more willing to accept genetically modified foods than those in Europe. In addition, there is the question as to how much more consumers are willing to pay for green products; a common argument is that the polluters should pay for the consequences of their actions, yet, of course, unclean industries are ultimately a product of consumer demand (Wyburd, 1993).

Traditionally, firms have viewed meeting environmental concerns simply as a cost. For example, the American Petroleum Institute has argued that conservation measures cost 400,000 jobs in the oil industry in the 1980s (Kulkarni, 2000) (of course, this argument does not take into account jobs that may have been generated in alternative energy production, or in monitoring or pollution-reduction equipment). However, as noted earlier, it has become 'good business' for firms to take the environment seriously, which would include the promotion of products that reduce waste and use energy more efficiently. In the marketplace, firms have to respond flexibly to consumer pressures (Welford, 1995: 11). While critics have charged that 'green marketing' is often characterized by overstatement, there is little doubt that there are plenty of pressure groups and competitors willing to expose the false claims of others (Welford, 1995: 45).

The need for greater environmental concern is eroded by the tendency of firms to focus on short-term profits; however, it has become increasingly clear that firms may pay a heavy premium for this in terms of loss of trust by the community (Oyewole, 2001). It can be argued that the wasteful use of resources reflects an organizational culture of expediency and indifference, hardly conducive to promoting customer loyalty (Welford, 1995: 40). A loss of trust may result in debilitating conflicts between the firm and community organizations and regulatory agencies, with considerable attendant costs (Welford, 1995). Should the firm lack legitimacy, its future survival becomes questionable (Bansal and Roth, 2000). In contrast, a high-trust environment may be a valuable basis for rent generation over the longer term. Firms are coming under considerable social pressure to be seen as 'good environmental citizens' in terms of overall environmental policies (Rezaee, 2000).

There is little doubt that public opinion has become a powerful force in encouraging firms to take environmental issues seriously. Often cited examples would include Shell being forced to backtrack over the Brent Spar oil platform, and the conspicuous success of explicitly green firms such as The Body Shop. However, while there is little doubt that public opinion does matter, consumers and the community tend to have far less information at their disposal than does the firm. The latter will automatically have far more knowledge about the nature of the products it produces, the raw materials required, the process employed, and the wastes generated (Kulkarni, 2000). Short-term profit maximization may make it desirable to conceal as much information as possible from the community, especially if large-scale environmental shortcuts are employed. Firms may be reluctant to impart information so as not to give competitors an edge, as well as for simple opportunism (Kulkarni, 2000). In other words, an information asymmetry may encourage the firm to ignore environmental concerns (Andrews, 2000). 'Dirty industries' such as mining and oil have tended to form close-knit industry associations, working within peer groups; strong pressures mitigate against being environmentally innovative, so as not to 'ratchet up standards for others' (Bansal and Roth, 2000). As one oil manager remarked, 'the closer you get to the marketplace, the more careful you must be what you disclose' (quoted in Bansal and Roth, 2000).

Moreover, firms are particularly likely to pollute poorer communities, where people may have less knowledge, and be less likely to object (Kulkarni, 2000). For example, in the United States, three out of five African and Hispanic communities live close to uncontrolled toxic waste sites (Oyewole, 2001). Meanwhile, the export of toxic waste to the third world has become a lucrative business. This issue is dealt with more fully in Chapter 6. These issues have led to calls for more rigid disclosure requirements, to level the playing field between firms and society at large (Andrews, 2000). Oyewole (2001) has suggested that it is critical that environmental justice be secured. This would entail fairness in environmental practices, without discrimination on the grounds of gender or race.

The increasing pressure on firms to be more environmentally responsible has led to a growing interest in environmental audits and standardized environmental management systems, with the objective of achieving fixed environmental yardsticks, and greater transparency (Fussel and George, 2000). While this has been associated primarily with industry, it has gradually spread to the service sector (Fussel and George, 2000). However, there is little doubt that the question of what constitutes environmental 'best practice' remains a highly contentious one, and varies greatly from one social context to another. Moreover, while many firms seek to develop comprehensive strategies for dealing with environmental issues, others will do the bare minimum to avoid 'trouble' from regulatory agencies or social pressure groups (Bansal and Roth, 2000). In other words, firms may simply seek to appease powerful stakeholder groups, or be environmentally responsible in order to realize notions of obligation, or as part-and-parcel of meeting some broader philanthropic agenda. The latter would entail doing the 'right thing' for 'feel-good' or moral reasons (Bansal and Roth, 2000).

5.4   Policy issues and pressures

In determining environmental policies, firms are not only subject to consumer and social pressures, but also the nature of the products and waste produced, as well as their specific demands on raw materials, their geographical locale, industrial sector, and state regulations (Andrews, 2000). As a result, the approaches firms adopt towards the environment are often fragmented and reactive, or even tokenistic (see Cartoon 4). Moreover, an atmosphere of confrontationalism between the state, firms and social actors may preclude the engendering of new synergies and the building of a collective future based on mutual understanding (Andrews, 2000). This has led writers such as Kleindorfer to suggest that more appropriate institutional contexts need to be developed, where environmental issues may be debated and tackled in a more constructive and holistic fashion (Andrews, 2000).

An alternative argument is that firms need to be more proactive; in developing environmental policies, the 'hand of management' should be visible, rather than merely ad hoc reactions to the 'hand of government' (Kulkarni, 2000). In other words, it can be argued that firms need to be more proactive in developing strategic self-regulatory mechanisms, rather than being prisoners of external demands (Maxwell *et al.*, 2000; Meyer, 2000). As writers such as Goodpaster have argued, firms do have an interest in the welfare of society, particularly in terms of securing a long-term role (Kulkarni, 2000). Indeed, it can be argued that an enterprise strategy which integrates the moral responsibilities of a firm into a clear vision as a basis for managerial policies and actions, should be extended to encompass ecological concerns (Stead and Stead, 2000). In other words, the ethical roots of what a firms stands for should be broadened to encompass environmental concerns (Stead and Stead, 2000).

'Our company's environmental policy is 100% recyclable.'

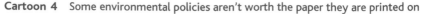

Cartoon 4   Some environmental policies aren't worth the paper they are printed on

It should be recognized that greening is a contested domain and open to multiple interpretations. As a result, environmental policies are inevitably 'contingent, local and variable' (Fussel and George, 2000). Many firms will simply concentrate on areas that are highly visible and where the benefits can clearly be measured, such as energy-saving initiatives, while steering clear of more complex policies that could affect profitability adversely (Meyer, 2000).

5.5 Environmental practices

While there has been a greater use of recycling techniques, many recyclable goods continue to be disposed of by other means, most notably in the world's largest economy, the United States. On the one hand, it can be argued that recycling ultimately makes economic sense, and that, particularly at the collection and initial processing stages, the recycling business is both lucrative and labour-intensive (Alexander, 2000). On the other hand, this fails to answer the question as to why so many apparently recyclable goods are disposed of by other means. In practice, recycling certain products – steel, certain types of plastic, and paper, are particularly profitable, but others are less so, while landfill disposal remains a cheap and convenient alternative (Goldstein and Madtes, 2000). This has led to arguments that landfill is artificially cheap, if the long-term environmental costs are considered, and recycling is not being properly costed in terms of the benefits it accrues. Currently, the United States only recycles 33 per cent of all goods; while this percentage is increasing, very slowly, outright waste disposal remains an economical alternative (Goldstein and Madtes, 2000).

This has led to suggestions that the scope of producer responsibility should be extended to encompass what happens to a product during its life cycle (Bellman and Khare, 2000). It is argued that this can be achieved through market-orientated costing and support, and by greater transparency at economic and technical levels. In other words, products need to be costed more realistically, including the costs of final disposal or recycling. This should be factored into pricing, in return for the producer taking care of the expenses associated with disposal or reuse. This would result in a more realistic – and ultimately more lucrative – market for recycling, while both producers and consumers would become aware of the real costs of using particular products (Bellman and Khare, 2000). However, if consumers are prepared to pay more for green products – and, in many areas, they palpably are – the potential exists for a win–win situation, with green firms securing continued profits, and the environment being protected (Oyewole, 2001). Indeed, a number of prominent firms, most notably within the European motor industry, have already assumed some responsibility for their products throughout their life cycles; however, they remain a small minority.

Finally, while it is easy – and potentially lucrative – for firms to claim sound environmental policies, there are a wide range of manners in which this may be measured (Wilks, 2000). For example, it could be claimed that a timber product is from sustainable plantations, when, as noted in Chapter 1, this may have entailed the destruction of indigenous forests and/or the devastation of river systems. However, there is increasing pressure for global standards. In 1996, the International Organization for Standardization developed the ISO 14000 criteria (Rezaeee, 2000). This provides voluntary guidelines for environmental management and auditing, and has already proved popular with commercial firms hoping to keep one step ahead of governmental regulation (Rezaee, 2000).

5.6   Philosophy and the environment

Both the Judeo-Christian tradition and classical philosophy place 'man' at the apex of creation, with a strong focus on the needs of *present generations* (Singer, 1995: 269; Aristotle, 1952). Even within this tradition, it can be argued that some conservation is necessary. For example, the well-being of present generations of humanity may be threatened by the effects of ozone depletion and global warming.

However, in practice, this school of thought has expressed little interest in providing specifics about which areas are worth protecting, and why. As Singer (1995: 269) argues, the 'remnants of true wilderness are left to us like islands amidst a sea of human activity that threatens to engulf them'; the wilderness has a strong scarcity value which cannot be discounted (Singer, 1995: 269). It is very difficult to calculate the long-term cost of loss of, say, an entire forest; certainly this more than just an aesthetic loss. It can be argued that a certain weighting should be given to the value of preserving an eco-system for its own intrinsic worth, in addition to the undoubted scientific, recreational and economic benefits that may accrue to humans in the future (Singer, 1995: 276).

Neo-liberals have deployed the classic utilitarian vision to see firms as orientated purely towards growth and material accumulation (Crane, 2000). If consumers are concerned about the environmental effects or health implications of a product, they will cease to buy it; 'good behaviour' is rewarded by the 'invisible hand of the market' (Browne and Kubasek, 1999). However, this assumes that consumers will have perfect knowledge, and that markets are truly functional, when, in the real word, neither is the case (Browne and Kubasek, 1999). Moreover, it can be argued that this vision is rather misplaced in the context of palpably finite resources, and pan-global and trans-generational pollution (Browne and Kubasek, 1999). Welford (1995: 5) argues that unrestrained free markets have failed to bring about an equitable distribution of income, to protect the third world, and have done little to protect the planet. Indeed, the capacity of the environment to supply raw materials and assimilate waste while maintaining bio-diversity and the overall quality of life is increasingly being undermined (Welford, 1995: 6).

In Western society, there persists a strong emphasis on the present and short-termism (Singer, 1995: 270). Neo-classical economics tends to discount future value (Singer, 1995: 271) However, some things, when destroyed, are lost for ever; a loss may be incalculable when the interests of not just one, but many future generations are considered (Singer, 1995). For example, many dams will last only a couple of generations before silting up, yet they inflict permanent damage on river systems, coastlines and, indeed, long-term agricultural potential. Singer (1995: 272) argues that, even if the possible future material benefits accruing from conservation are discounted, the generations to come should be left with the right to choose if, for example, they wish to gain fulfilment through spending time in wilderness areas (Singer, 1995: 272). Singer argues that utilitarian theory needs to be extended to take account of the future, rather than simply the immediate effects of actions. He argues that the interests of non-human sentient beings and future generations of humanity have particular rights which should also be considered (Singer, 1995: 286).

Recently, there have also been efforts to apply Rousseau's theory of the social contract to environmental issues. For example, Donaldson's social contract theory of business holds that while business benefits from – and indeed depends for its survival on – wider society, this does entail some necessary costs (Oyewole, 2001). Above all, firms must enhance the welfare of society, and adhere to basic standards of justice, including environmental justice. While some costs will be passed on to consumers in terms of higher prices, this will be considerably less than the costs of 'environmental victimization'. The latter would include increases in disease, birth defects and squalid living conditions; these are 'costs with negative results' (Oyewole, 2001). In contrast, greening will inevitably entail some costs too, but these would be 'costs with positive results', being beneficial to both the firm and the community in the longer term (Oyewole, 2001).

Others have argued that it is necessary to get beyond a 'homocentric' or 'species-ist' view that it is acceptable to damage the environment, as long as the people most immediately affected are compensated (Hoffman, 1997: 236). Up to the nineteenth century, it was commonly held that it was justifiable to deny slaves basic human rights (Singer, 1995: 60). Well into the 1950s, significant numbers of mentally impaired humans, and/or the very poor, were subjected to laboratory experiments and/or enforced sterilization in many of the advanced societies. Today, it is increasingly accepted that certain forms of conduct may be ethically unacceptable, even if a human being is not the recipient (Singer, 1995: 60). Mammals clearly have the capacity to feel pain, a capacity for suffering, even although this may vary from species to species, and, it has been argued that, with this, comes certain inherent rights, even if, at times, difficult trade-offs may be necessary (Singer, 1995: 59; Welford, 1995).

5.7   The hard green perspective

The hard green perspective has tended to depict itself as the 'free market' approach to the environment. Indeed, there are certain parallels between this approach and the vision of neo-liberal theorists such as Milton Friedman (1997), who have stressed the prosperity of the firm as providing the ultimate basis for general prosperity and progress. Neo-liberals would argue the firm has no moral obligations other than to its stakeholders, yet, through the relentless pursuit of profits – and sensitivity to market forces – environmental issues will appear on the agenda when wastage becomes overly costly or consumers prove reluctant to buy un-green products.

Similarly, hard green writers such as Peter Huber have suggested that conservation should only be based on incentives and signals from the market (Jackson, 2001). Environmental issues are the natural preserve of conservatives, who should be concerned with environmental issues within a broader agenda to promote 'progress'. Huber argues that, for example, the use of high-yield, pest-resistant crops will reduce demands on land, while nuclear energy is resource-efficient; it is necessary to place environmental issues in proper perspective (Jackson, 2001). The problem with this vision is, of course, that it is somewhat incomplete; for example, it is not just a question of what kinds of seeds are grown, but also what kinds of crops are produced, and whether they will be utilized in a wasteful way or not.

To Huber, environmental ethics should be firmly placed within the Judeo-Christian tradition; people should be put first under all circumstances (quoted in Jackson, 2001). The aesthetic value of the environment should be balanced against the needs of firms to pursue profits and the immediate needs of people (quoted in Jackson, 2001). Interestingly, in common with radical environmental activists, the hard environmental perspective is very suspicious of the role of science. Huber argues that environmental concerns – such as global warming – are the product of 'abstract computer models', which do not take into account the necessity for private gain and human welfare (Jackson, 2001). Huber's condemnation of such 'pagan' science and his religious absolutism stand in stark contrast not only to more progressive environmentalism, but also to businessmen and commentators who have promoted environmental concerns for pragmatic reasons.

5.8   The deep ecology perspective

To deep ecologists, it is only possible to have 'zero adverse effect' on the environment – or as little as possible – if there is a complete moral transformation within the firm (and society) and the elevation of environmental goals above the exigencies of profitability (Crane, 2000). It is virtually impossible to calculate in financial terms the loss, say, of an entire forest, not just in aesthetic terms, but as a distinct ecosystem. Deep ecology argues that the value of entire natural communities in terms of species diversity – and as a functioning whole – cannot be discounted (Singer, 1995: 276).

Deep ecology sees the community as consisting not just of people, but also of the physical environment around it – a 'land ethic' encompassing people, animals, plants, soil, water – or, collectively, 'the land' (Singer, 1995: 280). This is based on the assumption that all forms of life have some value in themselves, irrespective of their use to humans; this includes the overall diversity of life – and humans have no right to reduce this diversity other than to meet their vital needs (Singer, 1995: 281). A limitation of the 'deep ecology' viewpoint is gauging the worth of inanimate things, of entire ecosystems (Singer, 1995: 284).

It can be argued that existing reformist efforts have proved to be inadequate in staving off a mounting crisis, and that more radical measures are needed (Welford, 1995: 2). Too often, the approach adopted is one of 'business as usual' supplemented by marginal changes when the negative effects of environmental degradation are glaringly obvious (Welford, 1995: 2). Welford (1995: 3) argues that it should be recognized that economic activity is only part of wider processes that sustain life on earth. While the 'green revolution', involving more widespread use of new strains of seeds and fertilizers, resulted in increasing food production in the 1960s and 1970s, it has become increasingly obvious that faith in technological fixes is over-optimistic (Welford, 1995). This would include the loss of hardy native crops; 'sick plants that cannot withstand pests' without extensive use of fertilizers; erosion; and water contaminated by pesticides (Welford, 1995: 4). There is still insufficient evidence to conclude that the widespread introduction of genetically modified (GM) crops will be more beneficial than detrimental to humanity.

Welford (1995: 4) argues that, while it is hard for firms to refute the general need for environmental protection, it is considerably easier to respond in a piecemeal way with 'bolt-on strategies', in order to avoid having to face up to real challenges. There is little doubt that, for example, there has been substantial climatic change through human activity. This has led some writers to argue that 'we live in a post-natural world...we have crossed a threshold in the development of the planet'; the environment has already been irreparably damaged, and it is vital to conserve what is remaining (McKibben, quoted in Singer, 1995: 273). In contrast to the tradition focus of profits, there is need for organizations to become 'transcendent', treating green issues as paramount, seeing people as not above nature, but as one with it, environmental values being associated with sustainable development and long-term survival (Welford, 1995: 193).

The deep ecology perspective has traditionally been unpopular with firms; it has the attendant baggage of being associated with the 'beads and bangles brigade'. Even if managers may sympathize with much of the deep ecology vision, they are often to keen to couch environmental concerns within the discourse of securing long-term profitability (see Crane, 2000). On the one hand, it could be argued that the deep ecology perspective needs to become more business-friendly; as it stands, it argues that a fundamental moral overhaul is necessary, and that ecological problems can only be fully resolved through non-market solutions. Moreover, it can be suggested that it is overly prescriptive, without properly exploring what underlies the decision of firms to go green. On the other hand, it could be suggested that, if environmental concerns are simply reduced to cost–benefit issues, the broader ecological picture may become blurred (Crane, 2000). Indeed, it could be argued that deep ecology provides a much-needed moral high ground, even if firms have to operate within an atmosphere of compromise. Moreover, while some of what the deep ecologists have to say remains at the fringes of environmental discourse, many of their ideas have now entered the generally accepted 'mainstream' (see Welford, 1995). Increasingly, it is recognized that the world is a place where people live, rather than a 'preconstituted base for human action' (Attfield, 1999: 11; Weschler, 1999).

The need for more practical tools in the real world has led Peter Singer to argue that, given that people face a vast threat to their survival as a result of their destruction of the environment, any action resulting in further destruction of the environment is ethically dubious, and actions that are unnecessarily harmful are patently wrong. To Singer, ecologically insensitive actions, such as carelessly throwing out waste that can be recycled, is vandalism, and little more than the theft of 'our common property' of the earth's resources.

5.9   The 'middle ground'

It is often argued that environmental issues are necessarily at odds with the logic of capitalism (Prothero and Fitchett, 2000). Struggles between firms and environmental activists are seen as David and Goliath struggles, examples being the McLibel case (regarding McDonald's food products) and the Greenpeace-versus-Shell contestation. Invariably, this results in the mighty being humbled, or a new martyr being created (Prothero and Fitchett, 2000). In contrast to these arguments – and those of hard green theorists – there have been attempts to develop a more pragmatic perspective, allowing for more 'realistic' compromises than would be suggested by the hard green or deep ecology visions. It is argued that environmental problems are the inevitable result of development, and that some trade-offs are unavoidable. This would entail both changes in consumer attitudes – an even greater awareness of the importance and implications of buying green – and those held by managers – an acceptance that a narrow focus on profits may be detrimental in the medium and long term (Prothero and Fitchett, 2000).

In contrast to minimalist definitions of greening that would entail measures such as add-on pollution control, or perhaps basic environmental auditing, middle-ground approaches would entail auditing for sustainability and/or the firm taking responsibility for all stages of a product's life, from raw materials to ensuring its recyclability. However, this would fall short of deep ecology arguments for fundamental economic and social change (Welford, 1995).

Organizations need to see their survival and continued prosperity in the context of the exigencies of securing sustainability. There is a need to strike a balance between economic success and ecological protection, while it should be recognized that the two are not necessarily mutually reinforcing under all circumstances (Stead and Stead, 2000). The 'compromise perspective' is still an emerging one; it lacks the clear focus of the hard green and deep ecology alternatives. Its pragmatic nature has made for something of a fragmented vision; however, it focuses directly on the need to balance profitability with environmental concerns.

5.10 Morality and greening

This leads us back to the issue that was first raised in Chapter 1; if an action is visibly good for securing profits and for the firm, is it devoid of moral worth? The classical deontological vision would hold that this is indeed the case; actions are only ethical if they are for the 'right' motives. Indeed, it could be argued that the process of greening is part and parcel of the amoralization of social life; invariably, firms sell environmental awareness purely on the basis of profit (Crane, 2000). Thus the environment is reduced to little more than one of 'issue selling' and 'image management'. From a postmodern perspective, Zygmunt Bauman has depicted managers as being locked into a 'self-sustaining rationality' within the firm, with their moral responsibility ceasing once the customer's requirements are met (Crane, 2000; see also Bauman, 1993).

There is an emerging school of thought that business has an ethical responsibility to become more proactive in dealing with environmental issues than simply the bottom line (Hoffman, 1997: 232). Indeed, Hoffman (1997: 233) argues that business requires vision, commitment and courage, risk and sacrifice in providing much-needed moral leadership, transcending the view that protecting environment is desirable because, in many areas, it is demonstrably good for business. Welford (1995: 26) argues that truly sustainable development demands a global approach, a reconsideration of equity and a new stress on equality, and is based on firm moral foundations.

5.11 Environmental issues and the law

In almost all developed nations, there is a plethora of legislation governing environmental issues. For example, in the United States, this has resulted in an Environmental Protection Agency, which regulates air and water quality on behalf of the general public. However, national standards differ greatly between nations – typically Western European standards are more stringent than US ones (Currie and Skolnik, 1988: 305). In the third world, environmental standards and monitoring tend to be lax. This may have the effect of encouraging firms to 'regime shop' aggressively – in this case, relocating 'messy' activities to countries where controls are weak. Moreover, in some areas – most notably waste water treatment in the case of the UK – it may pay firms to pay nominal fines rather than clean up their act. However, here the situation is rapidly changing. Envirowise, a UK government-backed environmental body, has warned firms that they face increasingly hefty fines if they do not comply with eco-legislation (*Financial Times*, 30 June 2001). Eco-wise research has revealed that 75 per cent of small firms in the UK are unclear as to how environmental regulations affect their operations (ibid.). This has led to the establishment of the Environmental Business Network, which keeps firms up to date with forthcoming changes in the law.

5.11.1   Religion and the environment

Lynn White's seminal article in the journal *Science* (1967) posited that Judeo-Christian traditions and beliefs are the main cause of our current environmental problems. White argued that Christianity in particular is by far the most anthropocentric religion. He argues that the root cause of our environmental problems is the division between humans and nature. Anders Biel and Andreas Nilsson (2005) summarized White's thesis as follow: 'By establishing a dualism between humans and nature, Christianity made it possible to exploit nature in a mood of indifference to the feelings of natural objects. Modern technology is at least partly to be explained by the Christian dogma of human transcendence of, and rightful mastery over, nature'. Since White's paper was published, however, a number of studies have shown that the association between religion and environmental damage is weak, or even positive. For example, Naess (1989) reported that religious beliefs had a positive impact on the environment and were a cause of pro-environment behaviour. Similarly, Biel and Nilsson (2005) argue that different religious affiliations (which include different values) have different implications for individual attitudes towards the environment (Owen and Videras, 2007). Further, a distinction must be made between religious texts and the people who follow a religion when looking at the association between religion and the environment. For example, Muslims are instructed in the Qur'an to protect the environment and creations in all other forms, but corporations in Muslim countries may not adhere to these values. Rice's (1996) study of environmental behaviour in Egypt found that, while Islamic texts are pro-environment people in Egypt reported little concern towards the environment. Selected texts include 'no Muslim who plants a tree or sows a field from which a human, bird, or animal eats, but it shall be reckoned as charity' (saying of the Prophet Muhammad quoted in Rice, 1996). Despite Prophet Muhammad instructing his companions not to waste water, even when performing religiously mandated ablutions: 'Even if you take the ablutions in a fast-flowing river, do not waste the water' (quoted in Rice, 1996) and 'do not waste in excess, for God loves not those who waste' (Qur'an 6: 141).

5.12   Global warming: the ultimate challenge

Human activities have resulted in carbon dioxide content in the atmosphere being some 30 per cent higher than it was a hundred years ago (Wesley and Petersen, 1999: 171; Jamieson, 1992). The International Panel on Climate Change has projected dire consequences based on clearly visible existing trends, encompassing desertification, the melting of Arctic and Antarctic ice caps, rising sea levels, and increasingly unpredictable weather (Wesley and Petersen, 1999: 171). While some regions with cold climates could benefit, others will be very much worse off. Carbon dioxide emissions account for only part of the problem: deforestation has reduced the capacity to absorb excess carbon dioxide (Wesley and Petersen, 1999: 172). Currently, non-polluting energy sources account for only 10 per cent of the energy of the world. Most greenhouse gases are produced in the developed world, above all in the United States: energy consumption per capita in the latter is twice as much as in Japan, Britain or France (Wesley and Petersen, 1999: 172). As Gardiner (2006: 403) notes, global warming is both a resilient problem – that is, it will be hard and costly to deal with – and a deferred problem – its worst consequences will be in the future.

On the one hand, this would suggest that the developed nations – who can afford it most – should lead the way in cutting down on energy consumption, especially as there is considerable evidence that global warming will affect the poorest parts of the world the most (Brown, 2003). On the other hand, during the first Bush II term of office, a majority of the US Senate followed a view that those in the developed world have built their lives around a high-energy-consumption model – they have higher expectations, and curtailing the usage of hydrocarbons in the developed world would cause more misery than it would to those in the developing world, who have yet to develop such expectations and lifestyles (Wesley and Petersen, 1999: 179). The underlying argument that governments have special obligations to their own citizens (as opposed to humanity at large) has been heavily criticized by writers such as Singer and Pogge, who argue that nationality in the end has little morality, and that all people should have equal status as objects of moral concern (Wesley and Petersen, 1999:183). Similarly, Rawls argues that 'well ordered societies' have an obligation to assist the less fortunate in meeting 'basic human needs' (Wesley and Petersen, 1999:185; Brown, 2003). Of course, central to weighing up ethical concerns would be the relative importance assigned to entire ecosystems versus people, though there is growing evidence that the fates of both are inexorably connected (Brown, 2003).

As Michaelowa (2004: 1004) notes, sceptics of global warming fall into three camps. First, there are those who are clearly and openly funded by fossil fuel interests; the second consists of maverick amateur scientists, with no formal scientific training (Michaelowa, 2004: 1004); and the third consists of a small minority of often retired scientists: this camp overlaps heavily with the first (Michaelowa, 2004: 1004). In most cases, the usage of data is highly selective (Michaelowa, 2004: 1004). Notoriously, the Oregan Petition – supposedly signed by climate scientists urging rejection of the Kyoto protocol, and backed by an 'article' presented in a manner to make it appear to be a scientific, peer-reviewed paper – brings together members of all three groups. It contained signatures from individuals that appear to include such unlikely scientific experts as a former member of the Spice Girls pop group; more broadly speaking, there appeared to be no easy way of checking the credentials of signatories (see http://en.wikipedia.org/wiki/Oregon_Petition). Again, sceptics have been unable to reach a consensus among themselves between whether global warming is occurring, but is not important; and that nothing abnormal is happening at all. Gardiner (2006: 407–8) argues that global warming has proved to be morally corrupting; it has given rise to self-selective strategies, with comfortable data being preferred to the uncomfortable. While intergenerational ethics may demand action, present exigencies may work to defer it (Gardiner, 2006).

From a broadly utilitarian perspective, Danish academic Bjørn Lomborg assembled a panel of economists – the so-called 'Copenhagen Consensus' – to argue that 'money spent on counteracting global warming could be spent more effectively on basic healthcare in the developing world: *inter alia*, through the provision of drinking water and combating malaria'. There are two fundamental problems with this argument. The first is that it assumes a trade-off between global warming and poverty alleviation/primary healthcare: however, it could similarly be argued that global security could be better served through combating global warming than through wasting billions of dollars on supporting fruitless and devastating wars in the Middle East. In short, the Copenhagen Consensus assumes that there is an either/or trade-off for an imaginary pot of money for good works. Significantly, the support of many proponents of the Copenhagen Consensus for dealing with non-global-warming social problems appears to be purely rhetorical. Second, the Copenhagen Consensus ignores the interrelationship of problems: for example, global warming is likely to lead to the rapid spread of malaria.

Significantly, the Danish Committee on Scientific Dishonesty has heavily criticized Lomborg's methods, and his usage of source material, most notably his often cited work, *The Skeptical Environmentalist* (Michaelowa, 2004: 1005): they found that 'objectively speaking, the publication of the work under consideration is deemed to fall within the concept of scientific dishonesty', but that as he lacked expertise in the field, it could not be proved that Lomborg himself was dishonest; the Committee's decision was later challenged by the Danish government (Wikipedia, 2007).

An alternative strategy by opponents of action against climate change has been to make sweeping counter-claims (McCright and Dunlap, 2000). Indeed, there is a strand of thinking among critics of global warming that dismisses scientific evidence as simply a matter of opinion of equal validity to all others: a variation of the slippery postmodern 'you think the world is round, I think it is flat; we both have opinions and hence, as opinions, they are of equal value' argument. Those who deny climate change claim they are being censored when their views are challenged or deconstructed, while they continue to enjoy the uncritical support of large sections of the conservative media and certain oil companies: a letter written by scientists to Exxon Mobil asking the company to desist from funding lobbyists that promote climate change denial was held up as evidence of such censorship (Monbiot, 2007). More serious evidence of censorship has been the Bush administration's repeated interventions to water down government research that points to the reality of global warming (Monbiot, 2007).

What are the practical implications of global warming for business? Central to this is the 'tragedy of the commons': principled firms who take concrete steps to reduce their energy footprint or to promote less environmentally destructive products risk having less principled competitors seize a short-term competitive advantage (Gardiner, 2006). However, greater consumer awareness appears to have yielded real benefits to firms that have conspicuously promoted measures to reduce greenhouse gas emissions: the success of Toyota's Prius car represents a case in point. Again, a long-term trend to higher oil prices may make it more attractive for firms to take global warming seriously. However, in the end, there remains a central trade-off: firms may have to trade-off short-term profits against a long-term good that will shared by all.

5.13   Animals and ethics[1]

Another increasingly contentious issue is the use of animals in experiments and in intensive farming. The question of humanity's treatment of animals is a long-standing one. Charles Darwin highlighted the close evolutionary connection between people and animals, and because of this, was highly critical of the wide prevalence of deliberate cruelty towards animals (*Evening Standard*, 16 January 2001). Peter Singer has pointed out that a large proportion of animal experiments are unnecessary; for example, there is already a vast range of cosmetics available that have been proven as harmless to people, so further testing of cosmetics on animals is unethical (Singer, 1995: 66). Similarly, other experiments are often repeated ad nauseam. For example, H. F. Harlow of the Primate Research Centre in the United States proved that, if reared in conditions of maternal deprivation and isolation, rhesus monkeys could be reduced to a state of persistent depression or fear; these experiments – whose outcome may seem obvious – were repeated over a 15-year period, and continue after his death (Singer, 1995: 66). The benefit of the experiments – and similar research – is arguably slight to non-existent (Singer, 1995: 66); and the interests of the non-human beings are totally ignored (Singer, 1995: 67). Moreover, recent research has shown that the differences between people and animals are less absolute than was previously believed. Not only is there evidence that animals do form social communities of their own, but the DNA of the great apes is 98 per cent similar to that of people (*Financial Times*, 20 February 2001). Moreover, a number of gorillas and chimpanzees have been successfully taught the sign language employed by deaf humans and show evidence of relatively advanced consciousness and memory (Singer, 1995: 74). Singer argues that ethical conduct does not mean we discard partiality or personal relationships, but rather that we should be able to see the moral claims of those affected by our actions with 'some degree of independence from our feelings for them', be they people or other animals (Singer, 1995: 77). It can, of course, be argued that the battle against animal experiments is partially over; most Western governments have greatly restricted the scale and scope of animal experimentation, but certainly experimentation continues on a large scale.

In the United Kingdom, Huntingdon Life Sciences, which routinely engages in animal experiments, has been driven to the brink of bankruptcy by protests against its staffers and financial backers. Investors have increasingly been cautious about firms conspicuously engaging in animal experimentation; it is a line of business that is no longer as profitable as before (*Financial Times*, 16 February

2001). Again, however, it could be argued that such decisions are devoid of any moral worth, if they are motivated solely by concerns about loss of profits, rather than the well-being of the animals involved. Again, any excesses by animal rights extremists do not absolve companies and individuals from hard ethical choices and responsibilities.

Scientists involved in animal experimentation have often claimed that they are being unfairly subjected to public scrutiny, given that the scale of animal suffering in the farming industry is very much worse; some 2.5 million animals a year in Britain are subject to experiments, compared to some 700 million who are slaughtered for the meat industry (*Financial Times*, 20 February 2001). However, it could be argued that this does not make the lesser evil any more desirable.

Singer points out that edible crops produce a far higher food value than livestock farming; if grains are fed to animals, only 10 per cent of the nutritional value is transferred to the resultant meat (Singer, 1995: 63). In the West, excessive amounts of meat are consumed as a luxury item when alternative food sources are available. This has led Singer to pose the question in utilitarian terms: can a minor interest of those living in the advanced societies be reconciled with the major interest of those in the developing world who do not have access to enough food, or with the suffering of the animals involved? (Singer, 1995: 63). In other words, intensive meat farming is unnecessarily wasteful, especially given food shortages in large areas of the developing world: 38 per cent of the earth's grain crop is fed to livestock. In addition, livestock farming has led to the clearance of large areas of rain forest in Central and South America (Singer, 1995: 288). Moreover, factory farming is not just an issue of animal welfare; it has also led to pollution – intensive cattle farming, for example, is a major source of methane and other greenhouse gases, the depopulation of the countryside, and serious health problems (Harrison, 1993). However, it is only recently that the meat industry has come under popular scrutiny as a result of repeated health scares, ranging from salmonella outbreaks traceable back to battery-farmed chicken to the bovine spongiform encephalopathy (BSE) (mad cow disease) epidemic.

Again, however, it can be argued that mounting public pressure for changes in farming methods is a profoundly amoral process in that it is prompted primarily by the immediate personal health concerns of consumers, rather than a concern for the environment or the animals involved. Organic farming has proved to be increasingly lucrative, while Swedish meat exports have boomed as a result of the legal abolition of factory farming in that country. However, utilitarians such as Singer (1995) have argued that such debates are of little practical value; whatever the motivation, any reduction in overall suffering is desirable. None the less, even if one operated from the premise that the 'infliction of suffering on animals (should be prohibited) only when the interests of humans will be affected to anything like the extent that animals are affected', important changes would be necessary in society: new attitudes to wildlife and hunting for recreation, the trapping and wearing of furs, farming methods, and the range and choice of goods available (Singer, 1995).

5.13.1   The rights-based perspective and animals

Writing from a rights-based perspective, Nozick (1974) argued that not just people, but animals too had basic rights: even if bred solely for the purposes of slaughter, this did not deny animals having certain basic rights. While a species may benefit from large-scale agricultural production – in having their genetic material spread more widely – individual animals still had a right to be treated with a basic degree of humanity (Nozick, 1974). In other words, animals are morally relevant and should be included in moral calculations. Moreover, a narrow utilitarian view does not take into account 'utility monsters' – that people might gain so much pleasure from mistreating animals as to justify what objectively constituents mistreatment (Nozick, 1974).

Nozick acknowledges that an animal's felt experiences may be rather hard to gauge, but that a basic rule-of-thumb approach may be helpful: the needs of higher-order beings should be assigned more weight: none the less, different conceptions of life should be respected (Nozick, 1974). This approach is both minimalist (sentient beings have rights, but collectives do not) and founded on moral absolutes (certain forms of behaviour are simply not morally justifiable).

In contrast, from a classic Kantian point of view, humans only have duties towards animals, and not animals' rights (Larrère, 2002: 24). However, later writers in the Kantian tradition, such as Rollin (1981) have argued that there is indeed a relationship between the moral obligations people have, and the manner in which they treat animals. The usage of animals in turn should recognize their own nature: it is, for example, immoral to keep a bird in a cage without good reason: rational beings do have a capacity to make informed judgements as to what lies at the root of a species rights (Larrère, 2002). He acknowledges that domesticated animals may have different needs and desires from those in the wild, but that, at the core of all beings' nature lies a clear genetic code (Dawkins, 1990). All decisions have a moral basis, even when it comes to simple beings: for example, while killing flies to prevent the spread of disease may clearly be acceptable, it is significant that the wanton pulling of wings off living flies remains a popular benchmark for pathological sadism (Rollin, 1981: 58).

In reality, the degree of sentience does not translate absolutely: many individuals would assign more rights to their family dog than they would a convicted murder. Familiarity – and hypocrisy – make for stronger moral claims: domestic pets enjoy far more legal and customary rights than farm animals, or the poor for that matter (Francione, 1996). Regan (1983) argues that the way forward is to agree which practices are simply morally wrong (for example, battery farming), and which should simply be abolished. An alternative approach, suggested by writers such as Summer, have suggested that rights are about *autonomy* not *interest*: those incapable of exercising autonomy have no rights: however, critics have charged that this represents *anthropomorphy*, the projection of human concerns on to the animal world.

More minimalist rights-based accounts would suggest that individuals should be free to make their own moral choices, but that these should not be impinged on unnecessarily by others: for example, if intensive farming poses a health risk – as borne out by numerous health-related scandals involving the meat industry – this may impinge unnecessarily on the rights of others (Charlton *et al.*, 1993). More comprehensive rights-based accounts would stress the central notion of moral choice: concepts of right and wrong mould human behaviour, and go beyond immediate biological desire (Charlton *et al.*, 1993). Wanton cruelty towards animals – such as the endless repetition of animal experiments for which the results have been widely disseminated – is morally wrong. On the one hand, it could be argued that modern business has so many competing demands, that it is impossible to take into account moral issues in dealing with other species. On the other hand, one set of moral responsibilities does not absolve another: it is common practice for representatives of the status quo to argue that the interests of one disadvantaged group outweigh another, while visibly failing to do much about either: all injustice is morally inexcusable (Tannenbaum, 1991: 63).

5.13.2   Utilitarian alternatives

Early utilitarian writers, such as Jeremy Bentham and J. S. Mill, dealt explicitly with animal-related issues in their writings (Charlton *et al.*, 1993). More recently, the utilitarian tradition has diverged into two distinct strands regarding approaches to animals. First, more conservative utilitarians have argued that the untrammelled pursuit of profit is likely to result in the greatest social good. If consumers are concerned with the environmental or animal welfare cost of a product, they will cease to buy it, thus good behaviour by companies is being rewarded by the invisible hand of the market (Browne and Kubasek, 1999). However, this approach assumes that consumers possess accurate knowledge as to how a product was produced, and grossly discounts the future costs (in terms of the preservation of genetic diversity) (ibid.), and in organizations giving consumers an opportunity to act ethically (Ferrell, 1985). Moreover, the process of translating ethical concerns and attention into ethical actions – including buying ethically sourced products – is a complex and multidimensional process. Again, Welford (1995: 5) points out that the operation of unrestrained markets has failed to alleviate poverty, protect the developing world, or, indeed, the planet and other species.

More progressive utilitarian accounts promote a more holistic point of view. Singer (1995: 60) points out that, well into the late nineteenth century, many countries denied slaves basic human rights; only recently have some countries, such as Germany, formally accorded animals rights in terms of their constitutions. At least until the late 1950s, mentally impaired human beings, conscripts and the very poor were subjected to laboratory tests in many advanced societies: today, it is acknowledged that even if directed towards non-human species, certain forms of behaviour are unacceptable (Singer, 1995). For example, in 2003, the EU agreed to phase out the testing of cosmetics on animals, albeit that the ban only came into force in May 2009.

A key difference between utilitarian and rights-based approaches to the use of animals revolves around the basis of decisions. Rights-based approaches would see decisions made on profitability grounds as being devoid of any moral worth at all (see Rollin, 1981). For example, free-range eggs sell at a premium: as a result, many producers have been prompted to abandon battery farming to take advantage of this premium. Writing from a utilitarian perspective, Singer (1995) stresses that outcomes matter: even if done for the wrong (or non-ethical reasons) any overall reduction in suffering represents a positive good.

5.14   Summary

It is often assumed that poverty is a major cause of environmental degradation, when, of course, the bulk of damage to the world's environment is caused by the advanced societies (Brennan, 1993). Industrial growth and a rise in net incomes are not going to solve the great environmental questions facing today's world. There is little doubt that it cannot be business as usual; indeed, growing numbers of firms are stressing the importance of green issues. However, this is rarely couched in moral terms; a more common argument is that taking care of the environment makes increasing commercial sense. On the one hand, in many cases, this is undoubtedly correct, but on the other hand, it can be argued that there is a need for business to take environmental issues more seriously as an ethical concern. The deontological view that apparently ethical actions when prompted solely by commercial criteria are devoid of moral worth can be contested – the utilitarian response would be that it is surely better to have good actions than bad, no matter what the underlying motivation. None the less, there is a case for the argument that the sheer scale of environmental degradation, which has threatened the entire biosphere, requires a more radical change in attitude among commercial firms towards the environment; it can no longer be business as usual.

Discussion questions

- If firms take environmental issues seriously for public relations reasons, is their choice really devoid of moral worth?
- What do you think are the main ethical concerns associated with the usage of animals in the agricultural industry?

Case study

Closing case study

Global warming: business leading government in the USA

Along with controversial foreign policies, economic mismanagement, attitudes to torture, and unashamed incompetence, the Bush administration attracted considerable global opprobrium owing to its attitudes to global warming.

Case study

Continued

Many firms with close ties to the Bush administration, particularly in the oil and gas industry, did much to oppose any concrete action on global warming, and, in some notorious instances, actively promoted the activities of climate change denialists. Yet, ironically, it was during these years that many prominent US-based firms began to speak out against the dangers and challenges posed by global warming. Household names among these firms included Boeing, IBM, Whirlpool and General Electric. For example, General Electric saw new opportunities to profit from the growing demand for alternative energy technologies, especially as many countries were actively providing incentives for the usage of alternative energy sources. And many US energy utilities began to call for compulsory federal caps on emission levels; this would, it was felt, make for greater coherence than present uncertainties, and complex and uneven state regulations. Others prominent in this change included insurance firms, worried about high claims brought about by the increased incidence of natural disasters. Quite simply, to many insurance firms, global warming poses a direct threat to the way they price risk, and indeed, their entire business model. Institutional investors have also become more prominent in speaking out about global warming – and using this to guide their investment decisions – prompted by a range of concerns, ranging from the continued commercial viability of specific practices right through to broader ethical concerns. The Obama administration has placed global warming higher on the policy agenda, and it is likely that this will encourage many other firms to follow suit.

Questions

- If firms adopt policies to fight global warming for strictly commercial reasons, is this devoid of ethical worth?
- Do you think adopting policies aimed at contributing to reducing global warming could pose ethical dilemmas for the firm in other areas? What are these likely to be, and how might they be resolved?

Note

1. A fuller version of these debates is provided in Mellahi and Wood (2005).

References

Alexander, M. 2000. 'Economy Reaps Benefits from Recycling', *Waste Age*, 31,11: 24–5.

Andrews, C. 2000. 'Better Environmental Decisions: Strategies for Governments, Business and Communities', *Journal of the American Planning Association*, 66, 4: 453–4.

Anonymous. 2000. 'Environmental Work Is a Good Investment', *ENR Magazine*, 245, 1: 74–8.

Aristotle. 1952. *Politics.* London: Everyman.

Attfield, R. 1999. *The Ethics of the Global Environment.* Edinburgh: Edinburgh University Press.

Bansal, P. and Roth, K. 2000. 'Why Companies Go Green', *Academy of Management Journal*, 43,4: 717–36.

Bauman, Z. 1993. *Postmodern Ethics.* Oxford: Blackwell.

Bellman, K. and Khare, A. 2000. 'Economic Issues in Recycling End-of-Life Vehicles', *Technovation*, 20,12: 677–90.

Biel, A. and Nilsson, A. (2005) 'Religious Values and Environmental Concern: Harmony and Detachment', *Social Science Quarterly*, 86,1:178–91.

Blondel, A. 2004. 'The Logs of War', *Monde Diplomatique*, 1/2004. Available at: http://www.globalpolicy.org/security/natres/timber/2004/01logsofwar.htm.

Brennan, A. 1993. 'Environmental Decision Making', in R. J. Berry (ed.), *Environmental Dilemmas: Ethics and Decisions.* London: Chapman & Hall.

Brown, D. 2003. 'The Importance of Expressly Examining Global Warming Policy Issues Through an Ethical Prism', *Global Environmental Change*, 13: 229–34.

Browne, M. and Kubasek, N. 1999. 'A Communitarian Green Space between Market and Political Rhetoric about Environment Law', *American Business Law Journal*, 37,1: 127–69.

Business Week. 2004. 'Global Warming', *Business Week* 16,4. Available at: http://www.businessweek.com/magazine/content/04_33/b3896001_mz001.htm.

Charlton, A., Coe, S. and Francione, G. 1993. 'The American Left Should Support Animal Rights: A Manifesto', *Animals Agenda*, 1/2: 28.

Crane, A. 2000. 'Corporate Greening as Amoralization', *Organizational Studies*, 21,4: 673–96.

Currie, E. and Skolnick, J. 1988. *America's Problems: Social Issues and Public Policy.* Glenview, Ill: Scott Foresman and Co.

Dawkins, S. 1990. 'From an Animal's Point of View: Motivation, Fitness, and Animal Welfare'. *Behaviour Brain Science.* 13,1–9: 54–61.

Ferrell, O. C. and Gresham, L. G. 1985. 'A Contingency Framework for Understanding Ethical Decision Making in Marketing'. *Journal of Marketing* 49: 87–96.

Francione, G. 1996. 'Animals as Property', *Animal Law* 2,1.

Friedman, M. 1997. 'The Social Responsibility of Business Is to Increase Its Profits', in T. Beauchamp and N. Bowie (eds), *Ethical Theory and Business.* Upper Saddle River, NJ: Prentice Hall.

Fussell, L. and George, S. 2000. 'The Institutionalization of Environmental Concerns', *International Studies of Management and Organization*, 30,3: 41–58.

Gardiner, S. 2006. 'A Perfect Moral Storm: Climate Change, Intergenerational Ethics, and the Problem of Moral Corruption', *Environmental Values*, 15: 397–413.

Goldstein, M. and Madtes, C. 2000. 'The State of Garbage in America', *BioCycle*, 41, 11: 40–8.

Graybill, A. 2000. 'Losing Paradise: The Growing Threat to Our Animals, Our Environment, and Ourselves', *Library Journal*, 125,14: 244–6.

Harrison, R. 1993. 'Case Study: Farm Animals', in R. J. Berry (ed.), *Environmental Dilemmas: Ethics and Decisions*. London: Chapman & Hall.

Hoffman, W. 1997. 'Business and Environmental Ethics', in T. Beauchamp and N. Bowie (eds), *Ethical Theory and Business*. Upper Saddle River, NJ: Prentice Hall.

Jackson, D. 2001. 'Hard Green: Saving the Environment from the Environmentalists', *Forest Products Journal*, 51,1: 7–14.

Jackson, K. 1997. 'Globalizing Corporate Ethics Programmes', *Journal of Business Ethics*, 16,12/13: 1272–35.

Jamieson, D. 1992. 'Ethics, Public Policy and Global Warming', *Science, Technology and Human Values*, 17,2: 139–53.

Kulkarni, S. 2000. 'Environmental Ethics and Information Asymmetry among Organizational Stakeholders', *Journal of Business Economics*, 27,3: 215–28.

Larrère, R. 2002. 'Ethique et experimentation animale', *Nature Sciences Sociétés*, 10,1: 24–32.

Maxwell, J., Lyon, T. and Hackett, S. 2000. 'Self Regulation and Social Welfare: The Political Economy of Corporate Environmentalism', *Journal of Law and Economics*, 43,2: 583–617.

McCright, A. and Dunlap, R. 2000. 'Challenging Global Warming as a Social Problem', *Social Problems*, 47,4: 499–522.

Mellahi, K. and Wood, G. 2005. 'Business Failure in the Use of Animals: Ethical Issues and Contestations', *Business Ethics: A European Review*, 14: 151–63.

Meyer, H. 2000. 'The Greening of Corporate America', *Journal of Business Strategy*, 21,1: 38–43.

Michaelowa, A. 2004. 'Review: Energy and Environment', *International Affairs*, 80,5: 1004–5.

Monbiot, G. 2007. 'There Is Climate Change Censorship – And It's the Deniers Who Dish It Out', *Guardian*, 10 April. Available at: http://www.guardian.co.uk/commentisfree/story.

Naess, Arne. 1989. *Ecology, Community, and Lifestyle: An Outline of an Ecosophy*. Cambridge: Cambridge University Press.

Nozick, R. 1974. *Anarchy, State and Utopia*. New York: Basic Books.

Nozick, R. 1984. 'Moral Consciousness and Distributive Justice', in M. Sandel (ed.), *Liberalism and its Critics*. Oxford: Basil Blackwell.

Oyewole, P. 2001. 'Social Costs of Environmental Justice Associated with Green Marketing', *Journal of Business Ethics*, 29,3: 239–51.

Owen, L. N. and Videras, R. J. 2007. 'Culture and Public Goods: The Case of Religion and the Voluntary Provision of Environmental Quality', *Journal of Environmental Economics and Management*, 54,2: 162–80.

Prothero, A. and Fitchett, J. 2000. 'Greening Capitalism and Opportunities for a Green Community', *Journal of Macro Marketing*, 20,1: 46–55.

Regan, T. 1983. *The Case for Animal Rights*, Los Angeles: University of California Press.

Rezaee, Z. 2000. 'Help Keep the World Green', *Journal of Accountancy*, 1905,5: 57–67.

Rice, G. 1996. 'Pro-environmental Behavior in Egypt: Is There a Role for Islamic Environmental Ethics?', *Journal of Business Ethics*, 65: 373–90.

Roberts, T. and Sheail, J. 1993. 'Case Study: Air Quality', in R. J. Berry (ed.), *Environmental Dilemmas: Ethics and Decisions*. London: Chapman & Hall.

Rollin, B. 1981. *Animal Rights and Human Morality*. New York: Prometheus.

Rollin, B. E., 1990. *The Unheeded Cry*. Oxford: Oxford University Press.

Singer, P., 1990. *Animal Liberation*, 2nd edn. New York: Avon Books.

Singer, P. 1995. *Practical Ethics*. Cambridge: Cambridge University Press.

Stead, J. and Stead, E. 2000. 'Eco-Enterprise Strategy: Standing for Sustainability', *Journal of Business Ethics*, 24,4: 313–29.

Sztybel, D. 2000. 'Taking Humanism Seriously: Obligatory Anthropomorphism', *Journal of Agricultural and Environmental Ethics*, 13, 181–203.

Sztybel, D. 2001. 'Animal Rights, Autonomy and Redundancy', *Journal of Agricultural and Environmental Ethics*, 14: 259–73.

Tannenbaum, J., 1991. 'Ethics and Animal Welfare: The Inextricable Connection', *Journal of American Veterinary Medical Association*, 198: 1360–76.

Welford, R. 1995. *Environmental Strategy and Sustainable Development*. London: Routledge.

Weschler, L. 1999. 'Managing Green', *Public Productivity and Management Review*, 23,1: 105–8.

Wesley, E. and Petersen, F. 1999. 'The Ethics of Burden Sharing in the Global Greenhouse', *Journal of Agricultural and Environmental Ethics*, 11: 167–96.

Wilks, N. 2000. 'Be Seen to Be Green', *Professional Engineering*, 13,15: 40–6.

Wikipedia. 2007. 'Bjørn Lomborg'. Available at: http://en.wikipedia.org/wiki/Bj%C3%B8rn_Lomborg.

White, L. 1967. 'The Historical Roots of Our Ecological Crisis', *Science* 155: 1203–7.

Wyburd, G. 1993. 'Case Study: Industry', in R. J. Berry (ed.), *Environmental Dilemmas: Ethics and Decisions*. London: Chapman & Hall.

Ethics in a globalizing world

Chapter objectives

- Introduce and discuss critically different conceptions of what constitutes globalization.
- Discuss cultural relativism and universality of ethical practices.
- Explore the relevance of codes of ethics that aim to transcend national boundaries.
- Gain insights into current debates surrounding global trade and North–South relations.

Case study

Introductory case study

Companies can show the way to a more ethical world

As globalisation has weakened and marginalised political institutions, business is asked to fill the gaps. But it is being asked to lead the way towards a more ethical world without the authority or incentive to do so. Politicians need to become more confident about setting standards for business, based on an internationalist approach.

Firms find themselves invited to turn economic capitalism into a progressive force that spreads greater equality and quality of life. A business case can be made for such an explicitly ethical stance. Multinational corporations should be happy to be seen as powerful advocates for human rights and the environment.

Societies that are repressive, undemocratic, lawless and corrupt are unstable and bad for business; environmental damage makes business unsustainable.

There is a reasonable fear that multinational corporations will pursue profit regardless of other considerations, and duck their new ethical responsibilities. Ultimately companies must respond to economic indicators, even when they take the long-term view. So how can they show that ethical behaviour is good for business? And can new economic models emerge that foster democratic and societal control on business?

Government and society must set the ethics agenda for business; the question is whether they are ready. To answer it, we need to consider the role of the media. The media view of business is dominated by two features. First, bad news sells. Secondly, few mainstream journalists have direct experience in industries other than their own. There is a general assumption that industry is on the unethical make. A more constructive outlook would allow us all to be much more optimistic about an ethical future by creating more space for politicians, but also for industrialists, to lead.

Politics needs to recover its self-confidence, and to recapture some of the initiative from corporations at a time when governments' influence seems to be shrinking. Globalisation has opened the way to a new development model, with companies as the main vehicles for delivering social, environmental and economic progress. The question is how?

First, politicians and regulators should think beyond employment. While laudable, this is a very narrow aim that can often work against a more holistic view capable of producing real wellbeing. Secondly, governments could honour society's and consumers' desire for greater business ethics by positively discriminating in favour of ethically sound companies. Thirdly, they could define and articulate a more robust ethical framework in which corporations should operate.

All this would require real political leadership and a break with populism. Simple targets are required that can win popular support for companies which meet them. A general agreement on the role of business might even accelerate the rate of humankind's moral and ethical progress.

(*Source*: Andrew Mackenzie and David Rice, *Guardian*, 14 January 2002)

Question

Do you think, in the current global economy, governments should set the ethics agenda for business?

6.1   Introduction

Increasingly, firms are under pressure to compete in a global marketplace, given a general tendency to deregulation, reduced state involvement, and the increased mobility of investor capital. On the one hand, while holding undoubted risks, this process opens up new markets and opportunities, particularly for firms based in the advanced societies. On the other hand, with these opportunities comes a range of responsibilities and obligations: firms have the same duty to be ethical in both home and host markets. However, more contentious is the extent and range of ethical concerns that should be universal, and what forms of behaviour are acceptable in different national contexts, particularly given the exigencies of competition and pressures for development.

The first part of the chapter sheds some light on the globalization process and key ethical issues arising from the increasingly globalizing world economy. The second part discusses the impact of multinational enterprises (MNEs) on social and economic issues in both developing and developed economies. The third part of the chapter examines the impact, or lack thereof, of global codes of control on MNEs' behaviour. The fourth part discusses the role of local cultures and institutions, and limitations of universal ethical practices. The last part looks at recent developments in global trade and trade relations, and the roles they are playing in shaping the global economy.

6.2   Comprehending globalization

The concept of 'globalization' is an extremely loose one; there has been considerable debate as to its nature and implications (beyond the scope of this chapter). However, it is commonly assumed to result in a greater crossvergence in terms of state policies and workplace practices (Ralston *et al.*, 2007; Szaban and Henderson, 1998: 586). A central debate revolves around the extent to which national social formations can still be regarded as sites of institutions capable of determining political and economic outcomes for a population under consideration (Mellahi *et al.*, 2005; Szaban and Henderson, 1998: 586). For practitioners, globalization means operating globally without restrictions, as put by Percy Barnevik, President of the ABB international Group: 'I would define globalization as the freedom for my group of companies to invest where it wants when it wants, to produce what it wants, to buy and sell where it wants, and support the fewest restrictions possible coming from labour laws and social conventions'.

Keohane and Nye define globalization as a 'state of the world involving networks of interdependence at multi-continental distance' (quoted in Morrissey and Filatotchev, 2000). Late-twentieth-century globalization is particularly characterized by considerable diversity and interdependence in such networks. Globalization is not new: global trade has been around for thousands of years (McIntosh, 2000). However, what has changed is the size and scope of business organizations, the dramatic increase in private investment, and the ability to access information and communicate twenty-four hours a day (McIntosh, 2000).

A number of scholars, political actors and commentators regard globalization as *a deus ex machina* for many of the biggest challenges facing the world today such as poverty, political instability, inequality and global warming (Milanovic, 2002a, 2002b). They argue that globalization has only winners and no losers, and the surest route to deal with these problems is to globalize the economy (Cline, 2004). As put by Milanovic (2002b: 1) '[They believe that] the only thing that a country needs to do is simply to open up its borders, reduce tariff rates, attract foreign capital, and in a few generations if not less, the poor will become rich, the illiterate will learn how to read and write, and inequality will vanish as the poor countries catch up with the rich'. Cline (2004) estimated that free trade could potentially reduce the number of people in global poverty – that is, earning less than US$2 a day, by around 500 million over a period of fifteen years. However, accumulated evidence suggests that there is little doubt that the process of globalization is a contentious one (see Sklair, 1996): its benefits have, to date, been highly uneven. The economic performance of tropical Africa, and large areas of Eastern Europe, for example, lagged far behind the advanced societies in the 1990s (Morrissey and Filatotchev, 2000). At least 400 million people continue to lack the calories, protein, vitamins and minerals to sustain their bodies and minds in a healthy state (Singer, 1995: 218). The Worldwatch Institute estimates that about 1.2 billion people – 23 per cent of the world's population – live in absolute poverty: 'a condition of life so characterized by malnutrition, illiteracy, disease, squalid surroundings, high infant mortality and low life expectancy as to be beneath any reasonable definition of human decency' (Singer, 1995: 219). Indeed, the material conditions of many demonstrably worsened in the 2000s. Cline (2004) reported that about 2.9 billion people live in developing countries where the average per capita income is at or below the poverty line of US$2 per day.

These developmental problems have variously been ascribed to a lack of investment in human resource development and infrastructure, the role of global buyers and distribution networks, the fundamental inability of many third-world firms that previously enjoyed the backing of overly-protectionist states, and/or incomplete deregulation. However, it should be noted that, even in the advanced societies, many industries base their continued prosperity on protectionism or state intervention in some form or another (this could range from anti-dumping measures to lavish defence contracts awarded to local firms). In addition, it can be argued that transnational bodies such as the World Trade Organization (WTO) may exacerbate existing inequalities under certain circumstances; there is a need to 'consider the distribution side of globalization' (Morrissey and Filatotchev, 2000). The uneven – and unequal – process of globalization underscores the importance of central questions such as the universality of core ethical issues, and whether basic mores of behaviour can transcend legal and political boundaries (Payne *et al.*, 1997).

As McIntosh (2000) notes, topics such as global poverty are generally not seen as a major issue on the agenda of global business. However, it can be argued that, if business wants to promote a global economy and free trade, it has to be able to argue that the benefits will be felt by all the world's people, 'not just the few': 'poverty is not the business of business, but business should be part of the solution to resolve poverty, not part of the problem' (McIntosh, 2000).

6.3   The rise and impact of transnational corporations (TNCs)

As Jackson (1997) notes, TNCs have to contend with a 'layered array' of local, national and international rules and norms. TNCs control 80 per cent of the world's land cultivated for export-orientated crops, while many TNCs have a turnover larger than the gross national product (GNP) of entire nations and regions (Dobson, 1992). Western corporate culture has itself become increasingly transnational (ibid.). TNCs have often been depicted as agents of global uniformity, of economic and cultural hegemony, underscoring the importance of ethical issues in this regard.

Globalization has led to a greater awareness of the problems of corporate governance, and increasing pressures for reforms: even entire models of operation (for example, of the *chaebols* in Korea) have been questioned. The financial community has become increasingly aware of the need for greater self-regulation (Vinten, 2000: 173).

However, 'much of the need to encourage firm corporate governance... hangs on the supply of suitable director, shareholder, and perchance, stakeholder information' (Vinten, 2000: 177). The Barings Bank affair – resulting in the bankruptcy of a major financial institution as a result of the activities of a single 'rogue trader' – did not involve the violation of abstract ethical principles, but outright forgery and fraud (Jackson, 1997). It also revealed the intense difficulty firms may experience when they try to supervise remote operations, especially those where key decisions are delegated to a relatively small number of staff members. Moreover, it became evident that there was no systematic and comprehensive way of gauging corporate liability at transnational level (Jackson, 1998).

Even within countries, there is often considerable variation in laws and enforcement between provinces, states or regions (Payne *et al.*, 1997). Such variations are considerably greater at the international level: TNCs have to analyse, assess and amalgamate heterogeneous legal regimes (Payne *et al.*, 1997). They also face the problem of transferring domestic ethical norms into an international context, attempts that are often stillborn in the face of competing pressures, ranging from profitability to cultural variations.

Moreover, there is little doubt that many TNCS engage in regime shopping, locating contentious activities in countries where there are fewer legal restrictions, or where law enforcement is perceived to be weak or erratic. For example, in 1998, following protracted deliberations, the Irish Supreme Court found that US chemical manufacturer, Merck, had deliberately and wilfully discharged noxious chemicals in the hope that this would go unnoticed by surrounding communities (Dobson, 1992).

Oil companies operating in the Amazon basin routinely construct roads – even when transport alternatives such as water exist – opening up remote areas of tropical rain forest to clear-fell logging and slash-and-burn agriculture (Dobson, 1992). Third-world governments are often reluctant to challenge activities of TNCs, given the omnipresent threat of the latter relocating to countries where legal restrictions may be even weaker. In short, market pressures may undermine the scope of deregulation (Diller, 1999).

A firm may operate in a number of different countries, and may be faced with a range of ethical quandaries, even if it keeps scrupulously to the law in host nations. Indeed, Maynard (2001) argues that TNCs find themselves 'on the margins of morality', given the great diversity in historical, cultural and government mores in different nations.

In a large part of the world, basic human rights are still little more than a dream (Donaldson, 1991: 139). How TNCs should operate in such environments has been the subject of considerable debate: should authoritarian regimes be isolated and starved of investment capital, or should every effort be made to draw them into the global system, which will make it harder to retain anachronistic political institutions?

Moreover, even in democratic poor countries with reasonably good governance, a wide range of ethical dilemmas exist. This would include the growing of export crops in areas where widespread starvation exists (Donaldson, 1991: 139). Poor countries consume 180 kilos of grain per year per person, compared to 900 in the USA. The difference in the West is that most of the grain produced is fed to animals, to support a diet that contains far more animal products than in the diet of those in the South. Indeed, as Singer (1995: 220) notes, 'if we stopped feeding animals on grains and soybeans, the amount of food saved would – if distributed amongst those who need it – be more than enough to end hunger throughout the world'(Singer, 1995: 220). While many would shy away from so radical a solution, it is evident that even the cultivation of food crops in the developing world – and what is done with the produce – poses definite ethical dilemmas.

The above-mentioned issue of toxic waste is another issue: because of safety measures in the West, some of the world's poorest nations are used as dumping grounds for waste (Donaldson, 1991). This is achieved by means of legal loopholes, bribery, or simply large fees in countries where legislation is incomplete. It can be argued that even if a third-world government accepts responsibility for taking waste, it can still be extremely problematic: there are often inadequate safeguards to ensure that any benefits will reach the affected communities, or that adequate safeguards are adhered to (Donaldson, 1991).

In the end, TNCs have four moral agencies providing some boundaries as to what is acceptable conduct: internal in terms of managerial ideologies and corporate codes of ethics; other competitors; governmental agencies; and public pressure, especially given the activities 'of NGOs and offshore watchdog bodies'. However, competitors may often be reluctant to draw attention to unethical behaviour, as it may represent a useful form of internal cost-cutting in the future (Donaldson, 1991). In other words, firms may be reluctant to blow the whistle on unethical actions by others, in order to keep their own strategic options open. Meanwhile, host governments may be reluctant to question actions by investors if they face the threat that firms will simply relocate if confronted by greater regulatory pressure. There has already been a slow drift of firms from Thailand to China, because of the greater number of regulations (despite still being very modest) in the former.

However, parent governments (that is, of states where TNCs have their head office) may have considerably greater clout. There is little doubt that the US Foreign Corrupt Practices Act – which, seeks to combat the bribery of foreign officials – has had considerable influence. This has been both in terms of restricting what US firms may do, and in terms of US government pressure on other governments in order to 'level the playing field' and ensure that US firms do not compete at a disadvantage with foreign ones (Zagaris and Ohri, 1999). Indeed, a number of other Western governments have enacted measures to combat international corruption. However, the same governments appear willing to countenance – and indeed actively support – all manner of ethical lapses when it comes to arms exports: this would include the alleged bribery of governmental officials (examples would include the case of BAE Systems in South Africa and Saudi Arabia) and the sale of weaponry to oppressive governments with wretched human rights records (for example, Morocco, Pakistan, Saudi Arabia).

It can be argued that the practice of bribery is deeply embedded within certain national contexts; it is extremely difficult to design institutional mechanisms to combat something that may have been widely accepted as part and parcel of doing business for centuries (Zagaris and Ohri, 1999). In addition, there are many grey areas surrounding the payment of 'facilitation fees', semi-official taxes and the like, making enforcement of anti-bribery measures difficult. More invidious is a frequent lack of will. Firms can engage in a range of practices to conceal the payment of bribes, especially if they fear that a failure to make illegal payments may result in a vital loss of business (Zagaris and Ohri, 1999). None the less, Maynard (2001) argues that the threat of public exposure probably represents the greatest check on unethical actions by TNCs.

More contentious are suggestions that the practice of 'dumping' – where a foreign firm offers goods in a particular market at considerably less than the price for the same goods elsewhere, and sometimes at below cost price – constitutes an unethical act. Several governments – most notably that of the United States – have enacted anti-dumping measures. However, as Delener (1998) notes, the business practice of offering discounts is not generally seen as immoral. Indeed, predatory pricing by domestic firms to drive out competitors (local or foreign) is commonly seen as acceptable – an ethical problem only arises if the goods may constitute a health hazard, such as cigarettes, for example. Indeed, it can be argued that 'dumping' has few ethical implications, but simply represents a response to a situation where global over-production exists (Delener, 1998).

Proponents of the role of TNCs have tended to fall into two categories. First, there are the followers of the neo-liberal school (or modified versions of it). An example of such a follower, Dobson (1992), suggests that rather than attempting to decide what constitutes ethical behaviour, managers – who are simply agents – should leave the matter to their principles, who are best equipped to make ethical choices that are also economically optimal. In short, managers of TNCs face few ethical dilemmas, and should simply carry out the instructions of their principles, while seeking to maximize profitability. However, Dobson (1992) tempers his argument by suggesting that principles do not simply constitute shareholders (as is suggested by writers such as Friedman), but rather all relevant stakeholders.

Second, there are modernization theorists (in the broad tradition of writers such as Rostow), who argue that, given their undoubted economic muscle, as well as their role in shaping global culture, TNCs have the potential to bring about a considerably better world. For example, Buller *et al.* (quoted in Rallapalli, 1999) suggest that instead of being part of a problem, TNCs have the capacity to be part of a solution in promoting more ethical conduct because of their global influence. In short, they represent an essential part of the modernization process, and their activities will invariably contribute to modernization in both domestic and social life.

6.4   Global codes of ethics

It can be argued that attempts to deal with transnational ethical issues by unilateral or bilateral government actions leads to an unjust situation for both victim and perpetrator: enforcement is very difficult, and regulatory institutions will be incomplete (Jackson, 1998). Moreover, firms bound by the restrictive laws of a parent nation will be at an automatic disadvantage vis-à-vis those falling under weaker regulatory regimes (ibid.): ethical behaviour in a globalizing world requires global ethical commitments. Jackson (1998) argues that, given that TNCs have reaped the benefits of the globalization of markets, they should assume some of the responsibilities that comes with this, by binding themselves to internationally-relevant codes of ethics.

A range of international organizations – most notably trading blocs such as the European Community (EC) and the North American Free Trade Area (NAFTA), the International Labour Organization (ILO), the OECD, and the United Nations (UN), have all attempted to promote minimum ethical standards among firms operating in their member nations. However, such codes have tended to be very vague, in order to avoid disputes about what constitutes acceptable behaviour in different cultural contexts (see Payne *et al.*, 1997).

On the one hand, corporate social responsibility has become a global trend, not just the purview of the North (Leipziger, 2000: 39). For example, throughout Latin America, there has been great interest in corporate codes of conduct on labour standards. On the other hand, Latin-American firms (and, indeed, their Asian counterparts) are generally still less committed to independent monitoring than their Northern counterparts (Leipziger, 2000: 39). In part this reflects the persistence of corruption as a prerequisite for doing business in many regions, despite the general rise of an independent press and a stronger civil society (Leipziger, 2000: 40). Table 6.1 lists the ten least corrupt countries and ten most corrupt countries in the world, as perceived by business people. It is interesting to note that the nearly all perceived corrupt countries are going through a violent political transformation.

There are a number of international conventions to restrict corrupt practices, examples being the 1996 Inter-American Convention on Corruption, and the 1997 OECD Anti-Bribery Convention ('The Convention on Combating Bribery of Foreign Government Officials in International Business Transactions'). However, implementation and enforcement of these conventions remains extremely difficult. For example, while the Inter-American Convention

Table 6.1   Ten least and ten most corrupt countries, 2007

Least corrupt	Most corrupt
Denmark	Somalia
Finland	Myanmar (Burma)
New Zealand	Iraq
Singapore	Haiti
Sweden	Uzbekistan
Iceland	Tonga
Netherlands	Sudan
Switzerland	Chad
Canada	Afghanistan
Norway	Laos

Source: Transparency International, 'Corruption Perceptions Index 2007'. Based on a survey of business people's perception. Available at: http://www.transparency.org/policy_research/surveys_indices/cpi/2007.

requires signatories to prohibit domestic and foreign bribes and to actively combat the illegal enrichment of government officials, it lacks substantial mechanisms for monitoring and enforcement (Zagaris and Ohri, 1999). Meanwhile, while the OECD Convention obliges signatories to criminalize the bribery of officials, and provides the basis for international judicial co-operation. However, the governments that are party to the agreement continue to deal with corrupt practices in an uneven and not always transparent fashion (see Zagaris and Ohri, 1999).

In a review of international accords, which include ethical guidelines for TNCs, reached over the years 1948–88, Frederick (1991) found that the bulk of guidelines aim to shape practices with regard to employment relations, consumer protection, the environment, political participation and basic human rights. However, their moral authority was based on the competing principles of national sovereignty, social equity, market integrity and universal human rights. Deontological principles would suggest the primacy of questions of human rights, though utilitarians could argue that long-term environmental issues are of equal or greater importance. In practice, codes have tended to focus on the former, however (Rallappalli, 1999).

There is little doubt that growing numbers of TNCs do pay lip service to such codes, though there is little doubt that ensuring their operational acceptance is somewhat more difficult (Rallappalli, 1999). In addition, many TNCs have their own internal codes. However, there is considerable variability in such codes, though most are founded on rights-based principles, including an agreement to treat all employees fairly with regard to wages, working conditions and benefits (Maynard, 2001). Moreover, there is a general absence of protection for whistleblowers, while questionable behaviour can often be passed off as simply a product of cultural differences (Maynard, 2001).

Indeed, international codes of ethics remain dogged by inconsistency in scope and coverage, and the characteristic 'looseness' of implementation and assessment (Diller, 1999). Moreover, if they are to escape being protectionist, ethical codes have to actively seek to promote capacity development within the third world, and to actively offer support via concrete and targeted programmes (Diller, 1999). Payne *et al.* (1997) argue that an effective internal ethical code should incorporate not just moral, but also cultural and managerial concerns, and should go beyond being simply a public relations gambit aimed at proving 'one can shop without guilt'. They suggest that firms have specific duties, which encompass basic human rights issues, environmental protection, fair employment practices and consumer protection (Payne *et al.*, 1997). However, Getz (quoted in Payne *et al.*, 1997) asserts that firms have a more comprehensive range of obligations. This would include the need to promote local participation (and the use of local suppliers and local equity participation), reinvestment, refraining from corrupt practices and unlawful or improper political activity, keeping to the law, and engaging in technology transfers. Of course, the value of some of these enjoinders in contexts where the government is overly repressive – such as the former apartheid government in South Africa – can be contested. Perhaps, in such contexts, firms have a moral obligation to defy civil authority under certain circumstances.

Drawing on the rights-based view that underlies most international codes of ethics, Donaldson (1991) argues that there are a number of international rights that are fundamentally grounded. Such rights protect things of extreme importance and are subject to recurring threats, while the obligations imposed are fair and economically affordable, given the distribution of burdens generally (what Nickel calls the affordability–fairness criterion) (Donaldson, 1991). These could include the following international rights:

> The right to freedom of physical movement.
> The right to ownership of property.
> The right to freedom from torture; the right to a fair trial.
> The right to non-discriminatory treatment (for example, on grounds of race or gender).
> The right to physical security.
> The right to freedom of speech and association.
> The right to minimal education.
> The right to political participation.
> The right to subsistence.
>
> (Donaldson, 1991)

Other rights could include that of a basic standard of living, as might be prescribed by Rawls' difference principle (Donaldson, 1991). TNCs can honour some of these rights simply by avoidance (ibid.). None the less, there is little doubt that TNCs do have some obligations that go beyond abstaining from direct deprivation. For example, no firm can wholly neglect issues such as hunger, racism or political oppression (Vinten, 2000). However, many practices may be the subject of great controversy. For example, the aggressive promotion of high-yield seeds and fertilizers may increase food output, but may also lock peasants into a cycle of debt.

6.5   Cultural relativism and universals

The increasing role of transnational corporations makes some cross-cultural conflict inevitable (Buller *et al.*, 1997). Indeed, different social and cultural factors will result in very different ethical concerns. To Hofstede (1980), culture provides the basis for distinction between different groups and is reflected in the values and beliefs of a particular society; culture shapes what people see in a situation, and delineates appropriate behaviour. Hofstede (1980) argues that culture is a form of 'collective mental programming', and incorporates four dimensions, including the individualism/collectivism nexus, masculinity/femininity, power distance and uncertainty avoidance. Individuals' cultural make-up will, in turn, determine their approach to a range of ethical dilemmas.

International ethics involves an attempt to apply a specific set of moral values in situations involving two or more nations (Buller *et al.*, 1997). However, it can be argued that universal moral norms tend to be general and rather abstract; what constitutes 'fairness', for example, can be open to very different interpretations in different sets of cultural circumstances.

For example, a vigorous implementation of an equal opportunities policy may result in cultural condemnation, loss of customer and client contacts, and the eventual unprofitability of the entire firm (Mayer and Cava, 1993). On other hand, it is hard to maintain cultural particularism in a globalizing world, and the negative impact of 'doing things differently' should not be underestimated, nor the positive benefits from pursuing equity (Mayer and Cava, 1993).

Numerous different writers have suggested ways out of this quandary. Donaldson (1991), for example, from a rights-based perspective, suggests that, if an ethical contestation is based on economic concerns, TNCs should consider whether a particular practice would be permissible in the home country, if it were at the same stage of development as the host country. However, it could be argued that child labour, for example – which was tolerated in most Western countries a century or so ago – is unacceptable, whatever the economic circumstances.

Mayer and Cava (1993) argue that, without 'slavishly adhering' to Western equity legislation, the aim should be to promote equity in a low-key way: there is a need for some basic minimum principles and morals, without the 'ethical balkanization' that full-on relativism would entail. Values should be universally discovered to be shared, while universal standards should come out of experience – an example being the increasing global commitment to at least a form of multi-part democracy.

Donaldson goes on to suggest that, if the causes of an ethical dispute are not economic, then a practice is only permissible if it is necessary to do business in the host country and it does not violate fundamental international rights. Again, this could be contested. For example, De George (1986) suggests that each situation requires judgement and moral imagination (which would, of course, reflect the utilitarian approach). However, he further suggests that there is a need for practices, procedures and background institutions to reinforce ethical behaviour – people and firms need encouragement to make sound ethical judgements.

Jackson (1997) argues that, while cultural specificities must be acknowledged, there is a core of ethical values common to all societies. It is possible to encode this, but, in the end, the internal 'atmosphere' of the organization will largely shape its behaviour. Such an ethical core would, for example, encompass a rejection of overt racial discrimination (Jackson, 1997). However, even in this area, there is considerable room for contention. This would include the extent and scope of affirmative action programmes, and the degree to which other forms of discrimination may be unacceptable. For example, in many conservative societies in the developing world, a far higher degree of gender discrimination is enforced than would be acceptable in the first world. Less morally contentious issues would include a rejection of slavery, theft, outright deception, fraud and the like. Jackson (1997) asserts that, given that many ethical concerns are shared, ethical codes can rise above national parochialisms. Indeed, conduct can be guided by the Kantian enjoinder never to simply treat people as a means to an end, without taking into account their personal needs and rights.

Hamilton and Knouse (2001) developed a framework to help managers deal with cross-cultural ethical conflicts. Figure 6.1 provides a step-by-step process to help managers reach the most appropriate decision.

The framework is based on four principles or decision rules: Is the questionable practice in the host country less ethical than the MNE's usual practice? Does the questionable practice violate the MNE's ethical minimums? Does the MNE have leverage in the host country to follow its own practices? And do the host country's background institutions have prospects for improvement? Figure 6.2 provides a detailed explanation of the framework illustrated with examples.

6.6   Thinking about global trade and relations

As Moody (1997: 6) notes, despite globalization, 'the world remains a very uneven, fragmented and divided one'; indeed, 'the process of deepening international economic integration actually increases some aspects of fragmentation and inequality between nations'. World systems theory holds that global capitalism must, of necessity continually increase production and trade, to guarantee the political conditions for this to take place worldwide, and to constantly re-stimulate consumer demand (Sklair, 1995: 62). This in turn led to the emergence of the 'more precise and research rich' concept of global commodity chains (GCCs), first propounded by Gereffi and Korzeniewicz (Sklair, 1995: 40). Producers, intermediaries and buyers are seen as forming part of the same global organization, in ever-increasing networks of GCCs (Sklair, 1995: 62). Of

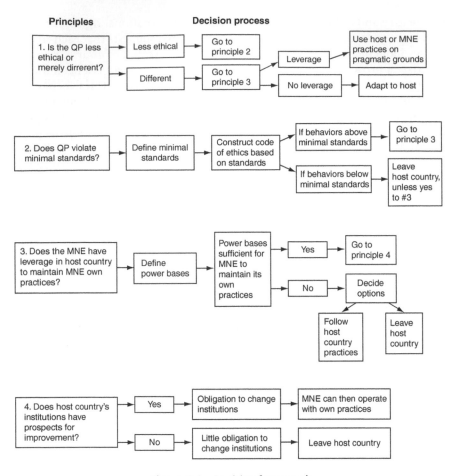

Figure 6.1   Decision framework

Source: Hamilton and Knouse, 2001, p. 80.

course, what really matters is who is the most powerful in the chain (Morrissey and Filatotchev, 2000).

GCC theory holds that transnational corporations (TNCs), or, failing that, end-users, represent the most powerful links in the chain (Szaban and Henderson, 1998: 587). While many of the underlying assumptions of GCC theory may be contested, there is little doubt that global inequality greatly increased during the 1980s and 1990s (Moody, 1997). Patterns of trade are likely to strengthen the strong and more powerful nations or regions, at the expense of weaker ones. This has led to periodic calls for a review of existing relationships, and for 'fairer trade', calls that have become increasingly part of mainstream discourse, and to which growing numbers of TNCs have been forced to pay at least lip service. However, there remains considerable debate as to solutions. Neo-liberals would

MNE should follow its own ethical practices rather than host country's questionable practices (QPs) if:

Decision Rule 1: Questionable Practices Are Less Ethical (Rather Than Different)

If QPs are not less ethical but only different, MNE can follow own or host country standards. If QPs are less ethical, then MNE must consider next three decision rules.

Examples: Bribes and corruption are less ethical; nepotism in hiring may only be different if justified by host country's background institutions.

Strengths: Prevents the cultural imperialism of assuming one's own values are superior by requiring an examination of the relationship of the questionable business practice to the legal, economic, and social institutions in which they are embedded.

Weaknesses: Requires reference to traditional ethical theories to determine whether practices are less ethical or different, so could challenge capacities of MNE manager or require an ethics consultant's expertise.

Decision Rule 2: Questionable Practices Violate Ethical Minimums

If QPs violate ethical minimums, MNE should not engage in these practices; if not, consult decision rules 3 and 4.

Examples: Murdering competitors and dumping toxic wastes are below ethical minimums; nepotism in hiring and paying bribes in some circumstances may not be below minimums for some corporations.

Strengths: Makes an important distinction between activities which are never acceptable no matter the beneficial consequences (places limits on what can be justified by cost/benefit analysis) and acts which can be considered.

Challenges businesses to examine what activities will likely raise ethical questions in their line of business and design a corporate ethics code to speak to those activities.

Weaknesses: Requires reference to traditional ethical theories to determine the ethical minimums. Could require ethics consultant's expertise.

Decision Rule 3: MNE Had Leverage In Host Country

If MNE has leverage, it should follow its own standards if (2) host country practices are less ethical and (4) host country has prospects for improvement.

Examples: MNE can refuse to follow host practices because it has access to needed hard currency, home country legal requirements or ability not to enter or to exit the market.

Strengths: Points out obligation of MNE to stakeholders in host country to contribute to improving the situation in their society, with the hopes of bettering the return for MNE employees and stockholders by helping create a more efficient market for its operations. Does not impose obligations on those without the power to act on them.

Weaknesses: Requires analysis of a number of economic, legal, political and social forces. Could require consultations with a variety of disciplines. Risk of special pleading in weighing exit and opportunity costs.

Decision Rule 4: Host Country Has Prospects For Improving

If the host country's practices have prospects for improving, and the MNE has leverage, then the MNE should operate in a way to contribute to that improvement.

Figure 6.2 Proposed decision rules for MNE managers drawn from Russian examples

Source: Hamilton and Knouse, 2001, p. 81.

Examples: If McDonald's can improve the business climate in Russia (or perhaps only in Moscow) by refusing to pay bribes, then they should do so. If Levi's cannot improve the forced prison labor situation in China, then they should exit the country.

Strengths: Emphasizes that obligation is contingent on possibility.

Weaknesses: Requires analysis of a number of economic, legal, political and social forces. Could require consultants from a variety of disciplines. Requires weighing the welfare of other stakeholder obligations against the obligations to improve conditions for stakeholders in host country and against possibilities for future benefits for employee and stockholder stakeholders if conditions in host country do improve.

Figure 6.2   Continued

suggest that this reflects market imperfection, and a failure to fully deregulate. Meanwhile, their critics would argue that a greater range of institutional mechanisms need to be erected to 'balance out' the flows of trade, in terms of national legislation, transnational conventions and accords, and via greatly strengthened international codes of ethics.

A broader question is whether the richer regions of the world have a duty to help the poor. This is an obligation that is distinct from questions of ownership and property: one can believe in property rights and the desirability of the market system, yet retain a sense of duty towards the poor (Singer, 1995: 234). The question emerges as to whether aid to the poorer parts of the world should be left to governments, rather than troubling firms or the conscience of the individual. As noted in earlier chapters, writers such as Friedman have suggested that the main obligation of the firm is towards those that own it: it is undesirable that management engages in philanthropic activity, in effect spending the money of others. However, only a handful of countries give more than 0.7 per cent of their GDP in aid to the world's poorer regions. Indeed, the USA gives only a sixth of 1 per cent (Singer, 1995: 241). Singer (1995: 241) suggests that there is no reason to believe governments will give more if individual contributions decreased, and an ethical obligation rests on all to improve the overall human (and, indeed, global) condition.

6.7   Summary

Globalization is a widely deployed and little-understood concept. However, it can be understood simply as the process by which national social formations – and the autonomy of national governments – have become eroded as a result of the unification of markets and of consumer taste, and the increasing global mobility of financial capital. The globalization of corporate activities is not a new process, but rather one that has been under way for over a century. However, there is little doubt that this process has been greatly accelerated, and opens up a range of ethical dilemmas for firms operating across national boundaries. These include the identification of ethical principles that are universal and should be upheld consistently (as opposed to culturally specific moral guide-lines), approaches to trade and competition, and, indeed, even the extent to which firms should be more proactive in alleviating global poverty. While, despite the proliferation of global ethical codes, clear solutions remain elusive, it is evident that firms are increasingly under pressure – from governments, NGOs, international organizations and the public at large – to take global ethical issues seriously.

Discussion question

- Do you think multinational corporations should adopt their ethical behaviour according to the norms of the countries where they operate or adopt a universal standards for ethical conducts regardless of the location?

Case study

Closing case study

Globalization and the spread of poverty

The two major reasons that tend to attract multinational companies to most developing economies are their cheap labour and weak environmental protection laws. Even being a huge market no longer forms the basis for being chosen as a manufacturing location. Thus countries that want to improve people's living standards through higher wages, increase social responsibilities of the government through high taxes, or increase environmental standards, tend to get punished. In other words, the labour-intensive and pollution-driven multinational companies tend to migrate to those other countries that still can guarantee cheaper labour and loose environmental control.

The Asian financial crises in the mid-1990s completely highlighted the economic danger a growing number of developing countries are today exposed to as they become completely coupled into the global economic system. The increase in labour costs and environmental awareness in South Korea and Thailand as the fastest-growing economies in Asia, coupled with the devaluation of China's currency in 1994, triggered multinational businesses to leave their shores *en masse* for the lower-income and less pollution-stringent China and India for their competitiveness. At the same time, Malaysia, based on the same logic, lost its production havens for computer hardware to neighbouring Indonesia. Indonesia later lost its gains to the Philippines, where salaries and pollution control seemed much lower. As the race continues, even the Philippines is being replaced by Cambodia and Vietnam for labour-intensive and pollution-driven industries.

Case study

Continued

The story is no different in Latin America, where most Western manufacturing giants move from one location to another in search of cheap labour and loose environmental control. One good example remains the speed with which most multinational companies moved production from Argentina to Brazil once wages and social costs of production became cheaper in Brazil. Even Mexico, with its outstanding policy of holding down wages and social benefits since the early 1980s with the opening of its economy to the world, is now losing that privileged position to neighbouring Central American and Caribbean countries that have far lower wages and weaker environmental protection laws. As has been the case in other globally-coupled developing economies, these countries now witness immense industrial growth without real economic growth, trickle down, multiplier or accelerator effects.

In fact, in this race to the bottom in most of these so-called developing world's superstar countries, real wages have lagged far behind productivity growth. For example, between 1994 and 1997, Indonesia witnessed an 11.5 per cent wage decline; the Philippines 6.0 per cent; and China 5.4 per cent, including the loss of their once guaranteed pension. Even Mexico's wages, which had been rising with productivity at 6.6 per cent annually between 1988 and 1993, were dragged far lower than productivity when adjusted to the inflation rate during the same period. At the same time, the governments of most of the so-called Asian tigers, particularly Malaysia and Singapore, have compulsory savings schemes. Tax policies are also put in place to drive down consumption, particularly to discourage the use of imported goods. For example, as of 1996, Indonesia had a 35 per cent vehicle tax, Brazil 36 per cent, Thailand 45 per cent and Malaysia 65 per cent in the form of excise duties. These policies are not new. They were successfully adopted in Japan for it to emerge as an economic superpower.

No doubt, with 770 million people, Africa will soon be joined in this league that globally exports poverty. While the ongoing World Bank and IMF visits to Africa are being undertaken to discover ways to ensure that Western multinational companies involved in extracting African mineral resources are not harmed by the so-called era of democracy sweeping the continent, the recent presidential and congressional visits to Africa translated into the passage of an African Growth Opportunity Act to prepare the ground for the inevitable landing of multinational companies to African shores. In fact, South Africa with its advanced infrastructure and industrial parks, is already enjoying the growth of multinational companies on shore. But the presence of the radical Mbeki, the president of South Africa, has not made life easy for these multinational companies. Making Nigeria and Ghana the new havens for the multinational companies has become inevitable, especially given the growing confrontational posture of China in the recent U.S.–China military relations.

As a result of this race to the bottom in a race that is guaranteed by cheap labour and weak environmental protection the highly industrialized countries in North America and Europe are losing their former industrial power to these less-industrialized countries. The consequences have been loss of jobs, social security benefits and quality of life. As a result, most Western governments are highly indebted from efforts to fill the financial gaps left by the new industrial gap. The fear of this trend has generated a lot of anti-globalization protest across the West, from Seattle to Washington D.C. and recently to Quebec. Unfortunately, the battle is being lost. To the extent that multinational companies have been able to finance elections and have their candidates elected, they have been able to penetrate very powerfully into the Western political system.

(*Source: Nigerian Guardian Online, 11 June 2001*;
available at: ngrguardiannews.com)

Questions

- Discuss the effects of the 'race to the bottom' in emerging and developing economies.
- 'Multinational corporations create jobs and economic growth in developing and emerging countries where they operate.' Discuss this statement.

References

Buller, P., Kohls, J. and Anderson, K. 1997. 'A Model for Addressing Cross-Cultural Ethical Conflicts', *Business and Society*, 36,2: 169–93.

Cline, W. R. 2004. *Trade Policy and Global Poverty*. Washington DC: Center for Global Development and Institute for International Economics.

De George, T. R. 1986. *Business Ethics*. London: Macmillan.

Delener, N. 1998. 'An Ethical and Legal Synthesis of Dumping', *Journal of Business Ethics*, 17: 1747–53.

Diller, J. 1999. 'A Social Conscience of the Global Marketplace', *International Labour Review*, 138,2: 99–129.

Dobson, J. 1992. 'Ethics in the Transnational Corporation: The "Moral Buck" Street', *Journal of Business Ethics*, 11,1: 21–43.

Donaldson, T. 1991. 'Rights in the Global Market', in R. Freeman (ed.), *Business Ethics: The State of the Art*. Oxford University Press.

Frederick, W. 1991. 'The Moral Authority of Transnational Corporate Codes', *Journal of Business Ethics*, 10,3: 165–78.

Hamilton, J. B. and Knouse, B. S. 2001. 'Multinational Enterprise Decision Principles for Dealing With Cross Cultural Ethical Conflicts', *Journal of Business Ethics*, 31,1: 77–94

Hofstede, G. H. 1980. *Culture Consequences: International Differences in Work-related Values*. London: Sage.

Jackson, K. 1997. 'Globalizing Corporate Ethics Programmes', *Journal of Business Ethics*, 16,12/13: 1272–35.

Jackson, K. 1998. 'A Transnational Court for Transnational Corporate Wrong-doing: Why the Time is Right', *Journal of Business Ethics*, 17,7: 738–57.

Keohane, O. R. and Nye, S. J., Jr. 2000. 'Globalization: What's New? What's Not? (And So What?)', *Foreign Policy*, 118: 104–19.

Leipziger, D. 2000. 'Corporate Social Responsibility: A Focus on Latin America', in M. McIntosh (ed.), *Visions of Ethical Business*. London: Financial Times/Prentice Hall.

Mayer, D. and Cava, A. 1993. 'Ethics and the Gender Dilemma for US Multinationals', *Journal of Business Ethics*, 12,9: 701–8.

Maynard, M. 2001. 'Policing Transnational Commerce', *Journal of Business Ethics*, 30,1: 17–27.

McIntosh, M. 2000. 'Introduction', in M. McIntosh (ed.), *Visions of Ethical Business*. London: *Financial Times*/Prentice Hall.

Mellahi, K., Frynas, G. and Finlay, P. 2005. *Global Strategic Management*. Oxford: Oxford University Press.

Milanovic, B. 2002a. 'True World Income Distribution, 1988 and 1993: First Calculation Based on Household Surveys Alone', *Economic Journal*, 112,1: 51–92.

Milanovic, B. 2002b. 'The Two Faces of Globalization: Against Globalization as We Know It', Unpublished manuscript (second draft), World Bank, Washington, DC.

Moody, K. 1997. *Workers in a Lean World*. London: Verso.

Morrissey, O. and Filatotchev, I. 2000. 'Globalisation and Trade: The Implications for Exports from Marginalised Economies', *Journal of Development Studies*, 37, 2: 1–27.

Payne, D., Raiborn, C. and Askvik, J. 1997. 'A Global Code of Business Ethics', *Journal of Business Ethics*, 16: 1727–35.

Rallappalli, K. 1999. 'A Paradigm for the Development and Promulgation of a Global Code of Marketing Ethics', *Journal of Business Ethics*, 18,1: 125–37.

Ralston, A. D. 2007. 'The Crossvergence Perspective: Reflections and Projections', *Journal of International Business Studies*; doi:10.1057/palgrave.jibs.8400333.

Singer, P. 1995. *Practical Ethics*. Cambridge: Cambridge University Press.

Sklair, L. 1995. *Sociology of the Global System*. Hemel Hempstead: Harvester-Wheatsheaf.

Sklair, L. 1996. 'Global Change: Regional Response (Book Review)', *Journal of Development Studies*, 33,1: 137–8.

Szaban, L. and Henderson, J. 1998. 'Globalization, Institutional Hegemony and Industrial Transformation', *Economy and Society*, 27,4: 5575–613.

Transparency International. 2007. *Global Corruption Perception Index 2007*. Available at: http://www.transparency.org/policy_research/surveys_indices/cpi/2007.

Vinten, G. 2000. 'Corporate Governance: The Need to Know', *Industrial and Commercial Training*, 32,5: 173–8.

Zagaris, B. and Ohri, S. 1999. 'The Emergence of an International Enforcement Regime in Transnational Competition in the Americas', *Law and Policy in International Business*, 33: 53–93.

Part 3
Ethical management in practice: ethics and key functional areas

Ethics, accounting and finance

Chapter objectives

- To understand the ethical challenges arising from changes in the accounting profession.
- To introduce the role of codes of ethics.
- To gain insight into the current ethical challenges in the practice of accounting.
- To gain insight into the current ethical debates surrounding the changing role of finance.

Case study

Introductory case study

Fury at private equity merger of AA and Saga

Two of Britain's best known brands – Saga, the insurance and leisure company for the over-50s, and the Automobile Association – are to merge, creating a financial services and motoring giant valued at £6.15bn.

The enlarged group, which will employ around 11,000 staff, is likely to be listed on the stock exchange in three to five years.

The surprise move brings together the three private equity houses that have separately owned Saga and the AA since 2004. Charterhouse, the owners of

Case study

Continued

Saga, will hold a 37.5 per cent stake in the new holding company, while CVC and Permira, who own the AA, will keep 42.5 per cent.

This gives private equity firms an 80 per cent stake in the combined company; management and staff at the two businesses will hold the rest.

More than 1,000 Saga staff will be able to cash in 75 per cent of their shares in the company after the deal, giving them a payout of almost £8,000 each. The rest will be rolled into the enlarged group.

The transaction, which has been financed by £4.8bn debt, £86m from staff and management and £1.4bn from private equity, values the AA at £3.35bn and Saga at £2.8bn. Private equity firms paid £1.7bn for the AA three years ago, while the Saga buyout was financed with £500m of equity and £800m debt.

Saga's chief executive, Andrew Goodsell, who will take over the helm at the combined group, which has yet to be named, said both companies will continue to operate in their separate fields. Tim Parker, head of the AA, is to leave to pursue other interests.

Earlier this year, Saga appointed Close Brothers to examine 'future ownership' options for the group, among them a return to the stock market. Stuart Howard, Saga's finance director, said yesterday that a flotation of the combined group was the most likely scenario in the medium term, and would give it a place near the top end of the FTSE. Mr Howard said the AA approached Saga about the tie-up six weeks ago. 'There is significant opportunity to grow Saga and the AA by having a single common management team,' he said. Much of the focus would be on growing the AA's financial business, he added. Though initially a holiday business, Saga now derives 80 per cent of its turnover from its financial services arm, which includes motor and home insurance. The AA's main business is roadside recovery, so there is room to develop its financial arm, Mr Howard said. He added that any job cuts would be limited and the focus would be on developing the businesses.

The £1.7bn buyout of the AA in 2004 led to 3,500 jobs being slashed, triggering a backlash from unions which have accused the industry of asset-stripping.

Paul Maloney, national secretary for the GMB, said yesterday that the union estimates that Mr Parker will walk away from the AA with £80m after this deal. 'This shows the extent to which we have entered into a casino economy,' he said. 'This money was made on the back of 3,500 sacked workers, cuts in the pay of the call centre staff, the elongation of the working day for the patrols and a decline in the service to the customers.'

He said the GMB wanted to talk to Saga about reversing the job cuts and improving working conditions at the AA.

Mr Goodsell said both companies have made significant progress under private equity ownership. 'We have taken a really close look and concluded that that there are significant advantages in combining Saga and the AA's experience, expertise, systems and negotiating power, while maintaining their separate and very distinct brands and personalities.'

(Karen Attwood, *Independent*, 26 June 2007.)

Questions

- Why is the GMB concerned about the effects of this merger?
- Do you think the union's concerns are legitimate? And, how does this tie in with the need of private-sector firms to make money for their owners?

7.1 Introduction

This chapter discusses business ethics in finance and accounting. Intensified competition on a global basis, together with radical changes in the accounting profession (Lawrence, 1998)– such as the rise of 'creative accounting' – have raised a number of well-publicized moral dilemmas for financial analysts and accountants. Finn *et al.*, (1994: 27) argue that many accountants believe 'unethical behaviour is on the increase' and that 'incentives and pressures in the marketplace may lead to even more widespread use of unethical behaviour to secure and retain clients'. Less publicized ethical concerns, but no less important, are the troubling conflicts of values that arise, or do not arise, for financiers and accountants.

This chapter is divided into three parts. The first looks at recent changes in financial management practices. The second deals with ethical financial practices – financial code ethics and how they are enforced, or not, in practice. The third part analyses the ethicality of current financial and accounting management practices, and the fourth part looks at the debate surrounding broader changes in investor behaviour, and looks at the rise of private equity, and the ethical implications of this.

7.2 Ethics and financial management

Over a decade ago, Dobson (1997) argued that 'it would be an understatement' to claim that the disciplines of ethics and finance have not been strongly associated with each other. According to Dobson, the two disciplines 'have been opposed to each other as mutually exclusive'. The latter is a result of several intertwined factors acting together. A number of writers examined moral dilemmas facing financial analysts and accountants. Drummond and Bain (1994: 185) state that 'anyone taking serious interest in ethics of business quickly comes to the conclusion that accountants have a key, if not a central, role to play'. This role, however, 'is becoming increasingly controversial'. Similarly, Hussey and Jack (1994: 186) note: 'Ask a group of customers whether business ethics has ethics and they are likely to laugh in derision. Ask a group of business executives the same about accountants, and the answer is not likely to be so different.'

One of the primary reasons for ethical concerns over financial and accounting practices is that practitioners of management accounting and financial management on the one hand have an obligation to the public and the state, and on the other hand to the organization or clients they serve. Dobson (1997) argues that 'the ethics of finance is underdeveloped compared to the fields of business ethics or professional ethics', because 'most financiers have not had a strong ethical formation', whereas ethicists 'lack an understanding of the technicality of financial management, and thus the situation perpetuates itself'.

Another cause of growing ethical concern in finance and accounting is the aggressive competitive environment and changes in the role of the profession. A survey by The Ethics Resource Centre/Society for Human Resource Management (1997) in the United States showed that 'meeting overly aggressive financial or business objectives' as the principal cause of ethical compromise. Activities that may undermine the integrity of the financial accountant include schemes to overstate a company's earnings and financial condition, wilfully and extensively falsifying corporate records, lying to auditors, coercing vendors into covering up practices, improperly applying accounting principles, making false disclosures, and repeatedly violating general accepted accounting principles.

In the USA, accountants and financiers claim that the accounting profession has been perceived by the public as being among the more ethical of business professions. Warth (2000: 69) note that 'CPAs' high ethical standards are the foundation for their trust in the mind of the public'. This is because the accounting profession has been founded on the notion that proper ethical behaviour is a cornerstone of providing professional services to the client (Finn *et al.*, 1994). Such ethical behaviour is enforced by professional ethical codes of conduct that every accountant and financier must adhere to as a condition for membership of professional organizations. Advocates of codes of ethics in finance and accounting argue that they are beneficial as a guide to professional conduct, and as a basis for making judgements with respect to ethical dilemmas. For example, CPAs who violate the code are subject to sanctions and the loss of their licence. Cottell and Perlin (1990: 18) assert that one of the defining characteristics of a professions is '[t]he capacity to regulate itself, often with the sanction of the law for those who violate acceptable norms of behaviour'.

Several researchers have explored the merits and demerits of strict ethical codes and standards that rely primarily on enforcement of procedures, and punishment in case of non-adherence, or a laissez-faire approach based on moral and ethical training to motivate accountants to behave morally without institutional monitoring (see Barry, 1999). Advocates of the latter argue that accounting and finance practitioners, like other professionals, should be left free to apply their skills, expertise and seasoned judgement, guided by moral conscience and not by rigid rules and regulations. Advocates of the former approach, however, further question the application of accounting and finance codes of ethics: are they legalistic documents – prescriptive – and therefore adhering to the codes is suffice for claiming that the practice is ethical? The jury is still out on the latter question, but in practice, it is observed that while the accounting and finance codes of practice may be described as rather prescriptive, accountants have generally discouraged a legalistic reading. Put differently, accountants and financiers are expected to abide by the spirit of the code and the professional ethic it prescribes.

For example, in the 1977 report by the Subcommittee on Reports, Accounting and Management of the Committee on Governmental Affairs, US Senate, the subcommittee stated: ' [it] agrees that disciplinary actions should be expedited, and should be based on failure to follow high professional standards, rather than violation of legal standards' (US Congress, 1977).

An ethical violation may be either a violation of a legal requirement or presentation of accounting information that may be misleading to potential users of financial information (Beckman *et al.*, 1989). In the performance of their duties, accountants are expected to adhere to personal standards that go beyond legal formalities. The Institute of Management Accounting (IMA) (*Strategic Finance*, 1999) lists five acts that practitioners of management accounting and finance have to adhere to:

Competence. Practitioners of management accounting and financial management have the responsibility to maintain appropriate level of professional competence; perform their professional duties in accordance with relevant laws, regulations, and technical standards; prepare complete and clear reports and recommendations after appropriate analysis of relevant and reliable information.

Confidentiality. They should refrain from disclosing confidential information acquired during the course of their work; inform subordinates as appropriate regarding the confidentiality of information acquired in the course of their work and monitor their activities to ensure the maintenance of that confidentiality; refrain from using or appearing to use confidential information acquired in the course of their work for unethical or illegal advantages either personally or through third parties.

Integrity. They have the responsibility to avoid actual or apparent conflicts of interest and advise all appropriate parties of any potential conflict; refrain from engaging in any activity that would prejudice their ability to carry out their duties ethically; refuse any gift, favour, or hospitality that would influence or would appear to influence their actions; refrain from either actively or passively subverting the attainment of the organization's legitimate and ethical objectives; recognize and communicate professional limitations or other constraints that would preclude responsible judgement or successful performance of an activity; communicate unfavourable as well as favourable information and professional judgements or opinions; and refrain from engaging in or supporting any activity that would discredit the profession.

Objectivity. They are responsible to communicate information fairly and objectively[*sic*]; and disclose fully all relevant information that could reasonably be expected to influence an intended user's understanding of the reports, comments, and recommendations presented.

Resolution of ethical conflict. When faced with a significant ethical issue, they should follow the established policies of the organization bearing on the resolution of the conflict. If the latter do not resolve the ethical conflict, they should consider the following courses of action: discuss the issue with immediate superior; if the issue is not resolved, submit the issue to the next higher management level or other relevant internal bodies. (For more details, see *Strategic Finance*, 1999)

It must be mentioned that ethical standards are not static but evolve as the business, economic, technological and social contexts within which they operate change (we shall explore this point in more detail later). For example, the American accounting profession has continued to monitor, revise and update its professional standards. In the late 1980s, the American Institute of CPAs (AICPA) conducted extensive revisions and adopted a revised Code of Professional Conduct (Anderson, 1985; Anderson and Ellyson, 1986; American Institute of Certified Public Accountants, 1988; Shaub, 1988). These revisions were sparked off by a US Congressional investigation of the accounting profession, which proposed legislation that would regulate the profession if the profession proved incapable of demonstrating more active self-regulation efforts. The above investigation revealed concerns by representatives of business and industry that the standards of ethical conduct for CPAs were not providing sufficient guidance for accounting professionals (Graber, 1979). In the revised code, the AICPA specified a set of general rules governing conduct as well as proper ethical behaviour for Certified Public Accountants (CPAs). The Enron scandal (see below) led to the passage of the Sarbanes–Oxley Act of 2002 (SOA) in the United States, to reduce the possibility of future scandals. However, critics have charged that 'the effectiveness of the SOA critically depends upon the focus and attention of the Public Companies Accounting Oversight Board (PCAOB) towards assessing the ethical climates of public accounting firms', and is, as such, no guarantee of future ethical conduct (Kaplan *et al.*, 2007).

7.3   Are ethical violations common within the financial and accounting profession?

This is largely an empirical question, but so far little empirical research has been done to resolve it in one way or another (see Finn *et al.*, 1994). There is, however, a large body of anecdotal evidence that seems to support an affirmative answer. Finn *et al.* (1994: 27) found that CPAs could be arranged in two groups. The first group consists of those who believe that unethical behaviour is already widespread, and that there are few, if any, deterrents to a continued growth of such unethical practices. They believed that the profession was ineffective in enforcing ethical standards, and that the partners of the CPA firms were similarly lax in enforcing ethical standardsinternally. They reported that some CPAs believed that unethical behaviour was condoned and could in fact improve one's opportunities for advancement in the profession (Finn *et al.*, 1988). The second group held a more positive view of ethical conduct. They believed that 'while unethical behaviour is not yet widespread, competitive pressures have led to an increase in unethical behaviour'. Understandably, the latter group called for tighter policing and the reprimanding of CPAs who did not comply with ethical standards.

7.4   Creative accounting and ethics

Prior to the 1980s, the caricature of an accountant was someone who was cautious and backward-looking, wore grey, and was unimaginative, boring and with no sense of humour. As a result of the changing nature of the equity market in the 1980s, however, the profession has changed beyond recognition. The changed conditions led to the birth of creative accounting, which is practised widely by both large and small companies (Paterson, 1995; Shah, 1996). Creative accounting is here to stay, because 'no amount of legislation, no code of best practice, and no system of accounting standards' can remove it (Pijper, 1994). In simple terms, creative accounting is the use of permitted cosmetic window-dressing accounting techniques to present a flattering picture of a company's financial situation. In some cases, creative accounting techniques are used to create a false impression while providing information that is not, in itself, untruthful. (For an extensive review of how creative accounting produces misleading information using real-life examples; see Pijper, 1994). Howard (1996) states that creative accounting is 'an example of hiding the truth while sticking assiduously to the rules'. It reflects pressure from executives who wish to create the impression of enhancing profitability and strengthening the balance sheet to ensure a healthy demand for shares (Whittington, 1995). The latter would subsequently reduce the need for external borrowing, and help to justify strategic moves such as acquisitions and/or defence against hostile takeovers. The accounting and finance profession responded with the development of a wide range of creative techniques, 'which broke with the caution of the past and seemed to spurn a predominant emphasis on the true underlying financial position of the company' (Hussey and Jack, 1994: 186–7). A well-publicized example is the technique used by the Polly Peck Group (see Howard, 1996). It is alleged that 'the company borrowed in Swiss francs at an apparently low interest rate, but Swiss franc appreciation against sterling meant that the real sterling cost of borrowing was much higher'. A 'loophole in accounting rules allowed this huge extra cost to be ignored in calculating the company's profit, which was made to look much greater' (Howard, 1996: 66).

Creative accounting is not always used to exaggerate profit. Sometimes it is used to minimize profit or to show a fictitious loss. Munk (1995) cites the example of Paramount Pictures' movie, *Forrest Gump*, which was made to appear – thanks to creative accounting – to make a loss rather than profit despite the over $657 million it made at the box office around the world. As a result, some parties in the movie-making process who were entitled to a portion of the net profit did not get their fair share (see Cartoon 5).

In the UK, creative accounting has been challenged by critics who describe it as 'fiddling with profits' (Griffiths, 1986); 'manipulation, deceit and misrepresentation', an 'accounting sleight of hand' (Smith, 1992); and potential

Cartoon 5   Creative accounting is like a box of chocolates, you never know what you're going to nett.

'abuse' (Naser, 1993). However, Breton and Taffler (1995), using a laboratory experiment in which a large sample of experienced investment analysts participated, found that creative accounting was not viewed as a serious problem. They stated that, contrary to conventional wisdom, there was is little evidence of window-dressing adjustments made by creative accounting in general.

Creative accounting has also led to the rise of 'opinion shopping' by companies searching for preferred ways of presenting their financial status. This could lead to a situation where companies select those accountants, accounting firms and financiers to produce their reports that are have the reputation of being sympathetic to certain irregularities, the most notorious being well-known financial 'beauty therapists'. In such an environment, financiers and accountants with a strong ethical will find it hard to attract and retain clients.

Century Business Services Incorporated represents a widely cited example of (un)ethical practices resulting from creative accounting (*Business Week*, 2000). This public company expanded to become the seventh-largest US accounting firm by acquiring small and medium-sized firms. The company's reported revenues nearly tripled in 1977, and doubled in 1988 (*Business Week*, 2000). But the company came under heavy criticism for controversial reporting methods that inflated its earnings. Critics claimed that, for example, some of the company's earnings were misrepresented, by being based on projected rather than actual (historical) growth. Other accusations included the selling of artificially inflated shares, and in at least one case, the company accounted for an acquisition before the deal was technically closed. After advice from the Securities and Exchange Commission, net income was reduced in 2000 by $16 million (*Business Week*, 2000). Accusations and controversies over its financial reporting methods resulted in a sharp fall in the price of Century shares. Though the company sought to revise its reporting methods and started reporting much lower expected income, the share price continued to fall. And the company's Chief Operating Officer resigned after a downward revision of the 2000 forecast. This case is of extreme significance – an accounting firm having problems over its own accounting system. The case of Century is an example of the aggressive use of creative accounting that patently went wrong (*Business Week*, 2000).

However, these and other scandals – such as that at World Com – were eclipsed by that of Enron in the United States. Enron managers persuaded the SEC and the auditors (Arthur Anderson) to agree to mark-to-market accounting, a technique whereby the entire revenue stream that could be derived from the spread between long- and short-term gas contracts would be recorded as earnings paid in advance: in essence, many years' revenue would be presented as a an upfront gain (Stewart, 2006). Moreover, this practice was extended to report as earnings the potential gains from new ventures, such as a new system for delivering home videos (Stewart, 2006). In other areas, profits were assigned to predicted revenue in markets where Enron hoped to set its own price: in other words, it was setting its own value to what it thought it could make in the future, and calling it profit (Stewart, 2006). The problem was exacerbated by the operation of a bonus scheme that rewarded managers for declared profits, rather than earnings, over and above the real cost of capital. Effectively, the money invested by Enron's shareholders was loaded with excessive risk, with managers benefiting from supposed earnings (Stewart, 2006). Loan proceeds were treated as capital inflows, ignoring the obligation of the firm to pay back its debts (Stewart, 2006).

Enron's collapse brought about the collapse of its auditor, Arthur Anderson. In fact, many of the transactions in which Enron engaged were reviewed by Arthur Andersen as being reliably reported in accordance with US GAAP; this led to a review of accounting standards:

> the US Congress passed the Sarbanes–Oxley Act (2002), which among other things mandated the Securities and Exchange Commission to study whether US Generally Accepted Accounting Principles (US GAAP) should be modified to focus on a principles-based rather than a rules-based approach to accounting standards setting... [indeed] a uniform application of the concept of substance over form would have provided investors and creditors with a more realistic view of the financial position and results of operations of Enron. (Baker and Hayes, 2004)

On the one hand, it could be argued that creative accounting was not a cause, but rather a symptom of Enron's underlying problems (Stewart, 2006): hence, a tightening up of accounting standards would solve many of the problems encountered in dealing with a 'rogue company'. On the other hand, it has been alleged that Arthur Anderson fundamentally violated the covenant between the practising accountants and the duties and obligations of their profession, in a manner that could reflect a deeper malaise (Briloff, 2004). Indeed, it can be argued that the concentration of the business of accounting – and associated revenue – in the hands of a limited number of giant accounting firms that also offer a range of management consulting services to their clients has invariably created serious conflicts of interest. Arthur Anderson's collapse has had the effect of further accelerating this trend towards excessive concentration, with a real danger that a further Enron-type scandal could not only derail the entire accounting profession, but also seriously damage the global economy. However, the accounting profession gives substantial amounts to fund political campaigns in the United States, favouring conservative politicians with 'light regulation' agendas (Dwyer and Roberts, 2004), which may block future attempts at greater regulation. It has been argued that the Enron experience reveals the persistence of a 'win at all costs' style of capitalism that will have seriously adverse consequences unless it is recognized and dealt with (Craig and Amernic, 2004).

7.5   Private equity, venture capital and ethics

The ethical challenges faced by the accounting profession represent only one facet of the ethical challenges posed by the dominance of finance-driven growth paradigms in the Anglo-American world: in other words, by financial services rather than manufacturing serving as the major engine of growth (Williams, 2000). From the 1970s onwards, changes in investor behaviour (less patient, more pro-active, expecting quicker returns) and associated governmental deregulation have driven a growing emphasis on maximizing shareholder value at the expense of other organizational objectives, often taking the form of 'downsize and distribute' policies (ibid.). This process has commonly been referred to as 'financialization' (ibid.), though the extent to which this really constitutes a coherent phenomenon may be disputed. The rise of financial services contributed to the superficially good economic performance of Britain and the United States in the late 1990s and early 2000s: it can be argued that it has forced firms to become more efficient. On the other hand, 'downsize and distribute' policies can have potentially devastating consequences for an organization's existing staff, customers, suppliers and other stakeholders, and indeed, may contribute to a series of speculative bubbles that invariably face deflation (Brenner, 2002). The financial crisis of 2008 pointed to the problems associated with excessive speculation and the extent to which beneficial effects in some areas have been counterbalanced by excessive risks in others.

An important trend in recent years has been the increasing importance of venture capital and private equity. While often conflated, the two in fact represent very distinct phenomena. The former focuses its attentions on organizations in the start-up phase and those in the early phases of their life cycle, and involves investors working with existing management in order to realize the fullest potential of any innovations in technology, design or focus. In contrast, private equity focuses its attention on more mature organizations. Private equity investors seek to gain control and de-list existing, well-established organizations. Typically, such takeovers are heavily funded by borrowing, which is then assumed by the target organization. Appointed managers replace the existing management team, and set to work to release 'value'. The latter could include the sale (and, where appropriate, leasing-back of) property assets held by the organization, and more efficient deployment of staff, which may entail heavy staff cutbacks, and/or the paring back of benefits, and/or the intensification of work. Eventually, the organization is relisted on the stock market, with the private equity investors moving on to their next target.

There is little doubt that non-managerial buy-out private equity takeovers are likely to generate very different types of behaviour compared to managerial buy-outs (MBOs) (see Williams, 2000). Existing managers are likely to have closer personal ties to the organization's principle stakeholders, and in many cases will be less likely to sacrifice the fruits of many years' work on the altar of a quick cash return. The increased prominence of private equity in the UK has led to intense debate as to the desirability of such activity, particularly as the latter has been greatly aided by a favourable tax regime.

To its proponents, private equity provides a way of 'unlocking' stagnant assets. Firms are forced to become more efficient, focusing away from non-core activities, and back to the real rationale of their existence – releasing value to their owners. Indeed, it is argued that, in the absence of such activity, organizations become complacent, ineffective and ultimately uncompetitive. Moreover, the threats of a private equity takeover keeps management on its toes, and hence are more likely to serve existing owners better: it is assumed that the principal ethical obligation on managers is towards those who own the firm, rather than to any other stakeholder group.

Critics have charged that private equity takeovers can amount to little more than asset stripping, with investments that have taken many years to accumulate – in people, plant and land – being rapidly liquidated, with little thought to medium- and long-term organizational sustainability: this has led the Trades Union Congress (TUC) in the UK to challenge private equity players to confirm or deny whether they acknowledge any responsibility to existing staff or community (Barber, 2007). In effect, private equity players have been charged with acting in an essentially unethical manner, taking advantages of low taxes and easy debt to expropriate organizational resources, leaving a trail of misery in the form of broken implicit contracts with staff in their wake. There is relatively little detailed research on the specific consequences of private equity, in contrast to the considerable body of literature on management buyouts (and the combined effects of management and non-management buyouts) (see Bruining *et al.*, 2005; Wright *et al.*, 2007). However, a 2007 study by the Work Foundation revealed that, in most cases, the consequences were job losses (Thornton, 2007: 14). Dividing the two sides of the debate over private equity is a fundamental central principle: the ethical obligations of managers to owners, vis-à-vis those to other stakeholders, including staff and the wider community.

7.6   Summary

Since the 1970s, the accounting profession has changed itself beyond recognition, in line with broader changes in investor behaviour and the operation of markets. It has moved from being a mere reporter of facts relating to the financial health of the company to being a management tool that could be misused to project a different financial reality. In turn, the latter has fuelled concern over the ethicality of certain 'deceptive but legal' practices. Two schools of thought have emerged. The first advocates that financial and accounting codes of ethics are essential to maintain and enforce ethical practices, and strongly supports rigid but effective codes of ethics to which all accountants and financiers should adhere. The second school argues that 'straitjacket' laws and regulations cannot regulate the function. The latter, it is argued, will create a culture where accountants and financiers will adhere to the minimum required by a code of ethics that cannot cover all possible ethical issues. Thus, accounting professionals should be self-regulated. However, this viewpoint has become increasingly untenable, not only in the face of repeated financial scandals, but also as a result of new forms of investor behaviour; accounting is perhaps too serious a business to be left to the discretion of accountants.

Discussion questions

- Critically discuss the benefits and disadvantages, from a business ethics standpoint, of voluntary codes of standards governing accounting practice.
- Do you think the activities of private equity investors can, in any way, be seen as unethical? Give reasons for your answer.

Case study

Closing case study

Returning to lighter regulation?

Business interests, seizing on concerns that a law passed in the wake of the Enron scandal has overreached, are advancing a broad agenda to limit government oversight of private industry, including making it tougher for investors to sue companies and auditors for fraud.

A group that has drawn support from Treasury Secretary Henry M. Paulson Jr. plans to issue a report tomorrow that argues that the United States may be losing its preeminent position in global capital markets to foreign stock exchanges because of costly regulations and nettlesome private lawsuits.

Interest groups are trying to build political support to review long-standing rules that govern companies, as well as parts of the 2002 Sarbanes–Oxley law, which imposed stringent responsibilities on accountants, boards of directors and corporate executives. Some key members of Congress have recently expressed concern that U.S. companies may be over-regulated.

For example, Sen. Charles E. Schumer (D-N.Y.) joined New York City Mayor Michael R. Bloomberg (R) to commission a study by McKinsey & Co. on whether U.S. stock exchanges are losing listings to more lightly regulated overseas markets. Sen. Christopher J. Dodd (D-Conn.), who is set to head the Banking Committee, has expressed skepticism that the Sarbanes–Oxley law has led businesses to flee overseas but has signaled a willingness to hold hearings next year on how the legislation is working. The business groups are initially focused on getting rules changed at the Securities and Exchange Commission, the independent federal agency that oversees U.S. capital markets and companies. The growing bipartisan concern about over-regulation will help set the tone for deliberations at the agency, which is led by Christopher Cox, a Republican and former congressman from California.

'From our perspective, the more people talking about this, the better,' said David C. Chavern, director of the U.S. Chamber of Commerce's corporate-governance initiative. The chamber plans to publish its own study next year that attacks what it views as duplicative rules and overly aggressive enforcement by securities regulators. The renewed push to soften government oversight of business comes as the outcry begins to diminish over a series of financial scandals that erupted five years ago after Enron collapsed, costing thousands of employees their jobs and wiping out billions of investor dollars. The phony accounting at Enron and the bankruptcy of WorldCom months later prompted Congress to pass the Sarbanes–Oxley law.

The chamber panel studying regulation contains several prominent Democrats, including two members of President Bill Clinton's Cabinet — William M. Daley, who headed the Commerce Department, and former U.S. trade representative Mickey Kantor.

Lobbyists at the chamber are moving to line up meetings with Dodd, who is considering a bid for the presidency in 2008, and soon-to-be House Financial Services Chairman Barney Frank (D-Mass.). Frank recently spoke in general terms of his willingness to compromise with business on some matters to win concessions on minimum-wage legislation and housing reforms.

The current drive to roll back regulation pivots on a complex rule that requires companies to assess their financial controls to prevent fraud and mistakes. The provision, contained in Sarbanes–Oxley, has proved more expensive than regulators envisioned, particularly for small businesses.

With the encouragement of senior federal lawmakers, officials from the SEC and the Public Company Accounting Oversight Board, which sets rules and oversees accountants, are meeting to hash out an accord on scaling back the rule. How far they go, perhaps effectively exempting smaller companies, is raising intense concerns from those who think the rules are necessary to protect investors from fraud.

If they decide to exempt small companies, that would take out 'the guts of getting accounting and auditing straightened out' after years of cursory reviews by accountants helped fuel financial scandals, warned Charles A. Bowsher, former comptroller general.

But business groups are not stopping there. They were encouraged when Paulson gave a speech last week calling for 'a more balanced approach' to

Case study

Continued

regulation. The private panel is frequently called 'the Paulson group,' even though Paulson is not a member. Instead, the panel is directed by Harvard University law professor Hal S. Scott. Other members include R. Glenn Hubbard, former chairman of President Bush's Council of Economic Advisers, and Brookings Institution Chairman John L. Thornton.

The group's report tomorrow is to advocate raising the standard for charging companies with crimes, according to sources briefed on its content who spoke on condition of anonymity because the document has not been officially released. It also is to propose shielding accountants from fraud lawsuits under certain circumstances.

Many of the group's recommendations would require congressional action, and passage of new laws is uncertain in the last two years of the Bush administration, even with a growing concern over regulation among senior lawmakers.

University of Rochester President Joel Seligman expressed concern about any new limits on the ability of people to sue companies over accounting, saying it could 'handicap the ability of the SEC to be a vigilant watchdog.' 'To have this occur, so soon after the dramatic increase in fraud that led to Sarbanes–Oxley, would be deeply troublesome,' he said.

(Carrie Johnson, *Washington Post*, 29 November 2006.)

Questions

- Do you think attempts to relax the post-Enron tightening up on the regulation of accounting practice and financial reporting in the USA are unethical? Give reasons for your answer.
- To what extent does the 2008 credit crunch demonstrate that calls for lighter regulation were shortsighted?

References

American Institute of Certified Public Accountants. 1988. *Code of Professional Conduct*. New York: AICPA.

Anderson, G. D. 1985. 'A Fresh Look at Standards of Professional Conduct', *Journal of Accounting*, 160,3: 91–106.

Anderson, G. D. and Ellyson, R. C. 1986. 'Restructuring Professional Standards: The Anderson Reports', *Journal of Accountancy*, 160,3: 92–104.

Baker, R. and Hayes, R. 2004. 'Reflecting Form Over Substance: The Case of Enron Corp', *Critical Perspectives on Accounting*, 15,6–7: 767–85.

Barber, B. 2007. Statement by General Secretary on Private Equity. London: Trades Union Congress. Available at: http://www.tuc.org.uk/economy/tuc-12983-f0.cfm; accessed 12 March 2007.

Barry E. C. 1999. 'Economic Analysis of Accountants' Ethical Standards: The Case of Audit Opinion Shopping', *Journal of Accounting and Public Policy*, 18,4/5: 339–63.

Beckman, J. K., Byington, J. R. and Munter, P. H. 1989. 'Regulating Financial Reporting: The Debate Continues', *Business*, 39,1: 56–60.

Brenner, R. 2002. *The Boom and the Bubble*. London: Verso.

Breton, G. and Taffler, R. J. 1995. 'Creative Accounting and Investment Analyst Response, *Accounting and Business Research*, 25,98: 81–93.

Briloff, A. 2004. 'Accounting Scholars in the Groves of Academe In Pari Delicto', *Critical Perspectives on Accounting*, 15,6–7: 787–96.

Bruining, H, Boselie, P., Wright, M. and Bacon, N. 2005. 'Ownership Change and Effects on the Employee Relationship', *International Journal of Human Resource Management*, 16: 345–63.

Buckics, R. M. L. 1999. 'Exploring Ethical Decisions', *The Internal Auditor*, 56,5: 19–20.

Business Week, 2000. 'Creative Accounting at Century', February, 142.

Cottell, P. G., Jr., and Perlin, M. T. 1990. *Accounting Ethics: A Practical Guide for Professionals*. Westport, Conn.: Quorum Books.

Craig, R. and Amernic, J. 2004. 'Enron Discourse: The Rhetoric of a Resilient Capitalism', *Critical Perspectives on Accounting*, 15,6–7: 813.

Dobson, J. 1997. *Finance Ethics: The Rationality of Virtue*. Lanham, Md./Oxford: Rowman & Littlefield.

Drummond, J. and Bain, B. 1994. *Managing Business Ethics*. Oxford: Butterworth Heinemann.

Dwyer, P. and Roberts, R. 2004. 'Known by the Company They Keep: A Study of Political Campaign Contributions Made by the United States Public Accounting Profession', *Critical Perspectives on Accounting*, 15,6–7: 865.

Ethics Resource Center. 1997. *Introduction*, Kalamazoo, Mich.: University of Michigan.

Fedders, J. M. and Perry, L. G. 1984. 'Policing Financial Disclosure Fraud: The SEC's Top Priority', *Journal of Accountancy*, 158,1: 58–64.

Finn, D., Chonko, l. and Hunt, S. 1988. 'Ethical Problems in Public Accounting: The View from the Top', *Journal of Business Ethics*, 7: 605–15.

Finn, D. W., Munter, P. and McCaslin, T. E. 1994. 'Ethical Perceptions of CPAs', *Managerial Auditing Journal*, 9,1: 23–8.

Graber, D. E. 1979. 'Ethics Enforcement – How Effective?', *The CPA Journal*, 49,9: 11–17.

Griffiths, I. 1986. *Creative Accounting*. London: Sidgwick & Jackson.

Harris, Louis and Associates, Inc. 1986. 'How the Public Sees CPAs', *Journal of Accountancy*, 162,6: 16–20.

Howard, M. 1996. 'Downsizing to Destruction', *Management Accounting*, 74,7: 66–70.

Hussey, R. and Jack, A. 1994. *The Finance Director and the Auditor*. Bristol: University of the West of England.

Jones, D. G. B., Richardson, J. L. and Shearer, T. 2000. 'Truth and the Evolution of the Profession: A Comparative Study of 'Truth in Advertising' and

'True and Fair' Financial Statements in North America during the Progressive Era', *Journal of Macromarketing*, 20,1: 23–35.

Kaplan, S., Roush, P. and Thorne, L. 2007. 'Andersen and the Market for Lemons in Audit Reports', *Journal of Business Ethics*, 70,4: 363–73.

Lawrance, A. P. 1998. *Research on Accounting Ethics – Volume 4*. London: PricewaterhouseCoopers/JAI Press.

Mintz, S. M. 1997. *Cases in Accounting Ethics and Professionalism, 3rd edn*. New York: McGraw-Hill.

Munk, N. 1995. 'Now You See It, Now You Don't', *Forbes*, 155,12: 42.

Munter, P. and McCaslin, T. E. 1998. 'An Empirical Investigation into Factors Affecting Professional Conflict in Public Accounting', Proceedings of the American Accounting Association, Orlando, Fla., 15 August.

Naser, K. 1993. *Creative Financial Accounting: Its Nature and Use*. London: Prentice Hall.

Paterson, R. 1995. 'New Creative Accounting', *Accountancy*, 116,1227: 88.

Pijper, 1994. *Creative Accounting: The Effectiveness of Financial Reporting in the UK*. London: Macmillan.

Shah, A. K. 1996. 'Creative Compliance in Financial Reporting Accounting', *Organizations and Society*, 21,1: 23–40.

Shaub, M. K. 1988. 'Restructuring the Code of Professional Ethics: A Review of Anderson Committee Report and Its Implications', *Accounting Horizons*, 2,4: 89–97.

Smith, T. 1992. *Accounting for Growth*. London: Prentice Hall.

Stewart, S. 2006. 'The Real Reasons Enron Failed', *Journal of Applied Corporate Finance*, 18,2: 116–19.

Strategic Finance. 1999. 'Standards of Ethical Conduct for Practitioners of Management Accounting and Financial Management', *Strategic Finance*, 81,2: 24–90.

Thornton, P. 2007. *Inside the Dark Box: Shedding Light on Private Equity*. London: The Work Foundation.

US Congress. 1977. Senate, Subcommittee on Reports, Accounting and Management of the Committee on Government Affairs, US Government Printing Office, Washington, DC.

Verschoor, C. C. 2001. 'Strengthening the Ethics of Finance', *Strategic Finance*, 82,9: 20–1.

Warth, R. J. 2000. 'Ethics in the Accounting Profession: A Study', *The CPA Journal*, 70,10: 69–70.

Whittington, G., Grout, P. and Jewitt, I. 1995. 'Is Total Auditor Independence a Good Thing?', *Accountancy*, 115,1218: 75.

Williams, K. 2000. From Shareholder Value to Present Day Capitalism, *Economy and Society*, 29,1: 1–12.

Wright, M., Renneboog, L., Simons, T. and Scholes, L. 2006. 'Leveraged Buyouts in the UK and Continental Europe: Retrospect and Prospect', *Journal of Applied Corporate Finance*, 18,3: 38–55.

Organizational behaviour and human resource management

Chapter objectives

- To understand, and to be able to criticize, the case for human resource management (HRM) as a new way of managing people at work.
- To recognize some of the inherent tensions and contradictions implicit in HRM.
- To be able to differentiate between (i) business orientated; and (ii) academic, critical literature on HRM.
- To understand some of the different models of HRM, and to be aware of their ethical implications.

Case study

Introductory case study

The sweet factory and the ethics school

Kondo (1990) gives a vivid account of everyday life on the shop floor of a small family-owned sweet factory in Tokyo...she is sent to an ethics school with two other employees...Here is a brief description of the activities before breakfast each day. The day started at 5 am with a call to rise. Waking up late was regarded as unnatural, indulgent, selfish, slovenly. Cleaning came next and was a standard ingredient of spiritual education. Each cleaning task was to be

Case study

Continued

performed with a glad heart. The counsellors would lead the group in chants of 'Fight!' as they hosed down the toilets, emptied the tins of sanitary napkins, and scrubbed the floors. After cleaning, they jogged to the statue of the founder and after a rousing shout of good morning, they were lectured on an inspirational theme. A tape recorder played the national anthem as the flags were raised. They then had shouting practice where they were required to scream greetings at the top of their voices or shout 'I am the sun of 'x' company. I will make 'x' company number one in Japan.' Every word was rewarded by shouts of encouragement from the others and rounds of applause. The idea was to inculcate receptiveness and a willingness to greet and appreciate others and eliminate resistance toward responding positively towards authority. They ran for at least 2.4km as a rehearsal for the 7.5 km marathon scheduled for the end of the programme. Shouting and chanting was required during running. Speed was not the issue, it was more important to finish and not give up. Neglect of the body was seen as lack of appreciation of the gift of life. Ritual ablution ceremonies with cold water, in order to give thanks to water, followed. The morning classes were for reciting in unison phrases like 'Hardship is the gateway to happiness' and 'Other people are our mirrors'. Students would be given instructions on how to bow at the proper angle, have a pleasant facial expression, and use the appropriate language level.

(*Source*: Wilson, 1999)

Question

- Is this what you would think of as a 'school'? If not, what other kind of organization(s) does it seem like to you?

8.1   Introduction: different ways of interpreting the ethics school case

There are a number of ways of looking at this extract from Fiona Wilson's introduction to organizational behaviour. It can be understood in a fairly neutral way as describing a company's training programme to instil a customer ethic, and to encourage bonding among employees. Each of the exercises and the associated rituals could also be described as a way of forming corporate identity, or of 'managing culture'. To more sceptical eyes it may seem as though this is a form of brainwashing. The ethics school (and those running the organization) could be described as breaching the boundaries of individual liberty, or as contravening basic human rights – for example, the right to dignity at work. From the perspective of a Western European liberal democracy, some of the rituals do seem somewhat strange (what do they have to do with making sweets?)

and even a little chilling. To require sessions of orchestrated screaming at work seems frightfully un-British, for example. In the ethics school it can seem even more unsettling and oppressive to the individual that these sessions are scheduled shortly after hearing the national anthem, since this can appear to be another way of legitimizing domination and subordination. On the other hand, in any country in the developed or developing world, there will be family-owned businesses run by petty tyrants that are vehicles of worse oppression. Perhaps one could argue that, unlike the case of the petty tyrant who is head of the family firm, there is some rationality at work in this ethics school. It could also be argued that what takes place in this ethics school differs by only a matter of degree (if at all) from what happens on some of the more exotic training courses inflicted on Western executives. In 2006, for example, a training consultancy – Si Group – ran a fire-walking exercise in South London designed to build confidence among Deloitte's staff. One senior accountant burnt her feet so badly she had to take two weeks off work, and Si Group was fined £3,000 and had to pay over £4,500 in costs (Thomas, 2006).

From all these different perspectives (training programme/a way to manage culture/a form of brainwashing/an abuse of human rights/cultural relativism/no worse than other apparently bizarre practices), the case of the ethics school prompts us to consider the duties owed by organizations to their employees. It also prompts us to reflect on the way in which those employees are managed. The type of behaviour expected in Kondo's ethics school may seem completely inappropriate if we compare it with the typical practices of a contemporary Western factory. However, such behaviour is not far removed from what might be expected in other communities or organizations. Consider, for example, the devotion required in a monastery, or the strict discipline and obedience to a regime expected in different ways by a school, a prison or a hospital (Foucault, 1979). As well as acknowledging some cultural relativism, we might allow for some trans-organizational relativism. We might also acknowledge that even in cultures that are (stereotypically) less deferential and more individualist than Japan, collective screaming is acceptable or even normal in some settings: among the temporary communities at a football match or rock concert, say.

Kondo's case study reveals that our notions of what is appropriate or acceptable when it comes to organizational behaviour, and managing people in organizations, can be dramatically different in different cultures, in different communities and in different types of organization. In the workplace, we may also have more flexible standards of appropriateness regarding certain activities. Consider, for example, a training course, where we might allow that learning something new involves moving beyond established boundaries. We could also be more flexible in acknowledging that at certain stages of one's career within an organization, periods of greater and lesser intensity are both natural and appropriate. Consider the cases of an induction period for graduate trainees, and a mid-career assessment centre to determine who is fit for promotion, for example. In both of these cases the organization may reasonably be expected to test or train employees in a more intensive way than in the course of their daily work.

One could even make an ethical case for this difference – it could be argued that it would be unfair to promote someone who was not able to cope with the demands of a more senior position (assuming, of course, that the assessment centre was a valid and reliable way of evaluating these demands).

The case of the ethics school also prompts us to think about what similarities there are in the management of people across different organizations and cultures. For example, if we find the idea of orchestrated screaming and flag saluting offensive, or un-British (or un-French or whatever) why might we think it acceptable for Western firms to expect their employees to undergo the rites of passage and cult-like rituals associated with some training programmes – whether it's paint-balling to build teamwork, or fire-walking to develop inner strength and confidence? Aren't these experiences rather similar, and if so, why should we be offended by one and not the other? It seems as though a more thoughtful reading of the case of the ethics school is encouraging a drift towards relativism: the denial of any absolute standards of rightful conduct. This is unsettling because it suggests that, when it comes to the management of people, what seems to be acceptable rather than unacceptable, or ethical rather than unethical, is at least partly subjective. We do not judge health and safety conditions in contemporary factories against the standards of the nineteenth century, for example. On the one hand this may seem obvious, but even if we think such standards would be totally unacceptable, as consumers, global capitalism means that we may continue to buy products manufactured in factories overseas where conditions are as bad as or worse than they once were in the developed world (Gibson, 2007: 68–73; Scholte, 2005). There are many ways in which we can blur the lines between what is acceptable and unacceptable, strange and familiar, ethical and the unethical. This should encourage us to take a critical perspective of even well-received ideas about how people are managed. There is always scope to question and consider alternative approaches since the management of people is inescapably enmeshed with ethical implications (Legge, 1998a). In terms of the themes of the opening chapter of our book, in our search for the science of the good we need to scrutinize the received 'truths' that dominate present-day thinking about how people are managed. The management of people is also the management of values and of meaning. As the Nietzsche quote in our opening chapter suggests, it is an arena where, 'a prejudice, a notion, an "inspiration", generally a desire of the heart sifted and made abstract, is defended . . . with reasons sought after the event'. We might even go further and suggest that, in the context of this chapter, those claiming to have the answers to how to manage people, 'are one and all advocates who do not want to be regarded as such, and for the most part no better than cunning pleaders for their prejudices, which they baptize "truths"' (Nietzsche, 1886/1973, 1(5)).

8.2   A new way of managing people?

Later in this chapter we look at the phenomenon of human resource management (HRM). HRM came to the fore in the 1980s and subsequent discussion of it can be separated into two strands of literature: a business orientated or managerial literature on what HRM is or should be, and how to do it (Dessler, 2000; Fowler, 1987); and an academic, largely critical literature that attempts to address or highlight failings in the HRM model(s) and expose the gap between the rhetoric of HRM and what happens in practice (Keenoy, 1999; Legge, 1995; Storey, 1995). The classical conception of the relationship between employer and employee was based on the notion of a free contract between the two parties, essentially for their mutual benefit (Hoffman and Moore, 1990: 269). Employers were expected to pay fair wages, and, in return, employees were to give their loyalty and obedience, and above all, a satisfactory performance (Hoffman and Moore, 1990). In modern organizations, however, the management of people is more complex and involves several stakeholders: the government, unions, shareholders, employees and management, to mention just a few (see Chapter 3). HRM management practices are affected strongly by the economic, political, technological, legal and social contexts within which they operate. These contexts pull the HRM function in different directions. While some writers argue for more protection of employees' interests and rights, others call for the protection of shareholders' interests at the expense of employees' rights and fair treatment. These debates take place amid a more turbulent economic environment.

HRM came to the fore as an ostensibly 'new' way of managing people to improve business performance (Beer *et al.*, 1984, 1985; Fombrun *et al.*, 1984; Hendry and Pettigrew, 1986; Walton, 1985). Before examining the business-orientated and academic approaches to HRM, it is important to set out the argument for a new way of managing people that in its own way has become a contemporary 'truth' about behaviour in organizations. The argument for a new way of managing people can be expressed as follows: the twentieth century and the opening years of the twenty-first have been characterized by rapid technological change and corresponding changes in the ease of transport, both of which have 'shrunk' the world. The early twentieth century witnessed mass production designed to deliver 'one size fits all' goods for a uniform, mass market. Henry Ford's Model T car was famously suited to the customer – who could have 'any colour they wanted as long as it was black' – in other words, no choice at all.

The advent of global consumerism challenged standardized production and, in turn, traditional ways of managing people. Since the 1960s, the influence of information technology has increased, with the advent and subsequent omnipresence of the computer and silicon chip. More recently, phenomena such as the internet, and global capitalism have led to the restructuring of society, the redefinition or abolition of national boundaries, and the emergence of new organizational forms (Scholte, 2005). Each *day*, $3 trillion dollars of currency is electronically traded on the international money markets. This is a sum greater than the wealth of any one state, and the amount traded has doubled in just over a decade (Progressive Policy Institute, 2007). The complexity (speed and anonymity) and scale of these transactions have led to various forms of insecurity across the globe. This is reflected in the corporate climate of today's multinationals, and through them to smaller companies everywhere. We now live in a business environment where prediction and control are ultimately unrealizable, because of the inter-relatedness, and instability, of the global financial system. This global instability has consequences for an organization's environment, and consequently how it has to manage its people. In times of uncertainty, the security of 'jobs for life', which some organizations historically have been able to afford employees, has gone for ever (Maund, 2001). Consequently, organizations have to look at new ways of encouraging employee loyalty and commitment. External uncertainties (such as those caused by complexity in the business environment), have translated into internal uncertainties (the problems of managing people within the organization).

One way to represent the effect of environmental complexity is using Ashby's Law of Requisite Variety. This was originally developed in the field of cybernetics but it has also been applied more specifically to look at behaviour in organizations (Morgan, 1995). Put simply, an organism (such as an organization) must be as complex as its environment to survive: the global environment is now more complex, and standardized production is not capable of meeting the needs of a diverse market which – in terms of the Ford Model T example – want black and every other colour as well. If we accept that it is appropriate to apply Ashby's Law in this context, it can give us a very powerful way of understanding the rise of new (post-bureaucratic, or sometimes post-Fordist) organizational forms, and of demonstrating the consequent challenges to effective people management. Seen in this light, HRM can be portrayed as the necessary 'silver bullet' (Legge, 1998b) to slay uncertainty and promote performance.

The case for a new mode of management is typically set out in the context of new technologies, changes in modes of consumption, the rise of post-Fordist and post-bureaucratic ways of working and global capitalism (globalization). However, even if we accept this is a fair description of the context, these changes have ethical implications that are very old and familiar. For example, let us suppose that we buy into the idea that traditional bureaucracies and hierarchies are no more and that we are all living in a knowledge economy (incidentally, not everyone does believe this, and it is certainly not the case that it is true for everyone, everywhere, as we suggest below). A critical (Marxist) perspective in this context would suggest that HRM (which is at the forefront of these new ways of managing people) is a fundamentally *managerialist* approach. That is, advocates of HRM are interested first and foremost in advancing the interests of managers and ultimately of a powerful elite, rather than those of workers or the masses. In these terms, HRM is basically a way of introducing changes to the way people are controlled – a necessity, given the changes brought about by global capitalism. This change is orchestrated in such a way that it serves the interests of those in power. Strategic HRM scholars such as Tsui (1987) have argued for the thesis of 'strategic fit' between HRM policies and practices, and overall corporate strategy. In a business environment characterized by relentless competition and a quest to achieve and sustain competitive advantage, the strategic role of the HRM function is to help the organization achieve its strategic goals regardless of whether HRM policies and practices are ethical or not. The key measuring criteria on this view is: do all practices help the company achieve a better than average return on investment? This prompts ethical questions relating to justice, rights and fairness.

A contrast to this Marxist analysis still prompts ethical considerations for HRM. Assuming that the scenario of the knowledge economy makes sense, this can also be used as the basis for recognizing the increasing importance and worth of the person in an organization. If 'knowledge workers' become increasingly prevalent and important, then organizational worth will reside in the work-force rather than in other factors of production (land, machinery, other fixed assets, financial capital and so on). Newer organizational forms will be increasingly dependent on their knowledge workers, largely through the way that they use information. Organizations and their employees will need to learn to remain competitive (Argyris and Schön, 1978; Pedler *et al.*, 1, 1991). Thinking about this in the context of one of the founders of ethics, in Aristotelian terms this is potentially a positive development. Learning is a uniquely human characteristic: reasoning is the difference that makes us human, and from that follows our ability to learn and our ability to behave (un)virtuously. It is what makes us individuals. In a post-bureaucratic era there would seem to be more focus on people as people, and individuals in organizations would seem to have greater power because of their valuable expertise.

There are some problems with this argument, however. First, it neglects the fact that bureaucratic structures and many elements of standardization continue to be highly cost-effective. Consequently, many of today's 'knowledge workers' may be difficult to distinguish from workers on a traditional (Fordist) mass-production assembly line. Consider the relatively recent phenomenon of the call centre, for example. Though call centre operatives may be providing a service (working in the knowledge economy), in effect they are often highly regulated and have to complete a certain number of calls in a given time. They may also have to stick rigidly to a standard script, and be monitored by having each call recorded (see Cartoon 6).

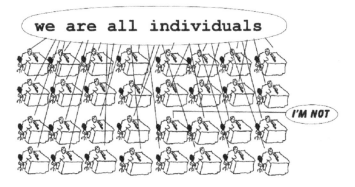

Cartoon 6   Spot the knowledge worker (apologies to Monty Python)

A second problem with a more positive take on the case for a new way of managing people is that the type of learning that is important to organizations is not really the kind of contemplative reasoning that Aristotle recognized as being uniquely human. Learning within organizations is typically learning for instrumental purposes – that is, for the benefit of the organization. It is very rare to find organizations sponsoring any forms of learning other than those that are believed to have a direct impact on the bottom line. Third, while in the developed world a greater proportion of people work in tertiary or quaternary sectors (that is, service industries and the knowledge economy), across the globe as a whole many people still work in agriculture and manufacturing (the primary and secondary sectors of industry). The danger of the high-flying rhetoric of a knowledge economy is that it ignores the fact that people somewhere still have to make things, and that often to compete in a global market this means that the cost of labour is ruthlessly driven down. The luxury that supports the knowledge economy has its roots in the systematic oppression of the majority of the world's workforce.

Reflective exercise

Should the business environment dictate how we manage people in organizations? What if the business context suggests some workers have to give up basic rights? Consider the 'business case' for slavery: 'if other people are using slave labour then their costs are low; we have to use it too otherwise we won't be able to compete'. What is wrong with this argument?

It is important to look at the case for a new way of managing people, because if we can find problems and contradictions in that case, then we are left with the same kind of uncertainty we feel when deciding whether Kondo's ethics school is appropriate or not. Unless there is a compelling argument for one best way, then it seems as though deciding on how we should manage people at work is always something that can be contested. Resisting the claim to 'truths' about the best way to manage people is an ethical endeavour, just as challenging taken-for-granted assumptions about the good is an ethical endeavour. As well as finding problems with the argument for a new way of managing people, there is a rich and detailed literature that identifies some of the problems and contradictions with the specifics of HRM itself. Before discussing briefly this academic and critical perspective on HRM, it is appropriate to start by looking at the descriptive, business-orientated or managerial literature on HRM. In that way, we shall have a clear idea about what we're talking about before moving on to criticizing it and examining the ethical implications.

The significance of a critical perspective on HRM is that this brings ethical issues into the foreground. It raises questions such as, what is the fair and right way to manage people, what sorts of expectations are legitimate from an employer, and what obligations can reasonably be expected of an employee. Though there is not enough space to do this critical tradition justice in this chapter, it is perhaps fair to say that its main theme is that HRM constitutes a new architecture of control, where traditional imbalances in power between the employer and employee are simply reconstituted or reinforced (rather than being abolished, or HRM being seen in any way as democratizing). This perspective allows us to be sceptical about claims that HRM is in some way necessarily liberating – as is implied, for example, in the title of Walton's (1985) influential paper 'from control to commitment in the workplace'. It also allows us to be sceptical about claims that HRM is genuinely new (and by association, in some way an improvement over the old). A Marxist analysis of work suggests that society is ordered in such a way that workers will be exploited increasingly under capitalism. The effect of capitalism in a global economy – what Scholte (2005) has called 'hypercapitalism' – means that workers are increasingly being turned into mere objects to be manipulated (Freire, 2003; Hanlon, 2007). In one sense, then, the label for this activity of 'human resource' management is remarkably transparent about such exploitation. The same could be said about its precursor, found in the title of the seminal text, 'managing human assets' (Beer *et al.*, 1984). There remain basic tensions between the liberating rhetoric associated with HRM and the ruthless pull of the bottom line. Advocates of HRM may well preach about high commitment management and an environment where people are the most important asset, but this is not reflected in terms of investment in those assets. Tom Peters, writing in the US context, stated that, 'investment in training is a national disgrace' (1989: 324). Michael Hammer, the architect of business process re-engineering, referred to this as the 'biggest lie told by most organizations' (Lancaster, 1995: 1). These tensions suggest that the unitarism (defined on p. 172) underpinning HRM is illusory, and that there can be very real differences between the interests of middle managers and their workers, and the interests of the board of directors.

8.3   What is HRM?

When discussing the academic and critical perspective on HRM, it is also important to acknowledge what the advocates of different versions of HRM have described. Though these advocates are many and varied, and there is no single real model of HRM, there are some similarities across various texts and authors. Because there is no one way of actually 'doing' HRM, it is difficult to talk about HRM as though it is a coherent phenomenon (Morrell, 2002a). This makes it difficult when thinking about the ethical implications of HRM, because there is no single place to stand in relation to HRM. A wide variety of management initiatives can fall under the banner of HRM, and some of these may even contradict one another. For example, some approaches to HRM place an emphasis on managing culture, communication and leadership striving for high employee commitment, while other approaches may entail widespread use of numerical flexibility and de-layering or downsizing – this distinction is sometimes referred to as the gap between 'soft' and 'hard' HRM, respectively (Morrell, 2002b). Additionally, it can be unclear how closely the actual effects of HRM initiatives relate to descriptions of these initiatives; in other words whether the realities of HRM in practice can match the various rhetorics of its advocates (Legge, 1995). In addition to these definitional and contextual complexities, we need to be aware that there are various interest groups, each with a stake or vested interest in 'HRM'. One way of making sense of this confusion is to look for conceptual frameworks (or models) which outline a particular version or interpretation of HRM (Morrell, 2002a). We can then take an ethical stance in relation to each conceptual framework.

The Harvard model, developed by Beer and his colleagues at Harvard University in the 1980s (Beer *et al.*, 1984), is perhaps the best-known model of HRM. It acknowledges the role of context-specific factors in the choice of HRM policies. These comprise situational factors (such as workforce characteristics, business strategy, the labour market), and stakeholder interests (such as shareholders, management, unions, employees, government). These influence the way in which HRM policy choices (for example, systems of pay) lead to HR outcomes (for example, commitment) and how they influence consequences over the long term (for example, organizational effectiveness, individual and societal well-being). An advantage of this model is the degree to which it emphasizes that HR initiatives need to fit the particular industry context, thus allowing for flexibility in terms of the choice of an HR strategy. This sets it apart from other, less flexible, models, which may have a more 'unitarist' conception of HRM, ignoring the role of different interest groups (briefly, unitarism is the belief that all the members of an organization share the same goals). From an ethical perspective, one advantage of the Harvard model is that it acknowledges that there may be differences in the interests of various groups. There is also a degree of flexibility built into the model, which suggests that it may discourage a dogmatic or ideological perspective on the employment relationship because, as circumstances change, the Harvard model suggests that our way of managing people should change too. This can also be a disadvantage, however, because it may encourage a more pragmatic approach to the employment relationship and there is certainly less emphasis on principle with a model that allows environmental factors to dictate how the workforce is managed.

Drawing in part on the Harvard model, David Guest (1987, 2000) has outlined a framework for assessing the effectiveness of organizations, based on the testing of propositions such as 'strategic integration', 'quality', 'flexibility' and 'commitment'. While the extent to which these propositions are open to testing remains a matter of debate, there is no doubt that his extension of the Harvard model is potentially useful in so far as it gives an example of how fairly abstract notions of 'commitment' and 'organizational effectiveness' might be operationalized (made concrete and testable), and be seen to interrelate. Guest's model of HRM places organizational commitment at its core, and to this extent it is also useful in terms of drawing a clear distinction between HRM and traditional systems of personnel management/industrial relations, which are said to centre more on compliance (Guest, 1989). None the less, it should be recognized that the belief that high commitment is key to organizational effectiveness remains an assumption that has received limited direct empirical support. More worryingly, despite considerable research interest over time (Boxall and Purcell, 2000; Guest *et al.*, 2003; Hope *et al.*, 2005; MacDuffie, 1995; Patterson *et al.*, 1997; Truss, 2001) the link between HRM and organizational performance remains contested. This is not least because, as noted above, there is no single thing that can be said to be HRM (Boselie *et al.*, 2005; Hyde *et al.*, 2006). Setting aside this rather sweeping challenge, Guest's account has a number of ethical implications. Starting with a less obvious inference, he has provided a way in which some of the claims of advocates of HRM may be tested by trying to make notions such as flexibility testable. This is important because it offers a way of challenging some of the rhetoric that surrounds HRM. Another, more obvious, ethical implication is that it forces us to examine the role of commitment in the employment relationship. On the one hand, it seems desirable that employers try to secure a commitment from their employees to the enterprise. This suggests that there is at least some consideration given to employee well-being – it is difficult to be committed to something without feeling positive towards it. On the other hand, though, the emphasis on commitment suggests a degree of encroachment by the organization into employees' personal feelings. Should it not be enough that people do their job well without expecting that they also be 'committed' to it?

John Storey (1992, 1995) proposed a 25-item checklist to differentiate the newer model of HRM from the older versions of personnel management/industrial relations (PM/IR). This offers a comprehensive way of thinking about the difference between HRM (as an ideal type) and PM/IR as a system of management. For each of twenty-five 'dimensions' of management, Storey's checklist sketches the difference between HRM and PM/IR. So, for example, in the dimension of 'conflict handling', for PM/IR we have 'reach temporary truces', whereas for HRM we have 'manage climate and culture'. Again, for the dimension of 'contract', for PM/IR we have 'careful delineation of written contracts', whereas for HRM we have 'aim to go "beyond contract"'. This offers another way of thinking about whether HRM is something new. It also suggests that some of the more important differences between these models are captured by Guest's emphasis on commitment. One argument for moving from a compliance mode to a commitment mode is that more and more work nowadays is carried out in the context of a knowledge economy. Since this work involves processes that cannot be observed directly (because they relate to intellectual capital) it is not enough to secure compliance; one must have commitment too. If we consider the example of someone building a wall, it is easy to see how many bricks they have laid in an hour, and by extension how much they could reasonably be expected to do in a week. In contrast, if somebody is designing a piece of software or providing a service to people, that cannot be observed directly or checked on intermittently with any degree of reliability. There has to be a new form of control or surveillance (Ouchi, 1979). Hence, returning to

Storey's checklist, there may be a need to manage climate and culture, and to ask people to go beyond contract, since we cannot specify in precise detail just how people should be served.

Karen Legge nicely identified some ethical implications of such a model (comparing and contrasting the old with the new). She pointed out that, whereas models of HRM were aspirational and setting out an ideal, the models of the old PM/IR way of managing the employment relationship were often caricatures. It is important to note this difference because this contrast was often used to support the change to a new way of managing (controlling) people. If this new way was simply rhetoric then this has profound implications. It can be argued generally that, however comprehensive a model may be, it is bound to be an oversimplification of what happens 'in real life', and as such, using a model may distract us from thinking about the inherent complexities involved in managing people. More specifically, the extent to which HRM models or theories are 'normative' (that is, accounts of how things should be) or 'descriptive' (that is, accounts of how things actually are) is problematic. One criticism levelled at comparisons between HRM as seen as a new and better way of managing people, and other traditional models such as PM is that they blur this distinction. Models of PM describe or caricature what is actually going on (are descriptive), whereas models of HRM are idealized or 'normative'. Writers such as Legge have argued there is little or no difference between the normative ambitions of PM and HRM. This is a fundamental challenge to the coherence of the argument for HRM because it suggests that HRM is not a new way of managing people at all.

8.4   Ethical implications of HRM

Karen Legge (1998a) noted that 'Thirty years ago, the answer to the question "Is HRM Ethical?" certainly in the mind of the lay person – would probably have been: "Of course personnel management is ethical. It's there to help people, isn't it?"' Personnel professionals, at least publicly, might have gone along with this and pointed to the supposed origins of people management in benevolent paternalism and social welfare. But if asked the same question today, would there be a more hesitant response? First, there would be some difficulty in presenting 'one consistent image' (Legge, 1996: 34). Several writers have examined the reasons for the rise of ethical concerns over contemporary HRM practices in considerable depth (Legge, 1996, 1998a, 2000; and Winstanley et al., 1996). One compelling reason would be that current HRM models, policies and practices partially reflect the macroeconomic and political environments of the 1980s and 1990s. These were characterized by global competition and cut-throat competition. They focused management concerns on survival and on achieving sustainable competitive advantage by obtaining higher-than-average returns on investment. Obviously, these exigencies would, in most cases, make managers unsympathetic to ethical HRM practices unless they were proven to help the company achieve its strategic advantage or at least not to damage it. In addition, in the UK, successive Conservative governments, and even the New Labour government, have given management a relatively free hand to improve the economy's competitiveness by doing what they see fit. Legge (1998a: 150) noted that:

> There was no 'other alternative', if a cure [for the British disease] was to be effected, then a strong dose of monetarism and market competition was in order, never mind if the side effects...threatened to kill the patent. Such medicine was seen as the *right* way to combat the evils of low productivity, high inflation and poor competitiveness.

As a result, the HRM function since the 1980s has embodied managerialist values focusing its aim primarily on helping the organization to achieve and sustain its competitive advantage at all costs. Keenoy (1990) describes the HRM function in the 1980s as a 'wolf in sheep's clothing'.

Because of the nature of the HRM function, HR managers must frequently make and implement decisions with ethical implications. This explains why HR managers may have reason to make the HR department the organizational locus of responsibility for ethical behaviour at work. During the process of making and executing HRM policies and practices, however, HR managers are often torn between strong conflicting pressures associated with the field (Hosmer, 1987), surveillance and at the same time upholding the right to privacy, making provision for whistle-blowing; and policing disloyalty, to mention just a few. HR managers face other dilemmas on a regular basis involving favouritism in employment – old boys' network, inconsistencies in pay (Heery, 2000), sex and race discrimination, and breaches of confidentiality, for example. Downsizing and outsourcing often lead to problems in maintaining employee motivation and a sense of well-being in the face of growing job insecurity. There is no easy way to deal with these dilemmas. Winstanley and Woodall (2000: 278) note that 'HRM managers must inevitably confront ethical dilemmas, and that some of these may be neither apparent nor easily resolved'. This explains the extensively debated widening cleavage between rhetoric and reality in HRM (see Table 8.1). In such a contradictory context, today's HRM managers and professionals are increasingly advised not to see their attitudes as dichotomous choices, but in some way to embrace 'paradox' as the simultaneous expression of diverse attitudes. HR managers are urged to strike a balance between these competing, and sometimes contradictory, values based on their reflection, personal experience and professional ethical codes of conduct. In her analysis of the ethics of HRM policy and practices, Legge (1998a) argues that, because people are used as a means to an end – achieving sustainable competitive advantage, HRM decision-making is firmly grounded in utilitarianism. She added that even the 'soft' model of HRM, which genuinely seeks to treat people in a humane way and would pass 'muster in terms of the deontologists', applied to all employees, has several embedded contradictions. Indeed: 'The contradictions embedded in HRM are illustrative of the Kantian dilemma that second-order moral rules can

Table 8.1   Sisson's model of rhetoric and reality in HRM

Rhetoric	Reality
Customer first	Market forces supreme
Total quality management	Doing more with less
Lean production	Mean production
Flexibility	Management 'can do' what it wants
	Core and periphery. Reducing the organization's commitment.
	Devolution/delayering. Reducing the number of middle managers
Downsizing/right-sizing	Redundancy
New working patterns	Part-time instead of full-time jobs
	Empowerment. Making someone else take the risk and responsibility
Training and development	Manipulation
Employability	No employment security
Recognizing contribution	Undermining the trade union of the individual and collective bargaining
Teamworking	Reducing the individual's discretion

Source: Legge, 1998a.

clash and that resolutions can often only be achieved by back-door admission of utilitarianism' (Legge, 1998a: 162).

A survey conducted by the Society for Human Resource Management/Ethics Resource Center (SHRM/ERC) (accessed from the website on 2 December 2009) in the USA showed that 47 per cent of the HRM professionals surveyed reported that they 'feel pressured by other employees or managers to compromise their organization's standards of ethical business conduct in order to achieve business objectives'. The list below shows that 'aggressive financial business objectives' are the main 'moralizing' factors – half of the HRM professionals surveyed felt pressure to compromise their ethical business conduct. Note that the first five key factors listed below are related to the survival and well-being of the organization, and not to individuals. Only 16 per cent felt pressure to save jobs. HRM professionals reported that they do not compromise their ethics for personal gain (4 per cent). They identified the following pressures:

Meeting overly aggressive financial business objectives	50%
Meeting schedule pressures	38%
Helping the organization survive	30%
Rationalizing that others do it	22%
Resisting competitive threats	18%
Saving jobs	16%
Advancing the career interests of my boss	15%
Feeling peer pressure	12%
Advancing my own career or financial interests	4%

Source: SHRM/ERC (DATE?) Ethics Survey Snapshot (http://www. shrm.org).

8.5   HRM and ethical codes of conduct

Many firms give the HR managers a key leadership role in establishing and maintaining their ethical code of conduct (Driscoll and Hoffman, 1998). This is often carried out through seeking – and providing – sources of ethical information and advice, as well as developing and executing ethical programmes (ibid.). As a result, certain aspects of HRM practices have become more formalized through the establishment of both a professional code of ethics within the HRM field, and the internal codes of conduct within many Western corporations. To outsiders, codes of conduct are the most visible sign of a company's ethical policy. In the UK, the ranks of companies gaining the IIP (Investors in People) status have swelled rapidly; the certification process includes a commitment to ethical HRM practices. Similarly, in the USA, the certification process is often linked to espoused goals of creating an ethical organization culture (Payne and Wayland, 1999: 300). Again, a survey of 1,500 American employees showed that the percentage of respondents reporting that their organization had in place a set of written ethical standards increased from 60 per cent in 1994 to 79 per cent in 1999 (SHRM, 2001). The survey also revealed that training on ethics increased from a third in 1994 to 55 per cent in 1999. Another survey of US employees, sponsored by the Society of Financial Service Professionals, reported that almost 90 per cent of respondents claimed that their companies have a written code of ethics and standards of conduct. According to the President of the ERC, Michael Daigneault, 'workplace ethics involves more than just applying the laws and regulations, ethical behaviour refers to standards of conduct such as honesty, fairness, responsibility and trust'. Evidence from the above survey suggests that written ethical codes of conduct have a positive impact on employees' behaviour only when top and line managers live by them and set good ethical examples. Otherwise, they build cynicism and scepticism, and companies would be better off not having them. This is because the ethical conduct of the organization requires the support of the top management.

None the less, Payne and Wayland (1999: 304) noted that HRM is 'still largely relegated to a role of serving strategic and control interests, defined mostly by owners, institutional investors and managers in work organizations, rather than conceived of as a force in helping shape alternative organizational potential'. Consequently, HRM practice 'inhibits the consciousness' of HRM managers towards 'potentially expanding ethical obligations' towards employees. They noted that while HRM managers may accept much of what is found in the ethical codes of professional organizations such as the Chartered Institute of Personnel and Development (CIPD) and SHRM, in practice, they lack the power and the ethical will to confront a powerful management paradigm geared towards competitive advantage at any cost. In brief, while the growing desire to make the HRM function more ethical by binding it to a moral code of ethics is understandable, it cannot, we believe, become an ethical function merely by producing a code of ethics.

8.6   HRM as practice

The main activities of HRM can be understood in terms of the CIPD framework that has been used by leading authors spanning the business-orientated and academic divide (Marchington and Wilkinson, 1996, 2002). Using this framework, HRM can be understood in terms of four main activities: employee resourcing (Taylor, 2005) (recruitment and retention, or getting the right people in the right place at the right time): employee reward (Armstrong, 2002) (pay, recognition and motivation); employee relations (Gennard and Judge, 2005) (managing the employment contract and relationship); and training and development (Harrison, 2005) (often expressed in terms of individual and organizational learning – though, as mentioned earlier, this learning is ultimately for the organization's benefit).

Ethical challenges for HRM in practice include such themes as discrimination, psychological testing, anti-union activity, work design, employment security, employee discipline, confidentiality, and employee privacy (Gandtz and Hayes, quoted in Payne and Wayland, 1999). Danley *et al.*'s survey of over 1,000 US HRM professionals reported that the 'most serious ethical situations' US HRM professionals face are: favouritism in hiring, training, promotion, pay and discipline due to friendship with top management; sexual harassment; inconsistent discipline practices; not maintaining confidentiality; sex discrimination in promotion; compensation and recruitment; non-performance factors used in appraisal; and arrangement with vendors or consulting agencies leading to personal gain (quoted in Payne and Wayland, 1999: 300).

8.6.1   Ethics in selection

8.6.1.1   Interviews

Firms use employment interviews widely in the selection process. Different types of interviews are used: structured, semi-structured, focused, and unstructured. For many years, academics and practitioners have attempted to develop scientific interviewing techniques to help predict a candidate's behaviour, attitudes and efficiency, and thus select the most appropriate person for the job. It is argued that these techniques will reduce bias and allow interviewees to reach a fair, efficient and objective decision. However, fairness is a vague term and hard to measure, especially when interviewing candidates from different ethnic groups and/or from cross-cultural backgrounds – members of different ethnic groups or different cultures behave differently during interviews and say things differently. In its narrowest sense, however, fairness refers to choosing a person according to job-related criteria. Choosing, or not choosing, a person because of his or her race, colour, look, gender, nationality and age is generally considered to be unfair (see Arvey and Sackett, 1993).

Pearn and Seer (quoted in Spence, 2000: 46) suggest the following measures to help avoid such discrimination and unfair recruitment practices:

- Interviews should be properly conducted along professional lines.
- Interviewers should be properly trained.
- Interviews should be as consistent as possible.
- Interviews should only be used to assess abilities which cannot be more directly and accurately assessed by other means.

Spence (2000: 55) lists three steps towards 'best ethical practice' in employment interviewing. Interviewers should:

Step 1. Acknowledge individual interviewer influence on interviewing and identify actual practices.

Step 2. Understand the reasons for those practices.

Step 3. Clarify and communicate with all participants in interviewing the preferred ethical stance of the firm.

8.6.1.2 Psychometric testing

Psychometric tests are often used in the selection process and considered as an 'important component' of the selection event (Baker and Cooper, 2000: 61). Baker and Cooper (2000) note that 'the ethics of occupational testing is one area of human resource management where there has already been established ethical debate'. Manese's (1986) book *Fair and Effective Employment Testing* highlights several ethical issues facing (and 'best practices' for) occupational testing in the North American context. Since this book was first published, the literature has grown rapidly. Perhaps this reflects the widespread usage of psychometric testing by Western firms as well, and the manner in which it is deployed. Saville and Holdsworth (1993) note that around 70 per cent of large firms use personality and cognitive measures in their selection processes. In some countries such Sweden, however, there is strong concern about tests and invasion of individual privacy (Baker and Cooper, 2000: 61). Advocates of psychometric testing claim that, if used properly and in a professional manner, it will help the firm to predict the performance and behaviour of employees better than interviews and other subjective techniques (Cooper and Robertson, 1995). According to Baker and Cooper, 2000: 60–1), psychometric tests, when used properly, can:

provide common and neutral language to discuss and understand differences between people;

provide powerful results in a short time span;

offer an idea of strengths and development areas and give a good starting point for open discussion;

provide focus for changing behaviour;

offer people the way to understand themselves better; and

generate objective, benchmarked, and impartial results.

(Beardwell and Holden, 1997).

However, several articles written by professionals and academics alike have raised concern over the use of psychometric tests in the selection process. These concerns range from employers not following the suggested guidelines of 'good practice' (Baker and Cooper, 1985; Commission for Racial Equality (CRE), quoted in Baker and Cooper, 2000), to the manner in which tests are carried out, and 'fairness, cross-cultural issues and biases of race and gender, test selling practice ... types of tests such as integrity and honesty tests, facets of testing practices and testing practices and disabled candidates' (Baker and Cooper, 2000: 63). Iles and Robertson (1997) highlight the negative impact of testing on individuals undertaking genetic, integrity, honesty and computer-based tests, because of intrusiveness and their impact on the individual concerned.

Baker and Cooper (2000: 66) note that the changing emphasis in HRM on strategic fit and achieving sustainable competitive advantage has opened a range of new ethical concerns. The testing process seeks not only to predict attitudes and behaviours, but also to tell whether the person would fit within the overall corporate strategic vision and structure. Iles and Robertson (1997) argue that, because of the strategic integration of the HRM function and the quest for 'strategic fit', tests have shifted from the traditional job/role and person fit to 'cultural values person fit'. For example, the results of the tests are widely used to help identify 'core' and 'periphery' workers.

Jackson (1997) reports cases where companies used testing not in a job selection process, but to justify who should go when downsizing takes place. Baker and Cooper (2000: 66) argue that using tests in this way 'is inappropriate because they are measuring constructs that were arguably not genuine occupational or job requirements. An example would be when existing data input clerks re-applying for similar jobs are rejected on the grounds of not displaying enough "creativity"'.

Baker and Cooper (2000: 68–9) examined testing from a range of different ethical frames of reference and reported the following from different frames:

- Utilitarianism: Mistakes and negative impacts on candidates are regrettable, but are acceptable as long as tests have utility for the system as a whole.
- A deontological approach: Stresses the regulatory process, and best practices and procedures to avoid harming candidates. A variation of this would be a perspective firmly grounded in Kantian 'universalism': emphasis is placed on testing processes and criteria so that tests meet the ethical principle of 'doing unto others as you would have done unto you'.
- Rights-based perspective: stresses egalitarianism, equity, fairness and equity of opportunity.

8.7   HRM as strategy

As well as considering the ethical implications of particular activities, HRM is distinctive (or at least advocates of this new way of managing people claim that it is distinctive) because there is also a commitment to greater alignment with business strategy. So, one claim within the new model of HRM is that these activities are brought under one umbrella and organized in such a way that they are mutually supporting (sometimes referred to as 'horizontally integrated'). An example might be that, if we want to encourage people to take risks (which might be part of our training and development or learning strategy) then we move away from reward systems that encourage conservatism (a fixed annual wage) to ones that reward entrepreneurship (additional bonuses for demonstrating innovation). As well as being horizontally integrated, these activities should be aligned with the main organizational business strategy (so they are also 'vertically integrated') (Marchington and Wilkinson, 2002: 9). An example might be that if as our main business strategy we want our organization to grow, then we concentrate on retaining existing staff and recruiting sensibly (the resourcing 'bit'), but in doing this we also look at what makes us a potentially attractive employer – for example, our terms and conditions (the relations 'bit') and pay package (the reward 'bit') as well as the opportunities the organization provides for growth and learning (the training and development 'bit').

The claim to be more in line with business strategy and more coherent is often contrasted with the more piecemeal approach of the old-fashioned model of personnel management or industrial relations (though how fair that comparison is, is open to debate, as we have shown). Leading academic authors such as David Guest (1987, 1997) have identified how managing for greater commitment is also a distinctive claim or aspect of HRM. For each of the associated activities (resourcing, reward, relations, training and development) advice can be found for those with responsibilities for HRM in terms of selecting the right staff, excellence in compensation (pay) management, managing culture and motivating staff, driving through organizational learning and so on. Though these kinds of topics have been popular among managers as long as there has been a management industry (Kaufman, 2007), a distinctive claim within the managerialist literature on HRM is that this newer model of managing people brings together these different activities under one function: the 'human resource' manager. There is a surface rationality to this since, if we accept that people are just one of a number of resources the organization brings to bear, than having somebody manage the 'human resource' makes as much sense as having an IT director (to manage the IT resource), a facilities manager (to manage buildings and associated resources), or an accountant (to manage capital): hence the title of Beer *et al.*'s (1984) seminal work, *Managing Human Assets*.

8.8 Conclusions: human beings – ends in themselves *or* resources – means to an end?

From an ethical perspective there is an immediate and basic problem with treating people in this way. Immanuel Kant, one of the most influential ethical philosophers, argued that in order to behave ethically we had to ensure that we never treated people as a means to an end. He based his moral philosophy on the idea that people were always ends in themselves. Though this may at times seem unrealistic in a business environment – where the end is to make money, or at least to stay in business – there are troubling consequences if we believe that people are only one of a number of resources or assets *a la* Beer *et al.* (1984). Some of the tensions inherent in colliding the two words 'human' and 'resource' are played out in critical perspectives on HRM (Legge, 1989; Noon, 1992). Some authors have even argued that the phenomenon of HRM is so beset with contradictions and internal incoherence that it is impossible to treat it as a distinct entity and instead that it should be seen as mere rhetoric or only understood through metaphor (Keenoy, 1999; Keenoy and Anthony, 1992).

Even looking at HRM in a fairly abstract way (and setting aside for the moment the difficulty of defining HRM), one can see there are ethical implications for this newer way of managing people. If the organization's needs change, then one implication of the HRM model is that this, above all else, should determine how we manage people across the board. So, rather than respecting people as ends in themselves, they are seen as a means to an end, another resource to be managed. One could say that this is true of any organization – there may come a point at which individual rights are sacrificed in order to preserve the goals and viability of the organization. However, the difference between HRM and the stereotype of the old-fashioned way of managing people is that management of the human resource becomes much more closely linked to business strategy. Simply put, the personnel department with its adherence to rules and procedures (the means) makes way for HRM with its eye firmly on the bottom line (the ends). Similarly, the focus on securing commitment has ethical implications (Legge, 1998a). Positively, it could imply people will enjoy work more if they are involved in it and invest in work outcomes. More troublingly, managing for high commitment could be seen as corporate brainwashing – the management of meaning. This is another, more subtle, architecture of control (Townley, 1993, 2004). More insidious than the (personnel management) insistence on adherence to agreement and contracts, HRM implies people go beyond contract because they are expected to be committed to organizational ideals and strategies (Legge, 2001). This could be a more subtle, and potentially therefore more dangerous, means of manipulation than the brazen devices of Kondo's ethics school.

8.9   A new way of managing people?

Some of the tensions identified in this chapter are apparent when we consider the way in which large companies extravagantly reward those at the top of their organization. In considering the case below it seems that even in a supposedly new business environment, the traditional divide between an elite class of capitalists (the 'fat cats') and a mass of workers holds true.

Case study

Closing case study

Pay for 'fat cats': why severance and golden parachutes are hot topics ...

Bob Nardelli's lavishly paid ouster as CEO from Home Depot has provided the latest material for headlines trumpeting controversial exit CEO packages – further stirring indignation among investors, the public, and some key politicians. Nardelli's departure on Jan. 2, 2007, triggered a payout of $210 million. But the embattled ex-CEO is far from alone in seeing his exit package flare up into controversy.

In what some may see as fitting symbolism, two of the most notorious examples of excessive compensation were anchored in Wall Street and Disneyland. The first involved Dick Grasso's $187.5 million compensation package after being forced from the top job at the New York Stock Exchange; and the second, the $140 million severance pay that Michael Ovitz received after 14 months as president at Disney. Both packages sparked lawsuits. Grasso is demanding a jury trial and has appealed a trial judge's ruling ordering him to return millions to the Big Board. In the Disney case, the Delaware court found that the directors had not violated their fiduciary duty – but also noted that the board's actions of 1996 fell short of today's expectations and best practices.

Excessive severance gives rise to shareholder complaints over 'pay for failure.' Strictly speaking, though, the 'severance' portion is often a relatively small part of the overall exit payout. Nardelli's, for example, includes $20 million in cash severance – a hefty sum in absolute terms, but less than 10 percent of the overall exit package. More glaring was the payment of $32 million in retirement benefits – for just six years of service at Home Depot. The balance of the exit payout included millions of dollars for bonuses, unvested deferred stock awards, unvested options, earned and vested deferred shares, and 'other entitlements' under his employment contract. As the company noted, the entire payout of $210 million consists of 'the amounts [Nardelli] is entitled to receive under his pre-existing employment contract entered into in 2000.' And that's the point. If payouts are egregious [stand out for their reprehensible nature], it is because of the decisions that the board made earlier – seven years earlier, in this case, when Home Depot directors recruited Nardelli, a runner-up in the three-way battle to succeed Jack Welch at General Electric Co. But it is the exit package that aggregates all the disparate elements of an executive's pay, bringing to light any and all past errors of judgment. It is a sharp and unrelenting glare, beaming in on a single, all-inclusive number: a $210 million payout for a CEO here, a package of $180 million there.

Severance agreements kick in when an executive leaves the company, but the company itself experiences no change in control. Golden parachute

Case study

Continued

arrangements, on the other hand, unfold after a change in control of the company, such as a merger or acquisition, which in turn leads to the loss of an executive's position or a substantial change in its terms...Excessive golden parachutes also draw fire from investors. Sometimes the executive gets her golden parachute even if she stays on in the same capacity in the new company – or when the deal is scuttled and the merger never takes place. Other times, the size of the payment itself generates controversy. Often there seems no earthly reason for such stratospheric payments. Other times, however, dispassionate analysis might argue that the payment, while large, was indeed deserved. Take, for example, the $164 million payment for severance and benefits that James Kilts, the head of Gillette Co., received when the company was acquired by Procter & Gamble Co. for $57 billion in 2005. Warren Buffett insisted that Kilts 'earned every penny.' As with severance payouts, golden parachutes draw attention because they reduce complex terms to a single, glaring number. Parachute payments inevitably raise a critical question for investors: did the executives have incentives to chase or make deals that are in their personal interests, but against the long-term interests of the company and its shareholders?

...Given the controversies over excessive exit packages, it's worth stepping back and asking what their purpose is. Proponents of severance agreements see advantages on both the front and back ends. A severance agreement can help in recruiting, because it mitigates the financial and reputational risks to the incoming CEO – especially if the new company is experiencing difficulties. And on the back end, when the executive's employment is terminated, the employment agreement will make the terms clear. That relieves both the departing executive and the board from having to negotiate severance terms on an ad hoc basis. Some observers also see a corporate governance advantage to an agreement that removes the need for board discretion on severance when the executive is forced out. Last but not least, severance agreements mitigate the risk that an ousted executive will file suit for wrongful termination.

But employment and severance agreements also have their detractors. Critics note, for example, that the employment terms should not outlast the dicey situation that gave rise to the severance agreement in the first place: have the risks to the company and its CEO subsided after time has passed – time in which the executive has been well paid? And not everyone agrees that severance and change-in-control agreements are needed in the first place. Rank-and-file employees have no such agreements, so why should executives? In the words of Kenneth D. Lewis, chairman and chief executive of Bank of America, 'I don't understand why a C.E.O. should have a safety net when others don't.' Jeffrey Immelt, chairman and chief executive of General Electric Co., also spoke out recently against multi-year employment agreements. In a November 2006 interview with the *Financial Times*, he 'argued that chief executives should not have multi-year contracts, which could lead to large pay-offs if they were dismissed...'

...some prominent companies and chief executives are working with no employment contracts. GE's Immelt is one. So, too, are the new chief executives of Exxon Mobil Corp., PepsiCo Inc., Pfizer Inc., and Wm. Wrigley Jr. Co., as well as the heads of Citigroup Inc. and Procter & Gamble Co. Other companies with no employment agreements for executives include Intel Corp. (which states that it has no executive employment agreements, severance payment arrangements or change-in-control arrangements), Cisco Systems (which also has no employment or severance agreements), Health Management Associates and home improvement company Masco Corp.

And the following chief executives voluntarily have given up their employment agreements:

- Bank of America's Lewis voluntarily canceled his agreement in December 2003. Bank of America has no employment, severance, or change in control agreements, according to its 2006 proxy statement.
- Wachovia Corp. CEO G. Kennedy Thompson voluntarily terminated his employment agreement in December 2005. Other executives at the bank, however, do have employment agreements.
- ConocoPhillips CEO James J. Mulva voluntarily gave up his employment agreement Oct. 1, 2004. All listed executive officers serve without an employment agreement.

Even with no employment agreements, differences between companies emerge in other severance and post-employment benefits. While neither HMA nor Masco offers employment agreements, their equity compensation plans include change-in-control provisions for cash payments and accelerated vesting, respectively. Senior executives at Exxon Mobil have no employment contracts, severance programs, or benefits triggered or subject to acceleration upon a change in control. The company, does, however, offer a defined benefit plan based on a percentage of final average salary and bonus. When CEO Lee Raymond retired in January 2006, he received a lump sum retirement benefit of $98.4 million.

> (*Source*: Taken verbatim from 'Exit Pay Best Practices in Practice', with the permission of Stephen Deane of the RiskMetrics Group, previously, Institutional Shareholder Services)

Comment on Case

In terms of the fourfold CIPD structure we introduced earlier (resourcing, relations, reward, training and development), this case study can be seen to be located in the 'reward' domain. However, it does have implications for the other practices too. Severance deals are part of the incentives that attract top talent, so in that sense this topic also relates to resourcing. The ability to

Case study

Continued

attract and retain exceptional chief executives and directors is also pertinent when we consider how HRM strategies should be integrated with business strategy, particularly if we consider how shareholders' opinions will be affected by large payouts. In a less obvious but perhaps equally important sense, there are implications in terms of how such stellar sums influence employee relations. In one sense, having extremely high pay for the chief executives of large multinational corporations is consistent with the notion in HRM that we have individualized contracts – the argument for this would be that chief executives need to be rewarded differently because they are exceptionally talented. For the wider workforce, however, if exceptional payouts to outgoing chief executives go hand-in-hand with organizational failures (which in turn have a negative effect on staff conditions, or even cause redundancies), employees may well feel that their relationship with their organization is compromised and consequently become de-motivated. This would compromise the claim of the HR department to be able to manage culture effectively, a well as damaging what is sometimes referred to as the psychological contract between employers and their organizations (this refers to a bundle of beliefs that each employee has relating to how they feel they should be treated by their organization; for example, with fairness, dignity, respect and so on) (Guest and Conway, 2001). A report in the HR magazine *Personnel Today* (Overell, 2004) in referring to the, 'great fat cat pay heist' neatly summarised this issue under the heading 'differentials disincentivise' and argued that 'Executive pay should never be isolated from pay in general [that is, pay among the wider workforce] because differentials are fundamental to the calculus of just reward.' From an ethical perspective, the topic of differential pay relates to basic notions of justice and fairness. If we think of it in terms of an Aristotelian framework of virtues and vices, some of these severance packages simply appear greedy. In contrast, the actions of those who voluntarily give up such packages could be described as (at least comparatively) virtuous.

Questions

- What is the case for paying executives a great deal of money?
- What are the ethical implications of this for management of the 'human resource'?

References

Argyris, C., and Schön, D. 1978. *Organizational Learning: A Theory of Action Perspective*. Reading, Mass.: Addison Wesley.

Armstrong, M. 2002. *Employee Reward*, 3rd edn. London: CIPD.

Arvey, R. D. and Sackett, P. R. 1993. 'Fairness in Selection: Current Developments and Perspectives', in N. Schmitt and W. Borman (eds), *Personnel Selection*. San Francisco: Jossey-Bass.

Baker, B. and Cooper, J. 1995. 'Fair or Foul: A Survey of Occupational Test Practices in the UK', *Personnel Review*, 24: 67–82.

Baker, B. and Cooper, J. 2000. 'Occupational Testing and Psychometric Instruments: An Ethical Perspective', in D. Winstanley and J. Woodall (eds), *Ethical Issues in Contemporary Human Resources Management*. Basingstoke: Palgrave.

Beardwell, I. and Holden, L. 1997. *Human Resource Management: A Contemporary Perspective*, 4th edn. London: Pitman.

Beardwell, I. and Holden, L. 2001. *Human Resource Management: A Contemporary Approach*. London: Prentice Hall.

Beer, M., Spector, B., Lawrence, P. R., Mills, D. Q. and Walton, R. E. 1984. *Managing Human Assets*. New York: Free Press.

Beer, M., Spector, B., Lawrence, P. R., Mills, D. Q. and Walton, R. E. 1985. *Human Resource Management: A General Manager's Perspective*. Glencoe, Ill.: Free Press.

Blyton, P. and Turnbull, P. 1992. *Reassessing Human Resource Management*. London: Sage.

Boselie, P., Dietz, G. and Bon, C. 2005. 'Commonalities and Contradictions in HRM and Performance Research', *Human Resource Management Journal*, 15,3: 67–94.

Boxall, P. and Purcell, J. 2000. 'Strategic Human Resource Management: Where Have We Come From and Where Should We Be Going?', *International Journal of Management Reviews*, 2,2: 183–203.

Cooper, D. and Robertson, I. 1995. *The Psychology of Personnel Selection*. London: Routledge.

Dessler, G. 2000. *Human Resource Management*, 8th edn. London: Prentice Hall.

Driscoll, D. and Hoffman, M. 1998. 'HR Plays a Central Role in Ethics Programs', *Workforce*, April.

Fombrun, C. J., Tichy, M. M. and Devanna, M. A. 1984. *Strategic Human Resource Management*. New York: John Wiley.

Foucault, M. 1979. *Discipline and Punish*. Harmondsworth: Penguin.

Fowler, A. 1987. 'Comment: When Chief Executives Discover HRM', *Personnel Management*, 19,1: 1–3.

Freire, P. 2003. *Pedagogy of the Oppressed*. New York: Continuum International Publishing Group.

Gennard, J. and Judge, G. 2005. *Employee Relations*, 4th edn. London: CIPD.

Gibson, K. 2007. *Ethics and Business: An Introduction*. Cambridge: Cambridge University Press.

Guest, D. 1987. 'Human Resource Management and Industrial Relations', *Journal of Management Studies*, 24,5: 503–21.

Guest, D. 1989. 'Personnel and HRM: Can You Tell the Difference?', *Personnel Management*, 21: 48–51.

Guest, D. 1997. 'Human Resource Management and Performance: A Review and Research Agenda', *International Journal of Human Resource Management*, 8: 263–76.

Guest, D.E. 2000. 'HR and IR', in J. Storey (ed.), *Human Resource Management: A Critical Text*. London: IT.

Guest, D. and Conway, N. 2001. *The Psychological Contract: Public and Private Sector Perspectives*. London: CIPD.

Guest, D. E., Michie, J., Conway, N. and Sheehan, M. 2003. 'Human Resource Management and Corporate Performance in the UK', *British Journal of Industrial Relations*, 41,2: 291–314.

Guest, D., Michie, J., Sheehan, M., Conway, N. and Metochi, M. 2000. *Human Resource Management and Performance: First Findings from the Future of Work Study*, Chartered Institute of Personnel Development Issue Series. London: CIPD.

Hanlon, G. 2007. 'HRM Is Redundant? Professions, Immaterial Labour and the Future of Work', Proceedings of the 5th Critical Management Studies Conference, Electronic Journal of Radical Organization Theory. Available at: http://www.mngt.waikato.ac.nz/ejrot/; accessed 22 August 2007.

Harrison, R. 2005. *Learning and Development*. London: CIPD.

Heery, E. 2000. 'The New Pay: Risk and Representation at Work', in D. Winstanley and J. Woodall (eds), *Ethical Issues in Contemporary Human Resource Management*. Basingstoke: Palgrave.

Hendry, C. and Pettigrew, A. 1986. 'The Practice of Strategic Human Resource Management', *Personnel Review*, 15,5: 3–8.

Hoffman, W., and Moore, J. 1990. *Business Ethics: Readings and Cases in Corporate Morality*. New York: McGraw-Hill.

Hope, H. V., Farndale, E. and Truss, C. 2005. 'The HR Department's Role in Organizational Performance', *Human Resource Management Journal*, 15,3: 49–66.

Hosmer, L. 1987. 'Ethical Analysis and Human Resource Management', *Human Resource Management*, 26: 313–30.

Hyde, P., Boaden, R. B., Cortvriend, P., Harris, C., Marchington, M., Pass, S., Sparrow, P. R. and Sibbald, B. 2006. *Improving Health through Human Resource Management: Mapping the Territory*. London: CIPD.

Iles, P. and Robertson, I. 1997. 'Impact of Selection Procedures', in N. Anderson and P. Herriot (eds), *International Handbook of Assessment and Selection*. Chichester: John Wiley.

Institutional Shareholder Services. 2007. 'Exit Pay Best Practices in Practice', Rockville, Md., USA, March.

Jackson, K. 1997. 'Globalizing Corporate Ethics Programmes', *Journal of Business Ethics*, 16,12/13: 1272–35.

Kaufman, B. A. 2007. 'The Development of HRM in Historical and International Perspective', in P. Boxall, J. Purcell and P. Wright (eds) *The Oxford Handbook of Human Resource Management*, Oxford: Oxford University Press, pp. 19–47.

Keenoy, T. 1990. 'HRM: A Case of the Wolf in Sheep's Clothing', *Personnel Review*, 19, 2: 363–384.

Keenoy, T. 1999. 'HRM as Hologram: A Polemic', *Journal of Management Studies*, 36,1: 1–23.

Keenoy, T. and Anthony, P. 1992. 'HRM: Metaphor, Meaning and Morality', in . Blyton and P. Turnbull (eds), *Reassessing Human Resource Management*. London: Sage.

Kondo, D. K. 1990. *Crafting Selves: Power, Gender, and Discourses in a Japanese Workplace*. Chicago: University of Chicago Press.

Lancaster, H. 1995. 'Re-engineering Authors Reconsider Re-engineering', *The Wall Street Journal*, 7 January: B1.

Legge, K. 1989. 'Human Resource Management: A Critical Analysis', in J. Storey (ed.), *New Perspectives on Human Resource Management*. London: Routledge.

Legge, K. 1995. *Human Resource Management: Rhetorics and Realities*. London: Macmillan.

Legge, K. 1996. 'Morality Bound', *People Management*, 2,25: 34–7.

Legge K. 1998a. 'Is HRM Ethical? Can HRM Be Ethical?', in M. Parker (ed.), *Ethics and Organizations*. London: Sage.

Legge, K. 1998b. 'The Morality of HRM', in C. Mabey, D. Skinner and T. Clark (eds), *Experiencing Human Resource Management*. London: Sage.

Legge, K. 2000. 'The Ethical Context of HRM: The Ethical Organization in the Boundaryless World', in D. Winstanley and J. Woodall (eds), *Ethical Issues in Contemporary Human Resource Management*. Basingstoke: Palgrave.

Legge, K. 2001. 'Silver Bullet or Spent Round? Assessing the Meaning of the "High Commitment Management"/Performance Relationship', in J. Storey (ed.), *Human Resource Management: A Critical Text*. London: Thomson.

MacDuffie, J. P. 1995. 'Human Resource Bundles and Manufacturing Performance: Organizational Logic and Flexible Production Systems in the World Auto Industry', *Industrial and Labor Relations Review*, 48,2: 197–221.

Manese, W. R. 1986. *Fair and Effective Employment Testing*. London: Quorum Books.

Maund, L. 2001. *An Introduction to Human Resource Management: Theory and Practice*. Basingstoke: Palgrave.

Marchington, M. and Wilkinson, A. 1996. *People Management*. London: CIPD.

Marchington, M. and Wilkinson, A. 2002. *People Management and Development: Human Resource Management at Work*. London: CIPD.

Morgan, G. 1995. *Images of Organization*. London: Sage.

Morrell, K. 2002a. 'Models of HRM', in T. Redman and A. Wilkinson (eds), *The Informed Student Guide to Human Resource Management*. London: Thomson.

Morrell, K. 2002b. ' "Hard" and "Soft" HRM', in T. Redman and A. Wilkinson (eds), *The Informed Student Guide to Human Resource Management*. London: Thomson.

Nietzsche, F. (1886) 1973. *Beyond Good and Evil*, trans. R. Hollingdale. Harmondsworth: Penguin.

Noon, M. 1992. 'HRM: A Map, Model or Theory?', in P. Blyton and P. Turnbull (eds), *Reassessing Human Resource Management*. London: Sage.

Ouchi, W. G. 1979. 'A Conceptual Framework for the Design of Organizational Control Mechanisms', *Management Science*, 25,9: 833–48.

Overell, S. 2004. 'Time to Thin Down Fat Cat Pay', *Personnel Today*, 17 February. Available at: http://www.personneltoday.com; accessed 20 August 2007.

Patterson, M. G., West, M. A., Lawthom, R. and Nickell, S. 1997. *Impact of People Management Practices on Performance*. London: IPD.

Payne, S. and Wayland, R. 1999. 'Ethical Obligations and Diverse Values Assumptions in HRM', *International Journal of Manpower*, 20,5: 297–308.

Pedler, M., Burgoyne, J. and Boydell, T. 1991. *The Learning Company. A Strategy for Sustainable Development*. London: McGraw-Hill.

Peters, T. 1989. *Thriving on Chaos*. London: Pan.

Progressive Policy Institute. 2007. 'Currency Trading Totals $3 Trillion a Day', *Trade Fact of the Week*, 14 March. Appropriate website accessed 8 October 2007.

Saville, P. and Holdsworth, R. 1993. *Equal Opportunity Guidelines for Best Practice in Occupational Testing*. Esher: Saville and Holdsworth.

Scholte, J. A. 2005. *Globalization: A Critical Introduction*. Basingstoke: Palgrave Macmillan.

SHRM. 2001. 'Business Paying More Attention to Ethics: Management Support Essential'. Available at: http://www.shrm.org/...les/default.asp?page=bna0614c.htm.

Spence, L. 2000. 'What Ethics in the Employment Interview?', in D. Winstanley and J. Woodall (eds), *Ethical Issues in Contemporary Human Resource Management*. Basingstoke: Palgrave.

Storey, J. 1992. *Development in the Management of Human Resources: An Analytical Review*. Oxford: Basil Blackwell.

Storey, J. 1995. *Human Resource Management: A Critical Text*. London: Routledge.

Taylor, S. 2005. *People Resourcing*, 3rd edn. London: CIPD.

Thomas, D. 2006. 'Firewalking Firm Fined after Accountant Has to Hotfoot It to Hospital', *Personnel Today*, 3 February. Available at: http://www.personneltoday.com. accessed 20 August 2007.

Townley, B. 1993. 'Foucault, Power/Knowledge and Its Relevance for HRM', *Academy of Management Review*, 18,3: 518–45.

Townley, B. 2004. 'Managerial Technologies, Ethics and Managing', *Journal of Management Studies*, 41,3: 425–45.

Truss, C. 2001. 'Complexities and Controversies in Linking HRM and Organizational Outcomes', *Journal of Management Studies*, 38,8: 1121–49.

Tsui, A. S. 1987. 'Defining the Activities and Effectiveness of the Human Resource Department: A Multiple Constituency Approach', *Human Resource Management*, 11: 601–18.

Walton, R. E. 1985. 'From Control to Commitment in the Workplace', *Harvard Business Review*, 63: 77–84.

Wilson, F. 1999. *Organizational Behaviour: A Critical Introduction*, Oxford: Oxford University Press.

Winstanley, D. and Woodall, J. (eds). 2000. *Ethical Issues in Contemporary Human Resources Management*. Basingstoke: Palgrave Macmillan.

Winstanley, D., Woodall, J. and Heery, E. 1996. 'Business Ethics and Human Resource Management – Themes and Issues', *Personnel Review*, 25,6: 5–12.

Ethics and marketing

9

Chapter objectives

- To introduce the importance of ethical issues in the practice of marketing.
- To understand the specific ethical dilemmas faced by marketing managers in their relationship with the customer.
- To explore the implications of codes of ethics for marketing.
- To introduce the practice of green marketing.

Case study

Introductory case study

Marketing to children: the case of Transformers Toys

From a marketing viewpoint, the birth of Transformers toys in 1984 was an orchestrated act of genius. It not only launched one of the most successful playthings ever, it propelled a massive change in toy selling. Today, marketing rules; toys and the entertainment industry have become two sides of the same coin. The groundwork of all that was laid with the birth of Transformers.

Hasbro, now the world's second biggest toy company, had licensed Diacron, a puzzle toy with cars and planes that transformed into robots, from the Japanese company Takara. The Japanese had tried to sell it on the American market for a year. When it failed, they handed licensing rights to legendary toy man Henry Orenstein, who took the toy to Hasbro.

Convinced it could still be a success, Stephen Hassenfeld, Hasbro's CEO, the man regarded by many as the architect of the modern toy industry, had made the decision to market the toy instinctively. Now Hasbro had to make it work. Just how was thrashed out in an after-hours car ride between Hasbro's Rhode Island headquarters and New York City: the toy company's marketing chief and the three heads of Hasbro's ad agency Griffin Bacal brainstormed for three and a quarter hours.

One after another, decisions emerged. The toys would no longer be three-dimensional puzzles but characters in a story, with cars (the Autobots) being the good guys, and planes (the Decepticons) the bad guys. Joe Bacal came up with the name Transformers against initial opposition from the others. A back-story was created: Transformers had all come from Cybertron, a distant planet, where civil war raged between giant alien robots, under siege and desperate for fuel supplies.

By the time they reached New York, Diacron was no longer a stand-alone puzzle. As Transformers, it had broken away from its role of toy as object. The play pattern was spelled out. So too was the inducement to keep buying Transformers merchandise – playtime now would need lots of characters and props.

The remaining problem was how to sell such a fantasy toy effectively on television – the use of animation in advertising in the US at that time was strictly controlled. The Griffin Bacal agency had the answer. They made Transformers the subject of a comic book, and then advertised that instead to create awareness of the Transformers brand: there were no guidelines for commercials for comic books, because comic books never advertised on television. Griffin Bacal's ingenuity drove a coach and horses through the rules. Now the commercials could include all the animation they wished.

There was one more ingredient. Over a decade before, the Federal Communications Commission had cracked down on attempts by toy companies to introduce toy-led programmes. But now, under the Reagan administration, that changed. Transformers was free to become a 'programme-length commercial'.

A watershed had been crossed. The old idea of basing toys on characters in books or movies or programmes was turned upside down. Now the toy came first. The borders between programme and product became forever blurred, and in 1984 the Transformers TV series was launched.

Transformers sold $100m worth of toys in its first year – the most successful toy introduction in history at that point. Despite ups and downs since, constant marketing-led initiatives – new TV series spinning off new toys – have ensured it has never been out of production, a triumph in a business where a successful toy is one that lasts more than a year [see Cartoon 7].

(*Source*: Eric Clark, *Guardian*, 4 May 2007; www.guardian.co.uk)

Question

- What do you think are the main ethical issues associated with marketing goods to children? Do you think Hasbro have crossed any ethical boundaries? Give reasons for your answers.

Case study

Continued

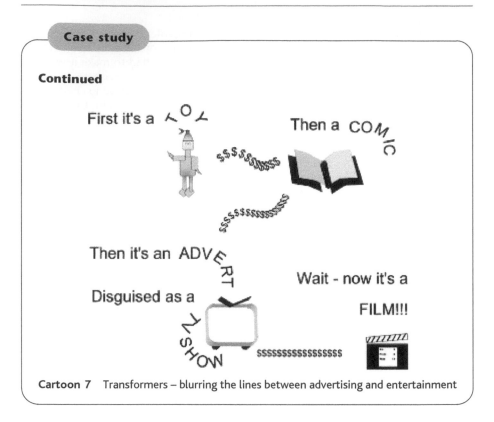

First it's a *TOY*   Then a *COMIC*

Then it's an *ADVERT*

Disguised as a *TV SHOW*

Wait - now it's a **FILM!!!**

Cartoon 7   Transformers – blurring the lines between advertising and entertainment

9.1 Introduction

As is the case with the discipline of business ethics generally, there has been a proliferation of research into ethics in marketing. This literature is a particularly fragmented one. None the less, a number of strands are apparent. These include debates surrounding the ethical duties (if any) of the marketing manager, the role of codes of ethics in marketing, and new forms of relationship between customer and client.

9.2 Advertising and ethics

Advertising constitutes the most visible form of marketing and today constitutes an essential component of trading (Harker and Harker, 2000). Critics of contemporary advertising have suggested that it has become increasingly pervasive, intrusive and pernicious (Laczniak and Murphy, 1993). While the origins of advertising can be traced back to the classical world, its different manifestations have greatly proliferated over the past thirty years or so. Indeed, advertising spending in the United States has expanded at a faster rate than the US economy as a whole (Laczniak and Murphy, 1993).

This has led postmodern writers such as Jean Baudrillard to suggest that our society has entered an age of what can be termed 'hyperreality'; differing forms of media have become so all-pervasive – and increasingly realistic – that the gap between image and reality is not always easily distinguishable (Friedman, 1992). While the scale and extent of this process may be disputed, there is little doubt that modern forms of advertising have permeated the most remote corners of the earth. Collectively, marketing managers have gained the power to shape the choices and lifestyles of the vast bulk of humanity. In turn, this creates a considerable range of responsibilities.

Marketing operates within a broader social context, and is shaped by, and reshapes, society (Laczniak and Murphy, 2006: 154). It is partially about economics, but not exclusively so: while what marketing managers do may be driven primarily by the 'bottom line', marketing incorporates a range of important ethical considerations (Laczniak and Murphy, 2006: 155). In practice, ethical considerations are relevant both at the micro level, in terms of the role of the marketing department within the firm, and more broadly – the role of marketing departments in wider society (Laczniak and Murphy, 2006: 155).

9.3   The relationship between marketing manager and consumer

In the essay 'De Officiis', the Roman philosopher, Cicero, argued that all vendors have a range of moral duties towards their clients (Singhapakdi *et al.*, 1999). However, what such duties are, and whether a particular set of duties is universal, is a somewhat contentious matter. Ferrell and Gresham argue that an individual's ethical framework is informed in a contingent fashion, reflecting individual, social and cultural environments (quoted in Singhapakdi *et al.*, 2000); what is deemed acceptable in one society may not be seen as such in another (Schlegelmilch, 1998). For example, in an Islamic country, the marketing of alcohol would be seen as an unethical act, but cigarette advertising – given the probability that less information may commonly be available on the hazards posed by smoking – less so. In contrast, in many Western countries, the reverse would be the case.

However, this does not free marketing managers from having to take into account a bedrock of common ethical norms; in almost all societies, the aggressive marketing of both cigarettes and alcohol to vulnerable groups, such as the under-aged, would be seen as an unethical act (Chonko, 1995). None the less, in advertising – as in most other fields – there are considerable grey areas as to what constitutes ethical conduct. And an ethical problem has first to be perceived as a problem for ethical decision-making to take place (Singhapakdi *et al.*, 1999). In practice, this means that marketing personnel have considerable leeway in deciding what constitutes ethical behaviour (Singhapakdi *et al.*, 1999).

To neo-liberals, the act of marketing entails no ethical duties other than those associated with the pursuit of profit. This would result in marketing being firmly embedded in what is assumed to be classic managerialism. The 'invisible hand' of the market will encourage firms to market in a suitable fashion – the products of firms that are touted in a distasteful or dishonest way to consumers will inevitably be eschewed. However, this approach is underpinned by the assumption of perfect knowledge (Beauchamp and Bowie, 1997). Consumers are not always aware of the hazards associated with a particular product, or may have uneven knowledge in this regard: hence, for example, consumer knowledge regarding the safety of a wide range of Chinese-made children's toys have appeared to repeatedly lag well behind their reaching the marketplace – and being widely sold. Consumers in countries with higher overall levels of literacy and formal education are in a far stronger position to make an informed choice than their less-well-off counterparts.

Moreover, advertisements may be – and, indeed, often are – deliberately pitched at groups that simply lack the capacity to make an informed choice at all, most notoriously the very young. A survey of representatives of US companies engaged in marketing products to the very young, conducted by Geraci (2004: 4), revealed that most respondents felt that it was acceptable to begin marketing products to children from the age of seven, although most agreed that the latter would only be able to make intelligent choices as consumers some five years later (ibid.); despite this, most said that they were happy with their industry's ethical standards (Geraci, 2004:14).

Furthermore, keeping one group of consumers happy may not be in the interests of wider society (Laczniack and Murphy, 2006: 158): for example, smokers may be very happy with a particular brand of cigarette, but all of society has to pay for the burden on the health system imposed by smoking-related illnesses. Again, it is likely that advertising targeting particular groups (for example, existing smokers in the case of cigarettes, over-18s in the case of alcohol) may spill over to reach other, unintended groups (and, in the case of unethical marketing, may have been deliberately designed to do so) (Laczniack and Murphy, 2006: 158).

There is little doubt that a minimalist ethical approach has often contributed to the poor image of the marketer as a 'vendor of snake oil', a tout or conman (Baumhart, 1961). This in turn, fuelled the rise of a consumerist movement, challenging the narrowly managerial view of marketing (Carrigan *et al.*, 2005; Higgins, 2000). There is little doubt that this forced the marketing agenda to change, to take on board the pressures of consumer lobbying; however, it can be argued that the good of the consumer can be reconciled with traditional marketing practice (Higgins, 2000). For example, Kotler suggests that marketing can play a vital role in facilitating a mutual benefit exchange; 'active and diligent' consumers reward the firm that opens up new opportunities for enriching their life-experience (Higgins, 2000). Thus, marketing can be seen as a force for enlightenment.

However, this raises two questions: the first philosophical and the second practical. With regard to the former, adherents of the mainstream philosophical traditions (with the possible exception of the rights-based approach) would argue that marketing managers should still subject marketing to certain ethical tests. For example, for utilitarians, advertising should make some contribution to overall happiness to be of some ethical worth, while to virtue theorists, advertising should be grounded in a learned body of desirable values and behavioural constructs (Murphy *et al.*, 2007). Second, there is the practical dimension of monitoring and enforcement. There are many cases where firms have benefited from palpably unethical practices. It can be argued that it is vital that consumers are supplied with sufficient information to make informed choices, and that certain basic norms of behaviour (such as the protection of the most vulnerable in society) should be upheld.

Traditionally, there have been three approaches to customer service: manipulative, courteous and personalized (Buckley, 2000). In other words, customers can simply be seen as people to be duped, directed, and/or refocused to encourage them to make certain purchases; as a person of value to be treated with respect; or as a partner in what is hoped will be a long-term relationship. However, recent work has pointed to the dyadic nature of exchange – exchange relationships are, in many cases, not one-off affairs, but each party is likely to be influenced and shaped by the other (Buckley, 2000; Singhapakdi *et al.*, 1999). This means not only that, for the firm, the views of the customer are crucial, but also that both have certain ethical responsibilities. A number of studies have indicated that substantial ethical gaps tend to exist between marketer and potential customer, even although such gaps might be extremely counterproductive in ensuring that custom is retained (Singhapakdi *et al.*, 1999).

Consumers are, of course, not always possessors of the necessary information to make an informed ethical choice. However, where there is widespread evidence – frequently aired in the popular media to the extent that it becomes common knowledge – to suggest that the consumption of certain products is unethical, then some responsibility must devolve on the consumer in a highly literate society, no matter how devious the vendor might have been. For example, there have been repeated exposés of the irreparable environmental damage caused by the unsustainable extraction of peat (for use in domestic gardens) and use of tropical hardwoods (to make cheap garden furniture, flooring and wood-based products). None the less, in the United Kingdom, considerable consumer demand persists both for peat, and for furniture constructed from tropical hardwoods of unverifiable provenance. Again, cheap flights and oversized 4 × 4 'mommy wagons' appear particularly popular among the middle classes, who are likely to be relatively aware of the disastrous consequences of global warming.

In short, the consumers have to make ethical decisions of their own, and must bear some responsibility for their actions (Singhapakdi *et al.*, 1999); evidence would suggest that many have been equally lax as a large number of companies in this regard. As with any other stakeholder grouping, it has been argued that consumers have a vital role to play in impelling firms towards more ethical conduct, and in monitoring compliance with basic ethical norms.

This does not, of course, excuse any ethical lapses by the vendor. It can be argued that, whatever the relationship between buyer and seller, the ethical decision-making process of the marketer remains crucial (Carrigan *et al.*, 2005; Singhapakdi *et al.*, 1999). While 'phoney smiles' (forced politeness and pretended interest in a customer personally to promote a sale) may not constitute an ethical breach, there are many grey areas. For example, some writers, such as

Ford, have charged that even the depersonalization of service in areas such as health care can constitute an ethical breach; the ability to rapidly gain the custom – and rapid turnover – of clients can easily be privileged over their long-term well-being (quoted in Buckley, 2000). The mixed track record of self-regulation, and indeed, the inability of many consumers to act ethically even when they possess knowledge as to the wider social and environmental damage incurred by using particular products, highlights the role of the state in upholding basic ethical standards, in the long-term interests of the community.

A further issue is that of pricing. For example, it has often been argued that some drugs are overpriced, given that they are vital to sufferers of certain illnesses; in practice, this means that the very poor may be denied treatment (Ferrell *et al.*, 2000). Marketing is, of course, not only about the use of the media, but also about pricing policies. Particularly contentious has been the pricing of drugs to treat AIDS, and attempts by major drug companies to block the distribution of generic alternatives. It is often argued that high pricing funds future research. However, a large proportion of advances in medicine continue to be made in publicly funded laboratories and universities; critics have argued that taxpayers continue to subsidize corporate gain at the expense of the most vulnerable.

Finally, in marketing, ethical dilemmas not only concern the firm and potential consumers, but third parties as well. For example, a local authority or charity may accept donations in return for helping to publicize a particular product or firm. Common examples would include those animal charities that display billboards advertising a particular brand of dog food on their premises, and/or include advertisements for such products in some of the media that they distribute. Such a relationship would be seen as mutually beneficial and unproblematic (provided, of course, that such food was of reasonable nutritional value).

More problematic was the decision by Guelph City Council (in the United States) to accept a donation from Imperial Tobacco Limited for its municipal theatre, naming the relevant facility after a well-known brand of cigarette in return (LeClair, 1998). This decision sparked off a protracted public debate, though the local authority in question stuck by its decision. In short, in addition to the seller and potential buyer, any third party that is in a position to provide publicity to the marketer faces ethical dilemmas as well. Such third parties would not only include charities and other 'deserving causes', but, of course, also the mass media.

9.4 Codes of ethics in marketing

Ethical issues in marketing concern both current practice, and *normative* issues – in other words, what *should* be (Hunt and Vitell, 2006: 143; Laczniack and Murphy, 2006: 156). Many countries rely on self-regulation as a means of ensuring 'fair play' in advertising, backed up by codes of conduct. While there is little doubt that certain forms of advertising can be misleading or harmful – an often cited example are cigarette advertisements aimed at teenagers – self-regulation frees governments of charges of controlling the freedom of speech (Harker and Harker, 2000; Laczniak and Murphy, 1993). However, the advertising industry has – in most cases –been unable to evade its responsibilities via self-regulation. Given the public nature of advertising, adherence to such codes of conduct tend to be closely monitored by government, social commentators and consumer groups (Harker and Harker, 2000). However, of course, the viability of self-regulation is heavily dependent on mutual co-operation and sufficient mechanisms to preclude free-riding rogue firms. In other words, there have to be mechanisms in place to preclude a less scrupulous firm from deliberately breaking an advertising code in order to gain a short-term competitive advantage.

A further issue is the question as to who should have the responsibility of drafting codes of marketing ethics. On the one hand, it can be argued that a code drafted by outsiders can result in low levels of commitment by the affected firms (Harker and Harker, 2000), but on the other hand, a code of ethics that is drafted unilaterally by the affected industry is likely to lack legitimacy, and be ineffective. Consequently, should an industry have the responsibility of drafting its own code of ethics, then wide-ranging consultation is necessary. Codes of ethics have tended to focus on areas such as the appropriateness of markets (for example, restrictions on the promotion of cigarettes or alcohol to children). However, in addition to expectations of a basic degree of truthfulness, there has been increasing political pressure for advertisements not to be overtly sexist or racist (Harker and Harker, 2000); in practice the former generally tends to be seen as more acceptable than the latter.

9.5   Ethical marketing strategies: cause-related marketing

Cause-related marketing (CRM) incorporates a charitable dimension within an act of exchange. Here the vendor undertakes to give a specified amount to a designated charitable cause for each good or specific service purchased by the consumer. In some respects, CRM represents a manifestation of classic corporate philanthropy (Higgins, 2000; Schlegelmilch, 1998). However, CRM does incorporate a more strategic dimension – giving is deliberately targeted, and closely linked to the performance of a particular product. The nature of sponsorship is thus firmly located within the realm of overall corporate activities. Higgins (2000) notes that CRM was sponsored by American Express in its 1981 promotion of the Fine Arts Group in California; since then, the scope of American Express's charitable giving has greatly expanded and the company's strategy has been widely implemented. However, critics have charged that CRM may not be sustainable, and may have weakened other forms of fund-raising, and, indeed, a tradition of free giving (Higgins, 2000).

Nonetheless, there is little doubt that many charities have benefited handsomely from CRM. This has led a number of charities to take a proactive role in persuading firms to make use of CRM, a good example being the RSPCA and Kellogg's breakfast cereals (Higgins, 2000). However, research has indicated that advertising agencies are likely to focus their efforts particularly on popular causes, such as illiteracy. More controversial – or uncomfortable – causes such as AIDS are widely shunned (Higgins, 2000). In short, for CRM advertising campaigns to be successful, the sympathy of target audiences must be gained; above all, causes must be unthreatening (Higgins, 2000).

A possible exception to this general rule would be the Benetton clothing advertising campaigns, which have focused on controversial issues such as AIDS, the death penalty, and clerical sexuality (Higgins, 2000). Benetton advertisements have repeatedly highlighted social taboos, including the depiction of dying people. Benetton's advertising managers have argued that the advertisements represent a sincere attempt to open debates on key social issues 'of our time'. However, by their very nature, advertisements tend to be closed-ended; they represent more of a (often sensationalist) one-off affair rather than the start of an informed debate. Indeed, to postmodern writers such as Baudrillard, such advertisements would simply represent a manifestation of a postmodern 'ecstatic age' – cheap sensation is privileged above substance (Friedman, 1992). The amoral gaze is all that is offered – voyeurism rather than steps towards meaningful change (Higgins, 2000).

There is little doubt that CRM is highly efficacious; surveys of consumers in the UK have revealed that 83 per cent of consumers have favourable images of brands associated with CRM (Higgins, 2000). While it is easy to dismiss CRM as a cynical marketing tool, research conducted by Teather has indicated that marketing managers engaging in CRM campaigns were motivated partially by sentiment; albeit that it was an effective marketing strategy, it resulted in, in the words of one marketing manager, 'a warm feeling inside' (quoted in Higgins, 2000).

However, a deontologist would, in many respects, be somewhat sceptical as to the moral worth of CRM (Higgins, 2000). To adherents of this philosophical tradition, acts are only of moral worth if they are motivated for the right reasons; if CRM is adopted to increase sales of a particular product then it is of no moral significance. Any claims to ethical status would be more easily be on utilitarian grounds; any act that enhances overall happiness is necessarily good.

Moreover, postmodernists would share the scepticism of deontologists. To Bauman, CRM quite simply removes moral behaviour from the hands of the 'other' (see Bauman, 1993; Higgins, 2000). In other words, charity giving is absolved by the act of exchange; rampant consumerism is given an acceptable moral face. In support of this assertion, Higgins (2000) cites the example of the American Express 'Charge Against Hunger' campaign. Through this campaign, alleviating the crisis of starvation was directly linked to consumerist acts such as the charging to a credit card of a meal in an expensive restaurant (Higgins, 2000); alleviating privation could be reconciled with wanton plenty. Similarly, an Exxon advertising campaign linked donations to environmental causes with fuel consumption, and, hence, indirectly, with the creation of pollution; existential discomforts could be reconciled with consumption (Higgins, 2000). To Bauman (1993), this would reflect the relentless instrumentalization of society, and its reduction to the pursuit of image at the expense of real moral worth.

9.6   Ethical marketing strategies: green marketing

The term 'green marketing' is often used interchangeably with 'sustainable' or 'environmental' marketing. Green marketing is an extremely loose concept. However, five broad approaches to green marketing can be identified; approaches which, however, are of very much broader relevance in providing a starting point for ethical marketing in the more general sense of the word. As Todd (2004: 87) notes, as visibly even if superficially 'green' products become increasingly fashionable, this leads to ethics becoming confused with aesthetics: products may be desirable not because they are ethically sourced, but because the consumer can appear – and to be seen to appear – to be environmentally conscientious. Genuine ethical marketing views consumers as part of the wider ecosystem; social change happens gradually, with consumers making ethical choices being part of the process of social change (Todd, 2004: 100).

'Fair play' approaches to green marketing argue that customers have a right to know what they are getting. This approach would be critical of attempts at 'greenwashing' (Crane, 2000b; Todd, 2004: 87). The latter refers to dubious environmental claims that are unverifiable (for example, claims that wood products have come from sustainable forestry operations, but with no independent corroboration), or patently false. 'Fair play' marketing would, for example, include clear labelling of cosmetic products that are not tested on animals (labelling certified by an independent monitoring organization), the absence of such a label implicitly denoting that such testing has indeed taken place. Consumers would thus be in a position to make an informed choice.

This has led writers such as Smith (2001) to propose a consumer sovereignty test (CST) – does the target market know the risks and/or damages associated with a particular product? An example Smith highlights is the case of tobacco, a product that probably does not make a significant contribution to environmental degradation, but which poses a very real health hazard. The latter information is less common knowledge in many areas of the third world where tobacco is promoted aggressively (Smith, 2001). Moreover, as noted elsewhere, tobacco is often marketed to teenagers, a group with 'reduced consumer capability'. Finally, tobacco, being highly addictive, reduces the capacity of even adult consumers who are fully conversant with the relevant health risks to make fully objective choices (Smith, 2001). Similarly, given that all sentient beings have a capacity for suffering, consumers should be informed if a particular product was tested on animals (Smith, 2001).

Second, there are approaches to green marketing that are simply 'managerialist'. Here, the consumer is seen as holding certain moral values with which the firm has to be seen to reconcile its activities in order to gain market share (Crane, 2000b). Ethical conduct is thus about placating the consumer, rather than necessitating a real change in corporate values.

Third, there is the reformist approach. This approach suggests that the firm's activities have to be realigned with legitimate stakeholder expectations and needs; however, again, any reform in activities would be promoted partially by self-interest (Crane, 2000b). In other words, the firm has to secure (and retain) a favourable image in the community in order to keep (and expand) its market share. Fourth, 'dialogic' approaches argue that a dialogue between firm and stakeholders to resolve competing concerns and interests is the best way forward: only the manner and format of the dialogue represents a universal ethical obligation, not the outcome or any core moral values held by a particular group (Nill, 2003: 103). Limits of this approach include disparities in knowledge and resources between different parties to the conversation, and cultural specificalities (ibid.).

Fifth, there is the reconstructionist approach. This is founded in the 'deep green' frame of reference discussed in earlier chapters. Reconstructionists would argue that the marketer has to respond proactively to growing evidence of irreversible environmental degradation (Crane, 2000b). Unregulated markets are, by their very nature, morally deficient; indeed, marketing is often part of the problem of environmental degradation, rather than part of the solution (ibid.). However, it can be argued that business can play a central role in ensuring sustainable development; as the 'deep green' perspective has become mainstream, it has increasingly taken into account the role and potential of business in helping to bring about a 'better world'. None the less, a fundamental rethink in marketing strategy is in order (ibid.).

'Deep green' marketing would adopt a minimalist approach in marketing products that were produced in a sustainable and humane fashion, an often-cited example being the Body Shop range of cosmetics. However, this would only be one dimension of 'deep green' marketing; the latter should entail not just the promotion of specific products in a certain fashion, but also aim to change wider social values. By focusing on environmental issues, 'deep green' marketing can help to raise consumer awareness of the major issues at stake. The 'deep green' marketing strategy does incorporate certain inherent contradictions. For example, would it ever be possible to market a motor car in a truly 'deep green' fashion? However, there is little doubt that many contemporary advertising campaigns do incorporate a 'deep green' dimension. Again, in the case of the motor industry (the above caveat notwithstanding), an example would be the Volkswagen advertising campaign that promoted the idea that motor cars should be fully recyclable, and that consumers should take recyclability into account when choosing a vehicle.

Finally, the interpretavist perspective would focus on internal issues, and the extent to which morality can become embedded in the marketing sections of 'green organizations' (Crane, 2000b). In other words, ethical issues should become part and parcel of the marketing process. Here William and Murphy suggest that virtue theories might provide a useful starting point: the question should be asked as to what kinds of perceptions the marketer is seeking to mould, and with what sort of organization should the virtuous individual wish to be associated (Murphy *et al.*, 2007; Smith, 2001). In other words, the extent to which 'green marketing' becomes an implicit assumption underlying marketing decisions. This is perhaps the hardest approach to follow; however, again, environmental issues have become squarely mainstream. Many consumer products now incorporate clear environmental information, either in advertisements and/or on the labelling of the product, as a matter of course (for example, 'GM free', 'Cruelty free', 'Recyclable', 'Made from recycled plastic and so on).

Whichever approach is followed, it is clear that firms have to take environmental issues increasingly seriously in advertising campaigns. Again, however, the question emerges as to whether this should be on the grounds of 'enlightened self-interest' or because it is the 'right' thing to do. Only the fourth and fifth of the above approaches would accord primacy to the latter and, as such, meet the deontological test of what constitutes ethical behaviour.

9.7   Conclusion

Ethics represents a choice between different courses of action; conflict and disagreement is natural in choosing the 'best option' (Keyes, 1997). Ethical theories provide useful guidelines for making decisions in marketing, but do not provide concrete solutions (Keyes, 1997). There is little doubt that trust is an important driver of long-term exchange relationships; in marketing, as in any other area, ethical conduct can be extremely good for business (Buckley, 2000). However, there is more to ethical marketing than simply what is in the long term an interest of business. Important questions include the nature and extent of consumer knowledge and the capacity for the consumer to make an informed decision, the role of third parties, and the extent to which marketing practice should be ethically grounded even if there seems to be little prospect of financial reward for good practice.

Discussion questions

- If green marketing pays, is a decision by a company to engage in green marketing devoid of any moral worth? Give reasons for your answer.
- What specific ethical challenges are likely to be faced by a company engaging in cause-related marketing?

Case study

Closing case study

Unhealthy eating in Italy

The stereotypical image we have of the Mediterranean diet as being a healthy one leading to a long life may be rather more of a myth than a reality according

Case study

Continued

to a government study by the Ministry of health in Italy. While components such as olive oil are associated with health benefits, apparently the diet of Italians is changing away from this to a more Western diet of carbonated drinks, meals high in sugar, and food that is fried or high in fats. Alongside other negative health behaviours, such as smoking and an increase in alcohol intake, this has actually led to a reduction in life-expectancy among some groups in Italy.

According to Tom Kinsgton, writing in the *Guardian* in February 2007, the situation has changed to such an extent that the Ministry of Health in Italy is even planning on different kinds of emergency intervention in the nation's diet and eating habits; for example, by sending supplies of fresh fruit into some of the nation's key institutions such as hospitals and schools. The evidence of shorter life spans seems clear, and the explanation does too: as a result of more drinking of alcohol, a diet becoming richer in processed food and an increase in cigarette smoking, the healthy Italian diet seems to be disappearing.

Kingston reported on a summary of the findings from a study by Walter Ricciardi, Professor and Chair of Hygiene and Public Health at the Catholic University of the Sacred Heart in Rome, who formed part of an Italian public health task force. As lead researcher in one relevant research project, Ricciardi summarized the implications of the research by saying that 'Bad food and smoking in the south is pushing the level of diabetes above the national average, while the south is also catching up with the north on tumours.' The regions in the South include areas surrounding Naples, long known as the orchard of Italy as a result of the rich soil near the (still active) volcano, Vesuvius. It is ironic that the natural abundance of some of the best fruit and vegetables in Europe is in an area where a more Westernized diet is claiming lives.

Writing in the *European Journal of Public Health*, Ricciardi (2006) identifies the role that governments should play in promoting positive public health: 'Population health should be presented as human capital, which is the basis for a solid economy and a happy population.' Unfortunately, of course, the influence of government is not the only factor affecting public health. Neither is it a predictor of what people choose to eat. Notwithstanding smoking bans and such interventions as emergency rations of fresh fruit, reduced prices for vegetables and an apparent commitment to public health, the Italian government faces many of the same problems as other Western governments.

One of the other major influences on people's consumption choices is the effects of the advertising industry. Another is the manufacturers who choose to put higher levels of fats and salt in products. These may taste more appealing, but the hidden costs of such changes may not show up for decades, and some fear that governments will have to pay the price by dealing with a rising tide of obesity.

(*Source*: Tom Kingston, *Guardian*, 17 February 2007; www.guardian.co.uk)

Question

- Can the advertising industry and food manufacturers be blamed at all for the health problems associated with poor eating in Italy? What ethical obligations (if any) should firms have in advertising foodstuffs.

References

Bauman, Z. 1993. *Postmodern Ethics*. Oxford: Basil Blackwell.

Baumhart, R. C. 1961. 'How Ethical Are Businessmen?', *Harvard Business Review*, 39,4: 6–31.

Beauchamp, T. and Bowie, N. 1997. 'Ethical Theory and Business Practice', T. Beauchamp and N. Bowie (eds), *Ethical Theory and Business*. Upper Saddle River, NJ: Prentice Hall.

Buckley, N. 2000. 'Review: Communicating with Customers', *Journal of the Academy of Marketing Science*, 28,2: 312–3.

Carrigan, M., Marinova, S. and Szmigin, I. 2005. 'Ethics and International Marketing', *International Marketing Review*, 22,5: 481–93.

Chonko, L. 1995. *Ethical Decision Making in Marketing*. Thousand Oaks, Calif.: Sage.

Crane, A. 2000a. 'Corporate Greening as Amoralization', *Organizational Studies*, 21,4: 673–96.

Crane, A. 2000b. 'Marketing and the Natural Environment', *Journal of Marketing*, 20,2: 144–54.

Ferrell, O. C., Fraedrich, J. and Ferrell, L. 2000. *Business Ethics: Ethical Decision Making and Cases*. Boston, Mass.: Houghton Mifflin.

Friedman, J. 1992. 'Narcissism, Roots, and Postmodernity', in S. Lash and J. Friedman (eds), *Modernity and Identity*. Oxford: Basil Blackwell.

Geraci, J. 2004. 'What Do Youth Marketers Feel about Selling to Kids?', *Advertising and Marketing to Children*, 4–6.

Harker, D. and Harker, M. 2000. 'The Role of Codes of Conduct in the Advertising Self-Regulatory Framework', *Journal of Macromarketing*, 20,2: 155–66.

Higgins, M. 2000. 'Cause-Related Marketing', *Business and Society*, 39,3: 304–22.

Hunt, S. and Vitell, S. 2006. 'The General Theory of Marketing Ethics', *Journal of Macromarketing*, 26: 143–53.

Keyes, B. 1997. 'Review: Ethical Decision Making in Marketing', *Journal of the Academy of Marketing Science*, 25,4: 362–4.

Laczniak, G. and Murphy, P. 1993. *Ethical Marketing Decisions*. New York: Prentice Hall.

Laczniak, G. and Murphy, P. 2006. 'Normative Perspectives for Ethical and Socially Responsible Marketing', *Journal of Macromarketing*, 26: 154–77.

LeClair, D. 1998. 'Review: A Pragmatic Approach to Business Ethics', *Journal of the Academy of Marketing Science*, 25,4: 364–5.

Murphy, P., Laczniak, G. and Wood, G. 2007. 'An Ethical Basis for Relationship Marketing', *European Journal of Marketing*, 41,1–2: 37–57.

Nill, A. 2003. 'Global Marketing Ethics: A Communicative Approach', *Journal of Macromarketing*, 23, 90–104.

Ricciardi, W. 2006. 'Ten Statements on the Future of Public Health in Europe', *European Journal of Public Health*, 16,5: 458–61.

Singhapakdi, A., Vitell, S., Rao, C. and Kurtz, D. 1999. 'Ethics Gap', *Journal of Business Ethics*, 21,4: 317–28.

Singhapakdi, A., Marta, J., Rallapahi, K, and Rao, C. 2000. 'Towards an Understanding of Religiousness and Business Ethics', *Journal of Business Ethics*, 27,4: 305–20.

Schlegelmilch, B. 1998. *Marketing Ethics*. London: International Thomson Business Press.

Smith, N. 2001. 'Ethical Guidelines for Marketing Practice', *Journal of Business Ethics*, 32,1: 3–18.

Todd, A. 2004. 'The Aesthetic Turn in Green Marketing', *Ethics and the Environment*, 9,2: 86–102.

Ethics and supply chain management

Chapter objectives

- To understand what constitutes ethical supply chain management.
- To examine the range of current ethical challenges facing the supply chain manager.
- To gain insights into the debate of child labour and sweatshops in the supply chain.
- To understand and examine conflicts of interest in purchasing.
- To gain insight into the relevance of environmental issues for supply chain management.

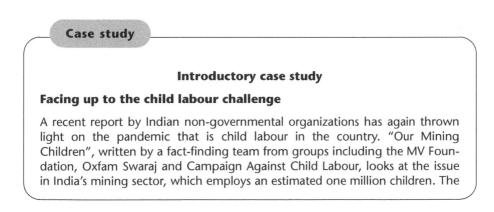

Case study

Introductory case study

Facing up to the child labour challenge

A recent report by Indian non-governmental organizations has again thrown light on the pandemic that is child labour in the country. "Our Mining Children", written by a fact-finding team from groups including the MV Foundation, Oxfam Swaraj and Campaign Against Child Labour, looks at the issue in India's mining sector, which employs an estimated one million children. The

Continued

team found about 200,000 of them working in the Bellary district of Karnataka state.

According to the latest (2001) Indian census, out of 210 million children aged between five and 14, an estimated 11.2 million are working. This accounts for about 5% of the estimated 211 million children working in the world and more than half the number of child workers in the Asia-Pacific region.

According to the new report, most of the children at Bellary's mines are involved in strenuous activities like digging and breaking stones. It says they are also engaged in the other processing activities of iron ore mining, without access to any safety equipment.

While the report heavily criticises companies employing child workers indirectly in their supply chains, a few companies are setting an example for the rest in tackling the problem.

Many companies have been seen, when discovering that child labour exists in their supply chains, to have been ignorant of the local social and economic conditions among their suppliers. Key among these conditions are often thin profit margins in poor communities where children often have to work to support a subsistence living.

In the case of many unscrupulous (or desperate) farm and factory owners and managers, the low level of their revenues can lead to the employment of cheap labour in the form of children.

Child labour experts say companies should address this on a basic level by raising their suppliers' profit margins and pushing them to employ adults, using audits to verify progress. However, corporate insiders point out that in many nations, the use of child workers is almost institutionalised, ingrained in local cultures through years of poverty, poor education and lack of strict law enforcement systems.

NGOs often acknowledge this, and the fact that the culture of child labour existed before the sourcing of products by multinational companies from poorer nations. However, both sides generally agree nowadays that, morally and reputationally, this excuses no-one from taking action on this most emotive of issues.

Regular third-party monitoring and social audits of supplier premises are necessary to ensure that buyers' social and environmental standards are enforced, say labour standards experts.

Swedish home furnishings company Ikea has a strict code of conduct, says its ban on child labour is 'non-negotiable' and makes suppliers sign up to the company's code of conduct to secure purchase orders.

Ikea requires all its suppliers to disclose all their production centres, which it then monitors through announced checks, while its auditors, KPMG, spring surprise inspections.

Factories found to be in violation of Ikea's code of conduct are put on probation for at least six months. During this time they are expected to put forward an action plan to ensure all child workers are placed in schools and that their education to the age of 14 is paid for. In some cases, suppliers are expected to compensate child workers' families for the income lost by placing them in schools. If all this is not done to the company's satisfaction, Ikea withdraws its business.

Complex outcomes

Partnerships, says the International Labour Organization, are imperative to finding collective solutions to the problem of child labour.

Back in the late 1990s, the organization's International Programme on the Elimination of Child Labour had success in eliminating child labour in the soccer ball industry of Pakistan's Sialkot district with the help of local NGOs, the district government and the Sialkot Chamber of Commerce and Industry. With ILO training in operational, auditing and reporting standards, the local NGOs are now better equipped to monitor progress. However, in this case, the end result was not what some might have wanted.

While child labour was virtually eliminated from the area's soccer ball production, that meant all workers had to be monitored. For cultural reasons, many women workers were not able to leave their houses and work in a monitored factory, and so lost their jobs. According to one source involved in the project, some 20,000 workers became unemployed so that child labour could be eliminated from the branded soccer ball industry in time for the 1998 World Cup.

To avert such an outcome, The India Committee of the Netherlands suggests companies should involve local community members or NGOs in the auditing and monitoring process. Locally known faces, used as part of the auditing process, can help win the confidence of workers, it says. The issue of homeworkers and associated problems of monitoring this informal economy is a well-acknowledged problem, but there are potential solutions beginning to emerge (see Box 1).

Box 1 Homeworker standards

Identifying and monitoring homeworkers in a company's supply chain is extremely difficult. Most homeworkers get paid less than half the legal minimum wage with no pay for overtime hours. They do not receive the benefits or protections of on-site workers. In many countries, such as India, homeworkers are not protected by national labour laws. Child workers form a large part of this homeworking community.

ILO Convention 177 and Recommendation 184 provide a guideline on what systems companies can put in place to protect homeworkers. These include records of workers' details being maintained by suppliers, including proof of age; workers being told their rights and taught how to keep records of hours worked; and overtime hours being paid at a premium rate.

Case study

Continued

> **Box 1 Continued**
>
> Companies including Hallmark Cards provide health and safety equipment and training to homeworkers while assessing their workplaces. The company provides homeworkers with details of complaint mechanisms like that of the Ethical Trading Initiative. These aim to provide a secure channel for workers to express their concerns about working conditions.
>
> The SA8000 labour code, one of the most comprehensive, requires suppliers to make frequent visits to the homes of workers to assess their working conditions. Some labour experts also recommend that companies encourage freedom of association and collective bargaining within homeworker communities.

Poverty is historically seen as the dominant cause of child labour in India. But this view is being increasingly challenged by NGOs such as the MV Foundation, which cites India's incompetently run education system as a principal challenge. Other barriers include bureaucratic hurdles for the poor to access and stay in schools, gender and caste discrimination and, more generally, the absence of a norm that children should not work but be in school.

Such systemic problems, the NGO says, can be overcome when people are confident that their local school is functioning. Today, as a result of the foundation's work, 700 villages in India's Andhra Pradesh state are child-labour-free and 320,000 children have moved from work to school.

Unicef, the United Nations Children's Fund, has collaborated with Ikea to address some of these challenges in the carpet industry of India's Uttar Pradesh state.

Ikea finances Unicef initiatives that aim to improve the educational infrastructure in communities and help children get back to school. Among these are 'alternative learning centres' or 'bridge schools' that aim to help older children who have lost study years through work to catch up with others of their age within 18–24 months. Ikea has invested about $1.5 million over a seven-year period towards these initiatives. Another $270,000 has been dedicated towards various health programmes run by Unicef and the World Health Organization to ensure children do not skip school because of ailments.

Though not bonded labourers per se, most children in Uttar Pradesh's carpet industry are compelled to work in order to repay debts taken by their parents from local moneylenders, usually at exorbitant interest rates.

In an innovative approach to tackling this, Ikea has helped the women in these communities to form self-help groups. These women are encouraged to make small financial savings that they can later use to inter-loan within the community and reduce dependence on local moneylenders. These loans, with support from some nationalised banks, are then used to finance micro-enterprises that in turn help fund children's education.

Ikea's technical team did a study of local skills in the area and found the women to be extremely deft at embroidery. So, the company has now started directly placing orders for cushion covers with these women, without the interference of any middlemen. As a condition of sale, these women must be a part of the self-help community.

While Ikea tackles the issue in its supply chain with the help of Unicef and local groups, members of the tobacco and chocolate industries are attempting to alleviate the problem collectively, with mixed results.

Tobacco moves

Global tobacco giants British American Tobacco, Philip Morris, Imperial Tobacco and Gallagher Group are members of the Eliminating Child Labour in Tobacco-growing Foundation (ECLT), established in 2001, with the help of the ILO and the International Tobacco Growers' Association.

As most tobacco farms are family run, children working on them are not bonded labourers. The first challenge the ECLT Foundation faced was one of awareness raising among the farmers about the need for educating their children.

Following this, the partnership has been involved in building schools and digging wells for farmers in countries including Malawi, Uganda and Tanzania. In a recent move, it has also announced the decision to extend micro-credit to tobacco farmers in Kyrgyzstan at low interest rates. This aims to ensure that some farmers are able to send their children to school rather than keep them on the farms.

The foundation says it is 'engaged in dialogue' with local governments and NGOs in order to 'enlist their support' towards addressing the problem. It has established partners on the ground, it says, to monitor the progress on the various initiatives it funds.

But of the tobacco companies involved in this initiative, only BAT reports on the progress of the foundation's work (at some length) in its annual corporate responsibility report. BAT makes detailed references to commitments towards addressing the problem of child labour in tobacco growing, while the other companies are reticent, publishing little information on targets and real achievements.

Out of the eight ECLT projects currently underway in various countries, BAT has directly run four of these – in Brazil, Mexico, Fiji and Pakistan. Under the programmes run in Brazil, BAT subsidiary Souza Cruz subcontracts to farmers with children only if they produce a declaration of school attendance signed by a teacher or headmaster. Breach of the condition ends the contract.

The role of lobbying

Peter McAllister, executive director of the International Cocoa Initiative funded by chocolate industry members such as Hershey, Mars, Cadbury Schweppes and

Case study

Continued

Nestlé and aimed at tackling child labour, says businesses should engage with governments on the issue. He says companies have an imperative to engage governments if they are not implementing national laws and international conventions on child labour that they have ratified.

McAllister says companies should identify influential NGOs and advocacy groups that could initiate conversations with governments to convince them of the risks of the child labour problem – the risks of business boycotts and the loss of an educated workforce.

He says companies have a range of tools, including staff training resources, database designing capabilities and policy framing skills, that they can offer to governments.

While the support programmes to eradicate child labour are ongoing in the cocoa farms of West Africa, industry-led certification systems that would measure progress and declare farms child-labour-free were not in place by the agreed date of 1 July 2005.

Jeroo Master, a child protection officer at Unicef India, says that if governments were approached through intermediaries such as Unicef or the ILO, officials may be less prone to hostility towards business's suggestions. Master sees the corporate role as 'helping with the capacity-building of government law enforcement mechanisms'.

While the biggest barrier to eliminating child labour remains the enforcement of national labour laws, international trade rules are beginning to factor in the issue of child labour.

Recently the European Parliament called on the European Commission to bring legal action against any European importers found using child labour. Members of the European Parliament also want the commission to make compliance with labour standards, including child labour norms, a condition in its own purchasing and contracting policies. MEPs want the commission to make tackling child labour a permanent element of bilateral trade deals with developing nations.

While the governments of the EU and the US (see Box 2) are looking at ways to tackle the issue via trade rules and political pressure, business clearly has its own important role to play in finding creative solutions to the problem of child labour.

Box 2 US action on child labour

The US has taken some legislative measures to tackle child labour. The Tariff Act of 1930 was amended in 2000 to ensure that the statute that forbids the importation of goods made with forced or indentured labour also applied to goods made with child labour.

According to the Trade and Development Act of 2000, the Office of the United States Trade Representative has to conduct a yearly review to ascertain if countries that receive trade benefits under the act's Generalised System of Preferences are implementing their commitments under the ILO's Convention 182 to eliminate the worst forms of child labour.

The US Trade Act of 2002 directs all US trade negotiators to 'promote respect for worker rights and the rights of children consistent with core labour standards of the ILO'.

Senator Tom Harkin of Iowa, who was instrumental in amending the Trade and Development Act of 2000 to reflect its current position on child labour, is also keen on reintroducing to Congress the draft Child Labour Deterrence Act, stalled back in 1999. If passed, the legislation would prohibit the importation of manufactured and mined goods that are produced by abusive child labour, heavily penalising companies that allowed this.

In a recent report to the US Department of State, Elliot Schrage, writing for the University of Iowa Center for Human Rights, suggested that companies participating in private voluntary initiatives that seek to improve supply chain conditions, such as anti-child-labour programmes, should be given favoured status on trade missions. The report also called for the US government to encourage federal agencies to buy products from companies taking part in private voluntary initiatives that seek to raise labour standards. It also suggested the government ask international financial institutions (IFIs) to require companies participating in IFI-funded projects to participate in qualified private voluntary initiatives as a condition of financing.

(*Source*: Poulomi Saha, and Tobias Webb in London, *Ethical Corporation*, 16 August 2005)

Questions

- Are codes of ethics forbidding suppliers from using child labour sufficient?
- Identify and discuss the best ways to tackle the use of child labour in the supply chain.

10.1   Introduction

Since the early 1990s, firms have increasingly adopted competitive strategies that focus on the core business. These strategies enable the firm to make the most of its core competencies and enjoy greater revenues by outsourcing its non-core activities to locations where the costs of production are low. This strategy also enabled the firm to operate with low investment in fixed assets and working capital, and low operational costs. However, the offloading of non-core activities means that the firm involves, and is dependent on, a large number of suppliers and distributors residing outside its traditional boundaries. For example, in 2004, Nike employed just over 24,000 direct employees located mainly in the USA, but its products were manufactured by over 8,000 suppliers employing around 600,000 workers in fifty-one countries. A large number of those suppliers, most of them located in developing countries, were fully dependent for their existence on Nike. This is because firms, especially large multinational enterprises (MNEs) such as Nike, tend to have exclusive suppliers. Take, for example, the Tae Kwang Vina factory in Vietnam, which employs over 10,000 employees, none of them working directly for Nike, but making only Nike products (Arnold and Bowie, 2003). Without Nike, the firm would not exist. This puts suppliers in developing countries in a weak bargaining situation vis-à-vis large MNEs. The high dependence of suppliers on the firms they supply creates a *respondeat superior* type of relationship between firms and their suppliers. This has led a number of people to argue that Western firms have an inherent responsibility for the actions of their suppliers and a duty towards the people employed by them. The weak bargaining position of suppliers vis-à-vis the main firm is not limited to MNEs and their suppliers in developing countries. In a number of sectors in Western developed countries, suppliers of big firms face the same dynamics. For example, most farmers in Western European countries have very weak bargaining power in their dealings with large supermarkets (Bloom and Perry, 2001). As a result, most large supermarkets deal with suppliers on a 'take it or leave it' basis, forcing them to drive costs down and operate on a very low profit margin.

In addition to the offloading of non-core business, in recent decades we have seen an increasing rate of globalization. As a result of intense competition in Western countries, firms are relying increasingly on international sourcing, in most cases, to reduce costs and sustain their competitiveness (Monczka and Trent, 1991). Most MNEs now have a global value chain through which their activities are dispersed worldwide. This is facilitated by the sharp fall in transportation costs, lower barriers to trade and investment in foreign markets, and significant improvements in information and communication technology (Mellahi *et al.*, 2005). As a result, products are no longer made and consumed within the same geographical area. Even the component parts of a product may, and often do, come from all over the world. Further, the different operations are located where they are more cost-effective and/or efficient. It is very common to find a firm carrying out design and marketing functions in the USA, outsourcing its manufacturing activities to a firm located in China, and outsourcing its after-sales and IT functions to a firm located in India. The global value chain creates longer and more complex supply chains, and thus also changes the requirements within supply chain management.

There has also been growing interest among a wide range of stakeholders, including the media, NGOs, investors and consumers, in how firms manage the ethical implications of increased global sourcing. For example, as firms moved increasingly from domestic to global sourcing, a number of rating agencies started to monitor the ethical and environmental performance of global supply chains. An example here is the General Index developed by Insight Investment and AccountAbility, which screens and scores the performance of major companies listed on the Financial Times and (London) stock Exchange index (FTSE-listed) companies in relation to key supply chain factors. This importance allocated to ethical issues in the supply chain is underpinned by the assumption that the choices firms make in the ways they organize and manage their supply chain are shaped, to a large extent, by the beliefs that managers hold about the importance of ethical practices both inside and outside their firms. Therefore firms could be seen as ethical or unethical based on the way they manage ethical practices within and between their networks of suppliers. As a result, it is now widely accepted that firms are responsible for processes and practices in their own companies as well as in their networks of suppliers and distributors. One could therefore argue that successful supply chain management involves a high level of accountability in managing (un)ethical practices in supply networks. As shown in the opening case study to this chapter, some companies excel at developing and managing an ethical supply chain (Argenti, 2004). This often, but not necessarily, leads to positive relationships among suppliers, producers and distributors, and promotes an ethical image (or at least a non-unethical image) that is crucial for developing and sustaining a competitive brand. As discussed in the case study at the end of Part 2, the key motives behind IKEA's great interest in the ethical behaviour of its upstream supply network are to limit the damage of being associated with unethical behaviour of its suppliers, receive favourable publicity from the ethical management of its supply chain, and develop a strong ethical supply chain network.

The purpose of this chapter is to identify the key ethical areas in supply chain management, to examine their challenges and controversies in terms of managing suppliers and purchasers, and to consider whether unethical management practices anywhere along the supply chain can be altered by the main firm, such that a more proactive ethical role by the firm becomes worthwhile. This chapter is structured as follows. The first section provides brief summary of the concept of supply chain management. The second section gives a general overview of the key ethical areas in supply chain management. The third section examines current ethical issues, focusing on supply chain and unethical work practices, such as child labour and sweat shops.

10.2 Understanding ethical supply chain management

Supply chain management is the oversight of materials, information and finances as they move in a process from supplier to manufacturer to wholesaler to retailer, and finally to the consumer. It involves co-ordinating and integrating these flows both within and among companies. Jayashankar *et al.* (1996) defines a supply chain as 'a network of autonomous or semi-autonomous business entities collectively responsible for procurement, manufacturing, and distribution activities associated with one or more families of related products'. Thus, a network of supply chain can be seen as 'the series of companies, including suppliers, customers, and logistics providers that work together to deliver a value package of goods and services to the end customer' (Maloni and Brown, 2006: 36).

The role of the main firm is to manage the network and facilitates the flow of raw materials and intermediate goods into final products, and oversees their distribution to customers (Lee and Billington, 1995). In brief, supply chain management is the management of the production processes from initial raw materials to the ultimate consumption of the finished product, linking across supplier–user companies. In this sense, the supply chain is the organizational crystallization of real material flows that form the life cycle of the product from the cradle to the grave (Green *et al.*, 2000). When a supply chain cuts across national boundaries, and is primarily concerned with the movement of raw or semi-processed commodities, it is sometimes referred to as a global commodity chain (GCC). GCCs were dealt with in greater depth in Chapter 6.

Supply chain management comprises the business processes that bring a product or service to market, including co-ordination, communication and collaboration among suppliers; manufacturing, materials, transportation and warehouse management; and procurement, distribution, wholesale, and service and sales channels. As firms outsource more parts and services to focus on their own core competencies, they increasingly expect their suppliers to deliver innovative and quality products reliably, on time and at a competitive cost. As a result, managing the supply chain has become an important factor in the quest to achieve sustainable competitive advantage. As noted above, logistics can no longer be narrowly defined from an internally-focused perspective, but from a holistic one, taking the whole supply chain into consideration. But how responsible is the company for those parts of the supply chain that are outside of its physical boundaries? In this chapter, we argue that while it is difficult, maintaining ethical standards throughout the supply chain is an important ethical cornerstone.

The central aim of ethical supply chain management is to have the right products in the right quantities (at the right place) at the right moment at minimal cost, translated into the interrelated issues of customer satisfaction, inventory management and flexibility *within an ethical framework*. Poist (1989), one of the early writers on ethical supply chain management, argued for taking social issues such as employee training, philanthropy, environment, urban renewal, workplace diversity, health and safety, and community issues, in addition to economic matters, into consideration when designing a supply chain. Slack *et al.* (2001) noted that operations management strategies must be ethical, as there are ethical implications in almost every decision in the area of operations management. Arnold and Bowie (2007: 135) argued that 'MNEs' managers have duties, both in their own factories and in their contract factories, to ensure that the dignity of workers is respected.' They added that 'MNEs have distinct duties regarding the employees of their contract factories because of the power they have over the owners and managers of such factories, and because of the substantial resources at their disposal.' This is because, Arnold and Bowie argued,

MNEs typically dictate to their contractors such terms as price, quality, quantity, and date of delivery. This imbalance in power means that they have the ability to either hinder or enhance the ability of contract factory managers to respect employees. For example, if MNE supply chain managers know, or have reason to know, that the factory cannot meet the terms of the contract while adhering to local labour laws, providing safe working conditions, or paying a living wage, then they are properly regarded as partially responsible for those disrespectful practices (p. 137)

10.3   Ethical challenges in supply chain management

This section first outlines the key ethical challenges and problems in supply chain management which may be expected to give rise to conditions where the firm has to expand its governance to maintain an ethical standard throughout the supply chain. The supply chain is made up of a complex network of firms and actors operating outside the boundary of the firm, ranging in the case of the food induxtry from labour and growers to restaurants and consumers (Maloni and Brown, 2006: 38); firms face different ethical issues in different parts of the supply chain.

Below, we discuss the different challenges at the suppliers, manufacturers and distributors levels.

10.3.1   Suppliers: labour conditions issues

To ensure the ethical integrity of their operations, firms must develop and implement an ethical approach to the management of people and labour conditions along the supply chain. The most important ethical challenge for Western firms outsourcing internationally is the maintenance of labour conditions that are legal and acceptable to Western customers. In this chapter we focus on child labour and sweatshops.

10.3.1.1   Child labour

In recent years there has been increasing interest in child labour in the supply chain. According to the International Labour Office (ILO), about 246 million children (aged between 5 and 14) – that is, one in six children – were involved in child labour in 2004, most of them working without any legal or regulatory protection (ILO, 2004). Child labour is hard to define. A research by Understanding Children's Work (UCW) – which runs a joint ILO, World Bank and UNICEF project on child labour – provides different types of work that are regarded as child labour. Figure 10.1 shows that child labour includes, but is not limited to, the involvement of children up to the age of 18 years in dangerous or hazardous work, employing children up to the age of 14 in full-time work and thereby restricting their educational opportunities, and any type of work in the labour market for those under the age of 12.

Up to age 18	Dangerous or hazardous work. Worst forms of child labour.	Full-time work	Part time work in labour market and vocational training	Household work if not interfering with school or health
Up to age 14 or 15 or age of completed compulsory education (if higher)		Full-time work in labour market		
Up to age 12 or 13			Any work in labour market	

Figure 10.1   Definition of child labour in international conventions

Note: Dark areas indicate the work defined as child labour; lighter areas indicate allowable or acceptable work.
Source: Grimsrud (2001).

Child labour is a difficult issue to deal with. Well-known firms such as IKEA, Adidas, Reebok and Gap which in the past were criticized by the media and pressure groups, for alleged violation of labour standards and use of child labour in their supply chain, have recently adopted a 'zero tolerance' strategy for the use of child labour, often in close consultation with their suppliers, combining regular monitoring of suppliers, training the suppliers regarding best labour practices, and providing financial help. The IKEA case shows that firms need to complement compliance strategies focusing simply on policing suppliers with consultative approaches involving suppliers and empowering them to take responsibility for their own workplaces. The task of crafting a 'zero tolerance' strategy for child labour entails answering a series of questions: how to monitor the strategy: how to get suppliers commitment to it: how to help suppliers develop needed competencies and capabilities without relying on child labour: how to respond to social and economic realities that force families to send their children to work: and how to help communities, and especially children, affected by child labour. An effective strategy to tackle child labour also means searching proactively for new or better ways to manage the supply chain. Evidence suggests that the poorer the community from which a firm sources its products and materials, the higher the chance for suppliers to involve child labour, and the more critical the need for its managers to develop strategies to deal with the situation. But as we indicated above, successful strategies for tackling child labour are the product of more than just the main firm's initiatives. Typically, suppliers, communities and NGOs have influential roles in developing and implementing the strategies. IKEA, for example, has a large number of staff whose responsibility is to oversee suppliers' compliance, and provide training and assistance to suppliers with regard to ethical work practices.

10.3.1.2   Sweatshops

Like child labour, sweatshops are very hard to define. Radin and Calkins (2006) argue that while one might recognize a sweatshop when one sees it, sweatshops are slippery and difficult to grasp, and as result it is hard to provide a precise definition for them. Radin and Calkins (2006: 262) describe sweatshops as 'work environments that violate laws and where workers are subject to: Extreme exploitation, including the absence of a living wage or long work hours; Poor working conditions, such as health and safety hazards; Arbitrary discipline, such as verbal or physical abuse; and/or Fear and intimidation when they speak out, organize, or attempt to form a union'. Arnold and Hartman (2006) provide a more precise definition of sweatshops that details the specific types of offences carried out in such factories. They define sweatshops as

> any workplace in which workers are typically subject to two or more of the following conditions: income for a 48 hour workweek less than the overall poverty rate for that country; systematic forced overtime; systematic health and safety risks due to negligence or the wilful disregard of employee welfare; coercion; systematic deception that places workers at risk; and underpayment of earnings.

Although a number of people question the unethicality of sweatshops (see Kristof and WuDunn, 2000; Martinez-Mont, 1996; Solar and Englander, 2007), it is generally accepted that the use of sweatshops is ethically and morally wrong despite the benefits they might bring to the people involved in them and the society in which they are found. Zwolinski (2007) defends the moral legitimacy of sweatshops by pointing to the *voluntary* nature of sweatshop employment by writing that

> They [people working in sweatshops] might not like working in sweatshops, and they might strongly desire that their circumstances were such that they did not have to do so. Nevertheless, the fact that they choose to work in sweatshops is morally significant. Taken seriously, workers' consent to the conditions of their labour should lead us to abandon certain moral objections to sweatshops, and perhaps even to view them as, on net, a good thing.

He argues that MNEs have a morale choice of not benefiting 'workers at all by not outsourcing their labour to workers in the developing world'; or benefiting 'workers to some extent by outsourcing labour to workers in the developing world without meeting the minimum conditions'.

In addition to the voluntary nature of sweatshops, writers who defend sweatshops also refer to their potential benefit, and the lack of alternatives, and argue that governments and NGOs in Western countries ought not to interfere in the issue by, for example, restricting or banning the importation of products made in sweatshop factories (Anderson, 1996). Further, they claim that anti-sweatshop activists such as boycott-sweatshop organization are misguided and may even harm the very people they are trying to help (Kristof and WuDunn, 2000). Zwolinski (2007) provided the following six arguments to defend sweatshops:

- Most sweatshop workers choose to accept the conditions of their employment, even if their choice is made from among a severely constrained set of options.
- The fact that they choose the conditions of their employment from within a constrained set of options is strong evidence that they view it as their most-preferred option (within that set).
- The fact that they view it as their most-preferred option is strong evidence that we will harm them by taking that option away.
- It is also plausible that sweatshop workers' choice to accept the conditions of their employment is sufficiently autonomous that taking the option of sweatshop labour away from them would be a violation of their autonomy.
- All else being equal, it is wrong to harm people or to violate their autonomy.
- Therefore, all else being equal, it is wrong to take away the option of sweatshop labour from workers who would otherwise choose to engage in it.

The anti-sweatshop camp argues that people in sweatshops are treated as means to an end not 'as ends valuable in and of themselves' (Radin and Calkins, 2006: 261). Santoro argues that MNEs

> are morally responsible for the way their suppliers and subcontractors treat their workers. The applicable moral standard is similar to the legal doctrine of *respondeat superior*, according to which a principal is "vicariously liable" or responsible for the acts of its agent conducted in the course of the agency relationship. The classic example of this is the responsibility of employers for the acts of employees. Moreover, ignorance is no excuse. Firms must do whatever is required to become aware of what conditions are like in the factories of suppliers and subcontractors, and thereby be able to assure themselves and others that their business partners don't mistreat those workers to provide a cheaper source of supply. (Quoted in Arnold and Bowie, 2003; from Santoro, 2000)

Furthermore, although people in sweatshop factories supplying MNEs are sometimes paid better than people working for local factories, and therefore one might argue that they are therefore fortunate to have such work, MNEs are *able* to improve working conditions and therefore they *ought* to put pressure on and work with their suppliers to comply with labour laws, improve working conditions, and pay decent wages in their global supply chain. There are many stories and much anecdotal evidence in the popular media about worker abuses in sweatshops. Take, for example, the toy industry. According to Clark (2007) nearly 80 per cent of all toys destined for the US market are manufactured in China under sweatshop conditions. For example, Barbie, a doll that is sold world over and makes over $3.6 billion annually in retail sales, is manufactured in Chinese sweatshops where workers work seven days a week, with an average working day of 11–12 hours and paid pitiful wages (*The Economist*, 2007). Rendon (2007) reported that only 35 cents (28 per cent of the retail price) goes to the Chinese manufacturer, including the cost of labour, for a Chinese-made Barbie which retails for just under $10 ($9.99). Similarly, in Bangladesh, employees in clothing manufacturing firms supplying major Western supermarkets often work 80 hours a week in 'death trap factories' earning as little as 5 pence an hour (*The Director*, 2007). Below are some widely reported examples of sweatshops and unethical working conditions:

- Thai 'slave labourers' sewing fashions for major department stores in the Los Angeles suburb of El Monte.
- Haitian workers earning six cents for every '101 Dalmatians' outfit that Disney sells for $20.
- Children in maquiladoras in Honduras and women in sweatshops in New York City sewing clothes for Wal-Mart's Kathie Lee Gifford label.
- Guess, the highly profitable designer-jeans company, failing to live up to an agreement to stop sweatshop conditions among its contractors in Los Angeles, then firing union supporters and shifting production to Mexico to thwart a union organizational drive.
- The use of child labour in Pakistan in the production of football balls by suppliers for the FIFA (see Cartoon 8).

Radin and Calkins (2006) argued that we should move from asking the question 'What's wrong with sweatshops?' to querying *why* sweatshops continue to exit despite the cruel and inhumane treatment of workers in sweatshop factories and the negative press surrounding them? Radin and Calkins (2006) argued that one of the main reason for the continuation of sweatshops is the absence

Cartoon 8   An Unethical Supply Chain – from 3rd world sweatshops to leisure in the developed world

of a definition of what is a 'sweatshop' and the lack of 'a bright-line distinction between acceptable and unacceptable treatment of workers' which makes it hard to agree on where to draw a line between appropriate and inappropriate work practices. Further, because of the benefits of sweatshops to people who work in them, and to governments and societies that benefit from them, sweatshops receive the approval of the very people anti-sweatshops activists try to defend. As put by Radin and Calkins (2006): 'They [sweatshops] endure because many of the vulnerable and victimized participate in the perpetuation of sweatshops. They do so because, as harmful as sweatshops are, they provide benefits that are not easily found in alternative work places.' Finally, some argue that actions by individuals and NGOs against sweatshops may backfire. In their *New York Times* article, Kristoff and WuDunn (2000) argued that in some cases boycotting not only failed to improve working conditions but led to the closure of the sweatshop and the dismissal of workers whose livelihoods depended on them.

10.3.2   Approaches to managing ethical issues at the suppliers' end

Firms can take one of four approaches in dealing with or managing the ethical conduct of their suppliers. The first form is the *unconcerned* approach. Managers who follow this approach take an, intentionally or unintentionally, immoral stand having no regard for their responsibility towards their suppliers and people who work for or are affected by them. This approach was prevalent in the 1980s, when managers tried to argue that it is not their responsibility to manage operations outside their boundaries, nor their responsibility to enforce ethical standards above and beyond what is legally required in the suppliers' home country. Firms adopting this approach may employ almost any supplier they believe can deliver the goods on time at the right quality and price regardless of their unsavoury unethical practices. Most large firms abandoned this approach under pressure from customers, NGOs and damaging media exposure. For example, when Nike's unethical practices in its overseas suppliers' network was exposed, initially the company declined to take responsibility. However, under persistent pressure from NGOs, the threat of a consumer boycott and significant damage to its brand, Nike made a U-turn and developed and implemented a diligent framework to monitor and assist its suppliers (see Emmelhainz and Adams, 1999; Maloni and Brown, 2006; Zadek, 2004).

The second form is the *damage control* approach. This approach is often adopted by firms that adopt the first approach but react to adverse reports that could tarnish the firm's reputation. Firms adopting this approach often make some window-dressing attempts to show that are doing something about the unethical practices of their suppliers. This include token gestures such as sending suppliers an ethical code of conduct but doing very little to enforce it, and companies are prone to turn a blind eye when suppliers bend the rules. While one might dismiss efforts to control damage arising from unethical practices in the supply chain as merely a public relations exercise, over time such efforts may help the firm to learn about the impact of (un)ethical practices and appreciate the benefits of such practices in the supply chain.

The third approach is *compliance*. Firms adopting this approach take a morale stand towards unethical practices and believe that forceful compliance is the best way to enforce ethical rules in the supply chain. Monitoring overseas suppliers, and enforcing ethical standards, involve three tasks (Emmelhainz and Adams, 1999):

- A 'code of conduct' specifying standards of employee welfare which suppliers are expected to adhere to. The code of ethics should be made visible and be communicated to all affected parties in the supply chain.
- A monitoring system to make sure that suppliers comply with agreed-upon ethical standards. This could take the form of visits, inspections, interviews with employees and so forth. An example of monitoring international suppliers is Cadbury Schweppes. The company conducted detailed consultations with its supply chain partners and other associate or joint venture manufacturers. The aim is to ensure that consistently high standards of human rights and ethical trading are encouraged across all areas from which it derives raw materials.
- Enforcement policies must be established. Marks and Spencer (M&S) (one of the most successful retailers in the UK before it ran into trouble in 1998) was accused in January 1996 by a British TV channel, Granada, in its 'World in Action' programme, of deliberately misleading its customers through labelling its St. Michael own branded products with incorrect country-of-origin stickers. Moreover, it was alleged that M&S had used under aged workers in the production process. M&S put a £1 million action plan by creating a 'hit squad' to audit its suppliers through randomly visiting foreign factories to ensure that they did not employ under-age workers. M&S also wrote to all its suppliers reminding them of the strict code of conduct and service obligations of being a part of M&S supply chain.

The fourth approach is the *embeddedness* approach. Here, ethical practices throughout the supply chain are deeply ingrained in the firm's values and norms. Firms adopting this approach work with suppliers and seek to gain their buy-in to the main firm's ethical standards and values. Firms work with their suppliers to help them observe ethical standards, and suppliers are encouraged and rewarded for embracing them.

10.4   Ethical issues in distribution and purchasing activities

Given the fact that the purchasing and sales functions are boundary-spanning functions, and have a significant influence on how other members of the supply chain network view a firm, ethical attitudes in purchasing and sales are imperative. Furthermore, because sales and purchasing functions are exposed to a firm's external environment, they may be under even greater pressure than other internal functions to deviate from the firm's accepted norms of behaviour (Ferrel and Gresham, 1985).

It is often argued that communicating ethics policies to suppliers effectively may act as a deterrent to purchasing personnel tempted to act in an unethical manner. However, as we have argued throughout this book, behavioural standards, such as a code of ethics, without associated sanctions are really little more than window dressing. Appropriate and enforced sanctions might not only have a positive effect on the behaviour of purchasing personnel, but also serve to demonstrate to those outside purchasing, including suppliers, that the company really cares about ethical practices. Below we discuss two ethical issues in purchasing: conflict of interest, and greening the supply chain.

10.4.1   Purchasing and conflict of interest

Carter (2000) notes that, in the current competitive business environment, pressures to increase sales on the outbound side and to lower costs and improve supplier performance on the inbound side continue to rise. Carter quotes a respondent as saying: 'As companies are pushing for improved performance, people will take greater risks and push the envelope ... the fear of losing your job is great.' Consequently, purchasing managers under strong pressure to deliver may be more likely to engage in unethical practices such as giving bribes, using obscure contract terms or exaggerating the seriousness of a problem when doing business with a supplier, in order to gain price concessions and to meet performance goals and expectations (Carter, 2000). Cooper *et al.* (1997) reported that the three most common ethical violations in purchasing are:

- showing partiality toward suppliers preferred by upper management;
- failure to provide products and services of the highest quality in the eyes of the internal customers; and
- receiving gifts or entertainment that influence, or appear to influence, purchasing decisions.

Handfield and Baumer (2006) listed conflict of interest behaviour as the most contentious issue in ethical purchasing. They noted that

> when an individual is hired by a company as an employee, officer, or member of the board of directors they enter into a fiduciary relationship with the company. At law, the fiduciary duties of employees, officers and directors require them to place the interests of the company above their own personal interests, fully disclose potential conflicts of interest, and abstain from activities that pose, or appear to pose, a conflict of interest. (p. 42)

Conflict of interest in purchasing is defined by the Institute of Supply Management (ISM) as 'any personal business or professional activity that would create a conflict between personal interests and the interests of the employer' (quoted in

Handfield and Baumer, 2006: 42). Handfield and Baumer warned that conflict of interest arise from both actual and perceived behaviours and situations. They argued that most companies define it as activities that are opposed to a firm's interests or gives the *appearance* of impropriety (ibid.).

One of the key activities or practices that give raise to conflict of interest is the giving and acceptance of gifts and gratuities. It has long been recognized that, in business, there is no such thing as a free lunch. In purchasing, it is considered as a device that facilitates preferential treatments for some suppliers and/or buyers (Rudelius and Buchholz, 1979; Turner *et al.*, 1994, 1995), or to put pressure on the buying firm to reciprocate. Turner *et al.* (1994) found that the acceptance of gratuities by purchasing staff is a significant concern of those in the profession as well as of upper management. Acceptance of gifts or gratuities has been forbidden by most professional associations, such as the American National Association of Purchasing Management (NAPM). Consequently, several (mainly large) companies have adopted a proactive attitude and developed a company policy that forbids the acceptance of gratuities and gifts (see NAPM principles below). Cummings (1979) argues, however, that purchasing in many firms continues to be dominated by 'do-as-I-say-not-as-I-do' attitudes. The latter is a result of double standards in several companies as the management often reprimands buyers for accepting gifts or favours from suppliers, yet rewards sales staff for their use of such 'sharp practice' in order to secure new contracts and accounts.

The NAPM Principles and Standards of Purchasing Practice refers to the ethical problems associated with accepting gifts. Here are just two such examples:

- Avoid the intent and appearance of unethical or compromising practice in relationships, actions, and communications.
- Refrain from soliciting or accepting money, loans, credits, or prejudicial discounts, and the acceptance of gifts, entertainment, favours, or services from present or potential suppliers that might influence, or appear to influence, purchasing decisions.

Handfield and Baumer (2006: 48) provided six steps to minimize conflict of interests in purchasing:

1 First, firms need to identify key areas of concerns for conflict of interest. Hot spots for conflict of interest change from one firm to another, and therefore firms need to identify their specific areas of concerns;
2 After identifying the areas of concern, firms need to develop well-defined policies and procedures to deal with them. Firms must provide clear definitions of key terms such as what constitute a gift, bribery, preferential treatment, a trade secret and so forth.
3 The next step is to communicate the policies and procedures throughout the organization and to ensure compliance.

4 The firm should provide top-down support to line managers and supervisors to help them deal with cases of interest.
5 The firm must provide training to help employees identify conflict of interests in purchasing and appropriate behaviour when they arise.
6 The firm should have periodic reviews to update its conflict of interest policy and procedures.

A number of firms developed ethical guidelines and policies to govern unethical behaviour in purchasing decisions. Below is an extract from General Motors' ethical policy in purchasing decisions.

GM's policy covering gifts, entertainment and other gratuities from suppliers

Both as a matter of sound procurement practice and basic business integrity, we at General Motors must make our purchase decisions solely on the basis of which suppliers offer General Motors the best value for the goods and services we need. We should avoid doing anything that suggests our purchase decisions may be influenced by any irrelevant or improper consideration, whether illegal, such as a kickback or bribe, or technically legal, such as personal friendship, favours, gifts or entertainment.

Consequently, it is General Motors policy that no General Motors employee accepts any gift, entertainment or other gratuity from any supplier to General Motors or bidder for General Motors business, including supplier units which are part of General Motors. This policy applies to all employees whether or not they are directly involved in purchasing activities.

There may be rare circumstances where to refuse a gift conceivably could be against General Motors' legitimate business interests, particularly in those countries where gift giving is simply an expected social courtesy and is not intended to corrupt or influence a particular purchase decision. There inevitably will be gray areas or situations where the applicability of this policy may not be immediately apparent. For example, very inexpensive mementos, such as 'logo' pens, cups, caps, or other similar items of nominal value, may be accepted subject to any more stringent policy which your business unit may adopt.

To help in interpreting this policy, several illustrations of its application to hypothetical fact situations are attached. In the final analysis, however, the best course is to decline any gift, entertainment or other gratuity from a supplier to General Motors. Any questionable situation should be discussed with your supervisor to determine how best to handle it. If there is a reason for you ever to accept a particular gift of any real value, it should be reported to your management and the gift always must be turned over to the Corporation for display, use or other appropriate disposition.

(Smith and Rothenberg, 1996)

10.5   Greening the supply chain

The topic of ethics and the environment was discussed in Chapter 4, and therefore this section focuses on issues related to the supply chain only. Greening the supply chain management consists of the involvement of purchasing and supply in activities that include reduction, recycling, reuse and the substitution of materials. It includes the examination of how intra- and inter-organizational factors both drive and constrain suppliers' and purchasers' involvement in supply chain activity. In simple terms, when a company imposes environmental conditions on the products and processes of its suppliers, it is called 'greening the supply chain'. As discussed in Chapter 4, companies cannot ignore environmental issues. Further, environmental standards should be met throughout the whole supply chain. The greening of the supply chain, however, poses several problems and challenges (Walton *et al.*, 1998). Many companies have developed screening protocols for their suppliers that probe deeply into their internal management and engineering practices. Others have been more aggressive and have incorporated environmental criteria into their procurement specifications. For example, Hewlett Packard has developed a quantitative supplier rating system that takes into account their environmental improvement policies and implementation plans, as well as their elimination of ozone-depleting substances. The key challenge is how to make the vendors and sellers abide by the same internal ethical standards?

10.5.1   The case of Nike

Nike has made environment performance a priority, reaching out beyond Nike-owned facilities to include manufacturing partners, suppliers and material vendors. In an effort to green its supply chain, in February 1993, the Nike Environmental Action Team (NEAT) developed out of Nike's efforts to coordinate specific environmental efforts around the world in the context of its business practices. NEAT's mission was to develop answers to the problems that Nike's business – and the sports industry as a whole – poses to the environment. Nike actively seeks partnership with ecologically-responsible suppliers who have made a commitment to sound business practices. Facilities not meeting Nike's environmental business standards are offered assistance through NEAT representatives.

To help track its contractors' progress in reducing pollution, Nike supplies all chemical vendors, equipment suppliers and manufacturers with an educational programme which includes an overview of Nike's objectives; its corporate environmental policy; a master substances list; legislation concerning products and packaging; executive summaries on all programmes so that factories/vendors know which ones apply to them; a sustainability assessment; and labour practices programme information. In addition, Nike has developed a programme for the Management of Environmental Safety and Health (MESH), to help its manufacturing partners develop objectives and targets to reduce and eliminate environmental impacts.

Nike's objectives include its efforts to:

- Integrate principles of sustainability into all major business decisions.
- Scrutinize its environmental impacts in its day-to-day operations and throughout every stage of the product life cycle.
- Design and develop products, materials and technologies according to the fundamental principles of sustainability.
- Promote Nike's practices throughout the supply chain and seek business partnerships with suppliers who operate in a manner consistent with Nike's values.
- Educate its employees, customers and business partners to support its goal of achieving sustainability.
- Turn awareness into action by integrating environmental responsibility into job responsibility.

Nike's efforts have been emulated by many other leading firms operating in a wide range of different sectors. Ironically, despite evidence of good practice in the environmental area, Nike has had to contend with allegations that at least one key South East Asian subcontractor has made use of sweatshop labour.

10.6   Conclusion

This chapter discusses the key ethical issues in the management of the supply chain. Nowadays, organizations focus on their core business and outsource non-core activities to suppliers and service providers around the world. We argued in this chapter that, while outsourced activities are outside the traditional physical boundary of the firm, firms are responsible for (un)ethical practices throughout the supply chain. Given the fact that partners in the supply chain are often outside the reach of corporate governance, ethics in supply chain management poses an additional challenge. The conflictual element inherent in the relationship between firms and their suppliers needs to be recognized and dealt with. At the suppliers' end, firms have to help their suppliers eliminate the use of child labour and sweatshops. While a number of scholars and commentators defend the use of sweatshops and child labour, we argued in this chapter that while one recognizes the potential benefits of such practices for people involved in, or affected by, them, large MNEs are able to assist their suppliers and communities in which they are embedded, and therefore they should work with their suppliers to ensure that products are sourced ethically. Firms face different ethical challenges at the purchasing end of the supply chain. Two key challenges are discussed in the chapter: conflict of interest and, in particular, the giving and accepting of gifts (bribery) and the greening of the supply chain. We argued that firms should be consistent in their ethical practices. Firms should not, for example, forbid their buyers from accepting gifts and gratuities that could influence their decisions, yet reward their sales department for doing exactly the same. In brief, the key argument of the chapter is that firms should not wash their hands of any unethical actions by their suppliers and distributors. Given the changing relationship of suppliers and distributors, with increasing amounts of collaboration and information sharing, where suppliers and distributors are becoming partners in the production process, firms have to be responsible for the behaviour of their suppliers and distributors.

Discussion questions

- Discuss the extent to which multinationals are responsible for the unethical behaviour of their suppliers?
- Are sweatshops really as bad as people in the West think they are?

Case study

Closing case study

Jonah Peretti's Nike media adventure

The email correspondence below took place between Jonah Peretti – a graduate student at the Massachusetts Institute of Technology (MIT), and representatives of Nike's 'personalize' service.

Nike offered customers the opportunity to have their own message or phrase sewn on to a pair of trainers (without wishing to sound like a 'plug', this service is still available on a range of Nike products; see http://nikeid.nike.com/). Peretti contacted Nike to ask for a simple message to be put on to a pair of trainers, but they declined. The personalized message that Peretti requested was the word 'SWEATSHOP.' The resulting exchange has been posted on dozens of websites and was circulated to an estimated 5,000,000 people by email. Both Peretti and spokespeople from Nike have confirmed that this exchange actually took place, and we have reproduced it in full with some minor editing to improve readability. You can learn more about it on the following sites: http://urbanlegends.about.com/library/blnike.htm; http://shey.net/niked.html; http://msbehaviour.blogspot.com/2005/04/nike-admits-worker-abuse-i-never.html.

From: Personalize, NIKE iD
To: Jonah H. Peretti

Subject: RE: Your NIKE iD order no 16468000

Your NIKE iD order was cancelled for one or more of the following reasons.
1) Your Personal iD contains another party's trademark or other intellectual property.
2) Your Personal iD contains the name of an athlete or team we do not have the legal right to use.

Case study

Continued

3) Your Personal iD was left blank. Did you not want any personalization?
4) Your Personal iD contains profanity or inappropriate slang.
   If you wish to reorder your NIKE iD product with a new personalization please visit us again at www.nike.com.

Thank you,
NIKE iD

From: Jonah H. Peretti
To: Personalize, NIKE iD

Subject: RE: Your NIKE iD order no 16468000

Greetings,
My order was cancelled but my personal NIKE iD does not violate any of the criteria outlined in your message. The Personal iD on my custom ZOOM XC USA running shoes was the word 'sweatshop.' Sweatshop is not: 1) anothers party's trademark, 2) the name of an athlete, 3) blank, or 4) profanity. I choose the iD because I wanted to remember the toil and labour of the children that made my shoes. Could you please ship them to me immediately?

Thanks and Happy New Year,
Jonah Peretti

From: Personalize, NIKE iD
To: Jonah H. Peretti

Subject: RE: Your NIKE iD order no 16468000

Dear NIKE iD Customer,
Your NIKE iD order was cancelled because the iD you have chosen contains, as stated in the previous e-mail correspondence, 'inappropriate slang'. If you wish to reorder your NIKE iD product with a new personalization please visit us again at www.nike.com.

Thank you,
NIKE iD

From: Jonah H. Peretti
To: Personalize, NIKE iD

Subject: RE: Your NIKE iD order no 16468000

Dear NIKE iD,
Thank you for your quick response to my inquiry about my custom ZOOM XC USA running shoes. Although I commend you for your prompt customer service, I disagree with the claim that my personal iD was inappropriate slang. After consulting Webster's Dictionary, I discovered that 'sweatshop' is in fact part of standard English, and not slang. The word means: 'a shop or factory in which workers are employed for long hours at low wages and under unhealthy conditions' and its origin dates from 1892. So my personal iD does meet the criteria detailed in your first email.

Your web site advertises that the NIKE iD program is 'about freedom to choose and freedom to express who you are'. I share Nike's love of freedom and personal expression. The site also says that 'If you want it done right... build it yourself'. I was thrilled to be able to build my own shoes, and my personal iD was offered as a small token of appreciation for the sweatshop workers poised to help me realize my vision. I hope that you will value my freedom of expression and reconsider your decision to reject my order.

Thank you,
Jonah Peretti

From: Personalize, NIKE iD
To: Jonah H. Peretti

Subject: RE: Your NIKE iD order no16468000

Dear NIKE iD Customer,
Regarding the rules for personalization it also states on the NIKE iD web site that 'Nike reserves the right to cancel any Personal iD up to 24 hours after it has been submitted'. In addition it further explains: 'While we honour most personal iDs, we cannot honour every one. Some may be (or contain) other trademarks, or the names of certain professional sports teams, athletes or celebrities that Nike does not have the right to use. Others may contain material that we consider inappropriate or simply do not want to place on our products.'

Unfortunately, at times this obliges us to decline personal iDs that may otherwise seem unobjectionable. In any event, we will let you know if we decline your personal iD, and we will offer you the chance to submit another.

With these rules in mind we cannot accept your order as submitted.

If you wish to reorder your NIKE iD product with a new personalization please visit us again at www.nike.com

Thank you,
NIKE iD

Case study

Continued

From: Jonah H. Peretti
To: Personalize, NIKE iD

Subject: RE: Your NIKE iD order no 16468000

Dear NIKE iD,
Thank you for the time and energy you have spent on my request. I have decided to order the shoes with a different iD, but I would like to make one small request. Could you please send me a colour snapshot of the ten-year-old Vietnamese girl who makes my shoes?

Thanks,
Jonah Peretti
[There was no response to this last request]

The website shey.net (referenced above) gives an interesting chronology of subsequent events, which included the manufacture and sales of the slogan 'sweatshop' through other manufacturers. One could argue that Peretti is brilliantly pointing out the hypocrisy of Nike – which seems to pay lip service to freedom, but curtails that freedom if it's considered likely to damage Nike's image. Alternatively, you could argue that Nike is one of the more ethical companies when it comes to managing the supply chain, and that some of the correspondence between Peretti and Nike's representatives is misrepresentative – Nike certainly does not allow its suppliers to use ten-year-old girls, for example. In an article entitled 'My Nike Media Adventure', Peretti set out his reflections on the experience. Writing in the weekly US periodical *The Nation* in April 2001, Peretti himself stated that, 'My guess is that in the long run this episode will have a larger impact on how people think about media than how they think about Nike and sweatshop labor. This larger lesson suggests an exciting opportunity for activists. The dynamics of decentralized distribution systems and peer-to-peer networks are as counterintuitive as they are powerful. By understanding these dynamics, new forms of social protest become possible, with the potential to challenge some of the constellations of power traditionally supported by the mass media' (http://www.thenation.com/doc/20010409/peretti). His commentary suggests that, as well as a global supply chain in the manufacture of products, there are complex dynamics involved in protest in our globalized world.

Questions

- Is Nike justified in refusing Peretti's request?
- What would be the implications of Nike agreeing to it?

References

Anderson, W. 1996. 'Kathie Lee's Children', *The Free Market*, 149.

Argenti, P. A. 2004. 'Collaborating with Activists: How Starbucks Works with NGOs', *California Management Review*, 471: 91–116.

Arnold, D. G. and Bowie, N. E. 2003. 'Sweatshops and Respect for Persons', *Business Ethics Quarterly*, 13,2: 221–42.

Arnold, D. G. and Bowie, N. E. 2007. 'Respect for Workers in Global Supply Chains: Advancing the Debate Over Sweatshops', *Business Ethics Quarterly*, 17,1: 135–45.

Arnold, D. G. and Hartman, L. P. 2003. 'Worker Rights and Low Wage Industrialization: How to Avoid Sweatshops', *Human Rights Quarterly*, 28,3: 676–700.

Arnold, D. G. and Hartman, L. P. 2005. 'Beyond Sweatshops: Positive Deviancy and Global Labour Practices', *Business Ethics: A European Review*, 143: 206–22.

Arnold, D. G. and Hartman, L. P. 2006. 'Worker Rights and Low Wage Industrialization: How to Avoid Sweatshops', *Human Rights Quarterly*, 28,3: 676–700.

Bloom, P. N. and Perry, V. G. 2001. 'Retailer Power and Supplier Welfare: The Case of Wal-Mart', *Journal of Retailing*, 773: 379–96.

Carter, C. 2000. 'Precursors of Unethical Behavior in Global Supplier Management', *Journal of Supply Chain Management*, 361: 45–56.

Clark, E. 2007. *'The Real Toy Story: Inside the Ruthless Battle for America's Youngest Consumers'*. New York: Free Press.

Cooper, R. W., Frank, G. L. and Kemp, R. A. 1997. 'The Ethical Environment Facing the Profession of Purchasing and Materials Management', *International Journal of Purchasing and Materials Management*, 332: 2–11.

Cummings, G. E. 1979. 'Are Purchasing Ethics Being Put to the Test!', *Iron Age*, 222: 21–4.

Denis, G. A. and Bowie, E. N. 2003. 'Sweatshops and Respect for Persons', *Business Ethics Quarterly*, 132: 221–42.

Denis, G. A. and Hartman, P. L. 2003. 'Moral Imagination and the Future of Sweatshops', *Business and Society Review*, 108,4: 425–61.

Denis, G. A. and Hartman, P. H. 2006. 'Worker Rights and Low Wage Industrialization: How to Avoid Sweatshops', *Human Rights Quarterly*, 283: 676–700.

Director, The. 2007. 'Stitched Up', *The Director*, 60,8: 52–4.

Economist, The. 2007. 'The Tale of Barbie and Li Mei', *The Economist*, 383,8527: 105.

Emmelhainz, A. M. and Adams, R. J. 1999. 'The Apparel Industry Response to Sweatshop Concerns: A Review and Analysis of Codes of Conduct', *Journal of Supply Chain Management*, 353: 51–7.

Ferrel, O. C. and Gresham, L. G. 1985. 'A Contingency Framework for Understanding Ethical Decision-Making in Marketing', *Journal of Marketing*, 49: 87–96.

Green, K., Morton, B. and New, S. 2000. 'Greening Organizations', *Organization & Environment*, 132: 206–25.

Grimsrud, B. 2001. 'Developing New Strategies for Understanding Children's Work and Its Impact: A Comparison of Survey Instruments for Collecting Data on Child Labour', *Understanding Children's Work* (UCW). Available at: http://www.ucw-project.org/pdf/publications/comparison_survey_instruments.pdf; accessed6 September 2007.

Handfield, B. R. and Baumer, L. D. 2006. 'Managing Conflict of Interest Issues in Purchasing', *The Journal of Supply Chain Management*, 42,3, 41–50.

Hartman, L. P., Arnold, D. G., and Wokutch, R. E. 2003. *Rising above Sweatshops: Innovative Approaches to Global Labor Challenges*. Westport, Conn.: Greenwood Press.

ILO (International Labour Organization). 2004. 'Facts on Child Labour'. Available at: http://www.ilo.org/public/english/bureau/inf/download/child/childday04.pdf; accessed 6 September 2007.

Kristof, N. D. and WuDunn, S. 2000. 'Two Cheers for Sweatshops', *The New York Times*, 24 September.

Lee, H. L. and Billington, C.1995. 'The Evolution of Supply Chain Management Models and Practice at Hewlett-Packard', *Interfaces*, 255: 42–63.

Maloni, J. M. and Brown, E. M. 2006. 'Corporate Social Responsibility in the Supply Chain: An Application in the Food Industry', *Journal of Business Ethics*, 681: 35–52.

Martinez-Mont, L. 1996. 'Sweatshops Are Better Than No Shops', *Wall Street Journal*, 25 June.

Mellahi, K., Frynas, G. and Finlay, P. 2005. *Global Strategic Management*. Oxford University Press.

Monczka, R. M. and Trent, R. J. 1991. 'Global Sourcing; A Development Approach', *International Journal of Purchasing and Materials Management*, 27,2: 2–8.

Poist, R. F. 1989. 'Evolution of Conceptual Approaches to the Design of Logistics Systems: A Sequel', *Transportation Journal*, 283: 35–9.

Radin, J. T. and Calkins, M. 2006. 'The Struggle Against Sweatshops: Moving Toward Responsible Global Business', *Journal of Business Ethics*, 662/3: 261–72.

Rendon, P.-M. 2007. 'Child's Play', *Marketing*, 112,16: 23–4.

Rudelius, W. and Buchholz, R. A. 1979. 'Ethical Problems of Purchasing Managers', *Harvard Business Review*, 57: 11–14.

Santoro, M. A. 2000. *Profits and Principles: Global Capitalism and Human Rights in China*. Ithaca, NY: Cornell University Press, p. 161.

Slack, N., Chambers, S., Harland, C., Harrison, A. and Johnston, R. 1995. *Operations Management*. London: Pitman.

Smith, D. C. and Rothenberg, A. 1996. 'A New Look at Ethics', *Ward's AutoWorld*, 1 August. Available at: http://wardsautoworld.com/ar/auto_new_look_ethics/; accessed 13 November 2009).

Solar, G. G. and Englander, F. 2007. 'Sweatshops: Kant and Consequences', *Business Ethics Quarterly*, January, 17,1: 115–33.

Swaminathan, J. M., Smith, S. F. and Sadeh, N. M. 1996. *A Multi Agent Framework for Modeling Supply Chain Dynamics*. Technical Report, The Robotics Institute, Carnegie Mellon University, Pittsburgh, Pa.

Turner, G. B., Taylor, G. S. and Hartley, M. F. 1994. 'Ethics Policies and Gratuity Acceptance by Purchasers', *International Journal of Purchasing and Material Management*, Summer, 30,3: 43–7.

Turner, G. B., Taylor, G. S and Hartley, M. F. 1995. 'Ethics, Gratuities, and Professionalisation of the Purchasing Function', *Journal of Business Ethics*, 149: 751–60.

Walton, S.V., Handfield, R. B. and Melnyk, S. A. 1998. 'The Green Supply Chain: Integrating Suppliers into Environmental Management Processes', *International Journal of Purchasing and Materials Management*, 342: 2–11.

Zadek, S. 2004. 'The Path to Corporate Responsibility', *Harvard Business Review*, 8212, 125–32.

Zwolinski, M. 2007. 'Sweatshops, Choice, and Exploitation', *Business Ethics Quarterly*, 17,4: 689–727.

Conclusion

Case study

Introductory case study

Samsung faces local difficulty

In November 2007, Kim Yong-chul, a lawyer working for Samsung, alleged that the firm engaged in regular bribery of government officials and politicians, and that he had personally taken part in the creation of a 7 trillion won ($7.5 billion) slush fund. The latter allegedly included money siphoned from subsidiaries, and hidden in a number of bank and stock accounts held in the names of various executives. Kim was forced to turn to the Catholic Priests' Association for Justice (CPAJ), who have supported him in seeking to publicize – and ensure action is taken as a result of – his allegations, after battling to attract media interest. This led to an independent investigation into the matter, which included allegations that then President Roh Moohyun took money from Samsung – as a form of 'congratulations' – when he was elected President in 2002.

Shortly thereafter, a presidential aid alleged that the company tried to bribe him as well. President Roh initially opposed any investigation of the firm, before giving way in response to pressure from the National Assembly.

These developments – only one of a number involving Korea's *chaebols* (large firms) – sparked off major debates as to whether Korea should hold its companies to global standards, or leave them alone, given their contribution to the growth of the country. In the end, the Samsung Group Chairman at the time, Lee Kun-hee, was convicted of tax evasion, but given only a suspended sentence. Prosecutors in Korea claimed a firmer line towards Lee would 'cause enormous disruptions...negative repercussions on our economy would be very big amid the extremely competitive global economic situation'. The conglomerate was cleared of bribery allegations.

(*Source*: Adapted from 'Dirty Laundry – World-bestriding Samsung Faces a Little Local Difficulty', *The Economist*, 29 November 2007.)

Questions

- It is often argued that, given the strong link between governments and big business, paying bribes is a fact of business life. Can there be any ethical justification for such an argument?
- What do you think are the ethical concerns associated with a government heavily supporting a big business group such as Samsung in a global economy?

There is little doubt that contemporary managers are faced with a vast range of ethical dilemmas. *Inter alia*, some of the most pressing questions fall into four broad areas: relations with employees; relations with the community; environmental issues; and the consequences of globalization. Let us examine each of these in turn.

11.1   Relations with employees

Firstly, in an age of flexibility and downsizing, the psychological contract between employee and firm has been greatly weakened. Jobs are no longer for life; conversely, firms can no longer expect the same degree of loyalty from employees. Moreover, there has been an increasing divergence between managerial and employee pay; the latter has tended to stagnate, ostensibly to ensure greater competitiveness and to reduce inflation (but also reflecting the reduced bargaining power of employee collectives). In contrast, in many industries (ranging from transport to higher education), managerial pay has increased exponentially, ostensibly to secure the services of the most capable. In practice, however, the relationship between managerial pay and performance seems, in many cases, extremely tenuous or non-existent. This raises a fundamental question, 'What remaining responsibilities do managers have towards their workforces'? Is it simply to ensure the continued survival of the firm, or is it to seek to reward all members of the organization fairly for the effort they expend? The latter may be justifiable in terms of a business case over the long term (it may lead to the creation of a loyal, productive and committed workforce). It can also be justified by an ethical case – because of a perceived moral obligation that managers may have towards their subordinates.

Whatever one's views on the matter, it is clear that the 'social question' within the firm has returned to the agenda. Cavalier managers of semi-moribund firms who have increased their pay to the brink of looting are being increasingly 'named and shamed' in the media. This happens even if the formal mechanisms for holding them to account are very much weaker in a globalized world. The weakening of these mechanisms is partly a consequence of global capitalism, but it also reflects both the product of over two decades of union decline (although there are signs of a limited recovery), and the reluctance of governments to take effective action, even in the case of organizations that are heavily subsidized by the state.

11.2   Relations with the community

Second, and related to the first of our four broad areas, we need to consider relations between managers and communities. The concept of 'stakeholder' has gained increasing popularity. Even if managerial notions of accountability to the workforce have seemingly diminished since the early 1970s, there are increasing pressures to be accountable to a range of other players. More specifically, community organizations have proved to be highly effective in bringing firms to account: examples would include the role of Greenpeace in forcing Shell to review the scuttling of a redundant oil rig: and a coalition of organizations forcing Nike to review its labour practices in South East Asia.

The rise of broadly-based community organizations – in part, a reflection of increased disillusionment with formal political processes – has resulted in a very real broadening of the discourse of management. Firms that fail to take into account the needs of key stakeholders – above all, the communities that will be most affected by its actions – face a range of pressures, from adverse publicity to fully-fledged consumer boycotts. However, it could be argued that firms also have a moral obligation to take into account those who have a direct or indirect interest in its activities. In other words, firms should take into account the interests of legitimate stakeholders irrespective of their capacity to make life difficult for management.

11.3   Environmental issues

Third, there is the question of the physical environment. The consequences of large-scale environmental degradation have become increasingly visible. These range from increasing global warming to the destruction of the ozone layer. There is a growing consensus around the need to take environmental issues more seriously, albeit that this has largely been prompted by concerns about health. Moreover, the deep ecology view, once the preserve of radical environmentalists, has now largely become mainstream. It is recognized that not just individual species need to be preserved, or specific cases of environmental degradation halted, but rather that entire ecosystems need to be conserved for both present and future generations. There has also been a growing recognition of the basic rights of all sentient beings: this has been reflected in increasing legal restrictions on animal experimentation and on farming practices.

While the conservative 'hard green' school, which sees the environment in terms of resources to be exploited for the primary benefit of humanity, remains influential – most notably in US governmental circles under the generally unmissed Bush II administration – but even here this position has been modified to take on board a broader range of concerns. There is little doubt that contemporary managers have to accord more attention to environmental issues than was the case a generation ago. This would reflect both consumer pressures and increased legislative strictures. However, while firms retain the option of regime shopping – and of relocating 'messy practices' to Third-World states, where both laws and civil society may be weaker – environmental issues have also permeated the core of ethical debates. In the past, environmental issues were firmly subordinated to the need to ensure human progress, but today conservation is seen as an inherent characteristic of sustainable development and growth.

11.4   Consequences of globalization

Finally, in what is related to each of the other areas there are the ethical dilemmas posed by globalization. As noted earlier in this volume, globalization is an extremely loose term, but it can be taken to encompass the integration of markets (and of consumer taste), rapid technological advance and interchange, and increasingly mobile financial capital. Firms are progressively more able to transfer operations between different national hosts, in search of less strict regulatory regimes, or simply to source cheaper labour. It can be argued that a little development is better than none, and that poor regions may benefit from such a process. However, in practice, it may exact unacceptable social costs, both to 'loser' regions and states who face capital flight, and, ultimately, to 'beneficiary' communities if the price is the wanton destruction of natural resources and massive social dislocation. Moreover, while free trade may open up new opportunities, it may also result in distorted pricing, entrenching the dominance of end-users in global commodity chains, with the producers of raw materials receiving only a tiny percentage of the end value. Again, these developments have led to a broadening of the ethical discourse: issues including fair trade (more specifically, 'fair' prices for primary commodities, most commonly foodstuffs) and global labour standards have increasingly become mainstream. Firms, however, retain the choice of becoming proactive in this area, or simply adjusting their behaviour when impelled to by consumer pressure and/or legislation in their 'home nation'. Regrettably, actions by firms often appear as reluctant responses to external pressures, rather than proactive efforts to ensure better labour standards and fairer trade.

The ethical dilemmas facing the transnational corporations are particularly pronounced. As noted earlier, there is often considerable variation in laws and enforcement between provinces, states, regions and continents. Moreover, transnationals are faced with the task of transferring what are often socially specific moral norms into a global context. However, contemporary theorists such as Singer (1995) note that ethics are universal. For example, to utilitarians, there is a set of behaviours that will, within a specific social context, increase overall happiness or diminish it; for deontologists, there is a set of behaviours that is objectively desirable and we would like to be at the receiving end of it outcomes. While the choice of philosophical tools may differ, managers of transnationals cannot escape ethical questions as easily as they may escape specific regulatory regimes; in a globalizing world, consumer pressure and the compass of transnational institutions cuts across national boundaries.

11.5   Corporate social responsibility

This brings us to the broad question of corporate social responsibility (CSR). This concerns businesses taking into account the socio-political and environmental impact of their activities, the monitoring of this process, and the promotion of best practice. As such, CSR links together a number of areas, such as marketing, environmental management, relations with stakeholders and so on, under a broad umbrella. CSR can become a component of overall organizational strategy, and, has indeed, in some notable cases, done so. Central to CSR is the notion of voluntarism – it is not about firms doing the right thing because they are legally obliged to do so, but rather because they choose do so, either of their own volition, or because they are encouraged by relevant government departments or NGOs that actively promote CSR agendas. CSR has become rather fashionable in recent years, with many firms seeking actively to highlight their policies, and to promote CSR guidelines and codes. The study and dissemination of CSR best (and worst) practice has also become increasingly popular. The coming of age of CSR would reflect a growing awareness of the environment, and the implications of trade with the developing world. However, while there is much that is positive about the CSR revolution, any effort to promote best practice on a voluntary basis remains just that, with an often uneven take up, and with CSR codes and policies in some cases coexisting with 'hidden' bad practices. And, like corporate social philanthropy, it can be used as a means of enhancing the image of the company, with CSR initiatives being the 'gift' of management, and on the latter's terms. A good test of how ethical an organization really is, is the depth and consequences of its CSR policies: is it simply 'window dressing' or really being responsible at the levels of both strategy and action?

11.6   Doing the right thing: philosophy and practice

To the bulk of philosophical perspectives on ethics, 'good' behaviour matters; it is, quite simply, desirable to do the 'right' thing. Even the seemingly relativist postmodern tradition, with its emphasis on the multifaceted power struggles that ravage organizations and society, does accord specific attention to the potentially undesirable consequences of domination and subordination. An argument might be made for moral relativism – that is, what is desirable for one society may be undesirable for another, but it can be argued that some actions are ethical and others not, regardless of the social context. In other words, some actions may result in the worsening of the human condition – and indeed, that of the entire biosphere – and some actions may result in an improvement. While the consequences of specific actions may be both seen and unforeseen, this does not absolve actors from the need to consider ethical issues. With the possible exception of the radical rights-based approach, with its belief that individual rights are paramount, and that regulation should be minimal so that these rights are not jeopardized, it is evident that philosophers are united in their belief that upholding ethical behaviour is a worthwhile end in itself. Indeed, ethical conduct should be seen as distinct from any other goals, such as the pursuit of profits.

This brings us to the question of unintended consequences. If an action has a positive outcome but was prompted by other motives – such as consumer pressures – is it ethical at all? This question is a particularly pressing one in advanced societies. Firms are under increasing pressure to be seen to act ethically in a range of areas, from environmental policies to marketing practices. To utilitarians, all actions that produce desirable outcomes (an increase in overall happiness) are ethical; there is little point in dissecting the rationale of key players. To deontologists and virtue theorists, actions are only ethical if they are prompted for the right reasons. In other words, by focusing only on outcomes, utilitarians can free managers and others from firmly placing their behaviour on a moral foundation (whether the latter is the product of rules or simply cultivated virtues). To the authors, there is merit in each of these perspectives. However, we do believe that increasing external pressures on firms to be *seen* to act ethically should not absolve managers from the responsibility to take ethical issues seriously for their own sake. In other words, managers should seek to infuse an ethical dimension into their actions, even in areas where popular scrutiny or market pressure may be slight. Decision-making should encompass an ethical dimension, even if it is simply an ad-hoc utilitarian cost–benefit analysis, but with these variables being seen in both financial *and* 'overall condition' terms.

But, if managers *should* act ethically, must they, under certain circumstances, be compelled to do so? The authors believe that, under certain circumstances, ethics are too serious a business to be left purely to managers. We share with Adam Smith a belief in the importance of co-operation and trust, and the indispensability of a basic degree of social solidarity, a belief Smith expounds at great length in his *Theory of Moral Sentiments*, but also touches on in *The Wealth of Nations*.

It has been argued that the distinction between unethical and ethical behaviour may simply be one between short- and long-termism. In other words, by acting ethically, firms are securing their long-term survival, wisely husbanding both their resources and those of the external environment to which it has access. In contrast, the 'unethical' short-termist will engage in behaviour that constitutes little more than 'slash and burn capitalism'. A proliferation of unethical short-termists would lead to a society where future living was jeopardized by the wanton destruction of natural resources. It would be a place with business activity being both a source of potential wealth to a few, but also the source of misery to many in surrounding communities. Business people simply have the choice of being 'rude and ignorant farmers' relentlessly squandering resources and goodwill to their ultimate ruin or 'skilled and scientific farmers' who act in such a manner as to ensure their own survival and the prosperity of the community at large (see Hobson, 1902).

While it could be argued that 'good farmers' will ultimately drive out 'bad', this discounts the perennial free-rider problem. In unrestrained free markets, firms can often seize a short-term advantage by acting unscrupulously. For example, the global dominance of Far Eastern textiles manufactures was partially built on extremely repressive labour policies and uncontrolled pollution. The same could be said for many 'respectable firms' operating in the West, if their activities a century ago are considered. However, the argument that 'robber barons' will ultimately seek respectability – that firms will inevitably clean up their acts, once their dominance has been secured, in order to promote stability within their sphere of operations – does not always hold water. Entire industries continue to be characterized by unethical practices, 'bad' firms often do drive out 'good' ones, while the elimination of excess in mature societies has often contributed directly to their reappearance on the periphery.

It can be further argued that the unethical/short-term–ethical/long-term distinction is unnecessarily crude. We have seen that unethical behaviour can, in some cases, pay, certainly over the medium term, and possibly also over the long term. Conversely, firms may seize a short-term advantage over competitors as a result of favourable publicity engendered by ethical behaviour. Even in a phase of aggressive growth, firms may benefit from being seen to be acting ethically, an example being the rise of the Body Shop chain of cosmetic stores in the United Kingdom. Moreover, an emphasis on the long-term does not absolve managers from very real ethical responsibilities. Fundamentally we also need to acknowledge the problem that the 'business case' for ethical behaviour is an amoral one – based on the profit motive. So, in an important sense, using this kind of justification for ethical behaviour is incoherent. The phrase 'good ethics is good business' is in fact a bribe to induce ethical behaviour – a bizarre paradox lying at the heart of much of contemporary 'business ethics'.

What, then, is to be done? To the authors, an important starting point is that institutions matter. The effects of particular financial, political, cultural and economic institutions are, as Richard Whitley (1999: 54) argues, particularly visible when the strength of a particular feature is either very high or very low. The institutional context is reflected not only in formal laws and regulations, but also in unwritten rules and norms governing human behaviour. All these shape the actions of managers. Laws designed to ensure ethical behaviour – be they strictures against pollution or minimum labour standards – can strengthen the hand of the ethical vis-à-vis the free-rider. They can also – by, say, linking good practice with access to markets – reward good conduct and penalize bad.

Above all, laws can help to promote greater social solidarity, which is one of the major outcomes of ethical behaviour on a sustained and comprehensive basis. A bedrock of ethical theory is a belief in the necessity of ensuring that one's actions are not aimed solely at one's exclusive benefit; even radical neo-liberals locate the pursuit of profit in terms of the need to promote general wealth. Social solidarity does not only result in reduced levels of disruptive conflict, but can also make the world a safer one in which to do business. Firms can count on a minimum degree of 'good practice' from their partners and clients, which will help to make a rapidly changing context more predictable, and facilitate long-term planning. Indeed, it can be argued that commitment to a firm is thus partially about commitment to the community at large.

However, managers can, through, ethical conduct, help to perpetuate the unwritten rules and strictures that underpin an institutional context. Ethics can be partially secured by laws, but must also be borne out through actions; institutions are partially reconstituted through human actions (Giddens, 1984). In other words, while the wider institutional context may shape the actions of individuals and collectives, these institutions in turn are continuously reconstituted through human actions (ibid.). Through a relentless search for loopholes – or simply by relocating – individuals and firms can undermine the most stringent legislation. Laws may 'help' managers on an ethical path, but ethics are ultimately about decisions and actions, about the effects of very human choices. We would argue that while ethical conduct may often be financially lucrative, managers have to take ethics seriously, not only to secure long-term profitability but also to help reconstitute an institutional context that underpins the very existence of the firm.

Case study

Closing case study

Top fashion brands accused over failure to ensure living wage

Big names hoodwinking public, War on Want says

Some of the biggest fashion brands in the (British) high street do not do enough to ensure the overseas workers who make their clothes are lifted out of poverty, a report published today claims.

The study, by the charity War on Want and the anti-sweatshop coalition Labour Behind the Label, has identified Matalan and Mothercare, two companies featured in a Guardian investigation into the pay and conditions of workers in Bangalore, India, as among the 'worst offenders'. It claims that they are failing to accept the need for overseas garment workers to be paid a 'living wage' by their suppliers, that they have no information available on pay levels, and that they failed to respond to questions put to them by the report's authors.

Case study

Continued

Today's report, Let's Clean Up Fashion, launched on the eve of London fashion week, criticises retailers including Marks & Spencer, Tesco and H&M, for what it claims is their 'unambitious' and 'disappointing' approach to improving the wages of those who make their clothes.

It also describes as disappointing the response it received from Arcadia [G]roup, which owns the brands Topshop, Topman, Dorothy Perkins, Evans, Miss Selfridge and Wallis. The report follows a Guardian investigation into allegations from workers in Bangalore who supply Matalan and Mothercare that they were paid as little as 13p an hour for a 48-hour week, wages so low they sometimes had to rely on government food parcels. Similar allegations over pay and conditions were made by workers who made clothes for M&S, Primark, H&M and Gap. At the time, Primark and Mothercare launched an investigation into the allegations, and the other companies said they required their suppliers to pay the legal minimum wage or above.

The investigation followed the Guardian's earlier report in which Primark, Asda and Tesco were accused of breaching international labour standards in Bangladesh. Asda responded by launching an inquiry. Primark expressed concern and Tesco said it could not take action because the Guardian, in order to protect workers, had not provided the names of the factories concerned.

The authors of Let's Clean Up Fashion contacted 34 of the biggest fashion brands to see what they were doing to improve wages for workers in their supply chains, to compare with a similar survey last year. But the report concludes: 'Only a couple of fashion brands will admit publicly that working conditions in their supply chains are significantly below what is desirable. The vast majority continue to hoodwink the public by telling them that everything is fine and the examples cited by campaigners and the media are just glitches.'

It adds: 'With a couple of notable exceptions, those that do admit the problems have little to show on the issues we raise. They tend to agree that something must be done on a sector-wide level, but then sit back and wait for it to happen.'

The report said it was most disappointed in those which were members of the Ethical Trading Initiative (ETI), a code of conduct which sets out basic rights for employees across the supply chain, but which 'seem not to have grasped the gulf between what most companies do on labour rights and what needs to be done to have a serious impact on working conditions'.

Bringing in a living wage for overseas suppliers is something which would currently be achievable for UK fashion firms, the report claims. Gap, New Look and Next are named as retailers with 'genuine plans' to address the need for better wages for overseas workers, while it concludes that Primark, which has pledged to be active in work on the living wage, has made 'a definite improvement' to its position on pay a year ago. It points to the 'stark contrast' between the large financial rewards given to some fashion firm bosses and the low wages paid to overseas workers.

Simon McRae, senior campaigns officer for War on Want, said: 'This report exposes retailers' empty rhetoric on ethical treatment for workers who make their clothes but remain trapped in poverty.' Staff in Bangladesh earn 7% of a UK living wage – even taking into account the cheaper cost of living. This compares with 9% of a UK living wage earned by the average garment worker in India, 11% in China and Vietnam, 14% in Thailand and 25% in Morocco.

The charity wants legislation to make UK firms enforce ethical labour standards throughout their supply chains.

Yesterday, Mothercare said it demanded that all its suppliers worldwide 'comply with our ethical sourcing policy and code of conduct, which conforms fully with the Ethical Trading Initiative'. It added that its wages policy complied with the ETI and stated that 'wages and benefits must meet, at a minimum, the national legal standards, local legal standards, or industry benchmark standards, whichever is higher'.

The designer Jeff Banks, speaking on behalf of Matalan, said that all factories supplying Matalan had to first complete an audit ensuring that wages paid were above the minimum wage. When asked about a living wage, he replied: 'If the minimum wage does not meet the living wage of an industry, that's something for that country's government. It's beyond our adjudication.'

War on Want quotes Arcadia Group as saying that it 'continues to support the principle of a living wage', but that such a concept is 'beyond the influence of one single brand or company'. An Arcadia spokesman added that it 'will also continue to support and participate in multi-stakeholder initiatives which endeavour to find a solution to the sustainable implementation of the living wage'.

M&S told the report's authors its minimum standards were that 'workers should be paid the minimum wages in their country', and Tesco said it would continue to work with local unions and NGOs to define 'the appropriate living wage country by country'. H&M said all employees at suppliers receive 'at least the minimum wage'.

(*Source*: Karen McVeigh, *Guardian*, 14 September 2007.)

Question

- What responsibility do retailers have to ensure fair labour standards are applied by their suppliers? Why?

References

Giddens, A. 1984. *The Constitution of Society*. Cambridge: Polity Press.

Hobson, J. 1902. *Imperialism: A Study*. London: Allen & Unwin.

Singer, P. 1995. *Practical Ethics*. Cambridge University Press.

Whitley, R. 1999. *Divergent Capitalisms: The Social Structuring and Change of Business Systems*. Oxford University Press.

Index

Printed and bound in Great Britain by
CPI Antony Rowe, Chippenham and Eastbourne